PRAGUE

Bohemia

Moravia

OLMÜTZ

WISCHAU

IGLAU

TREBITSCH

BRÜNN

POSORZITZ

AUSTERLITZ

PILSEN

POHRLITZ

BUDWEIS

ZNAYM

NIKOLSBURG

GÖDING

AUSTRIA

ZWETTL

SCHÖNGRABEN

HOLLABRUNN

XXXX
NAPOLEON (-dets.)
(116,000)

EGELSEE

STEIN

KREMS

STOCKERAU

(8,000)

WEISSENKIRCHEN

DÜRRENSTEIN

MORTIER

Res. MURAT (xxxx)

MAUTERN

TULLN

SIEGMARTSKIRCHEN

LANNES

GREIN

MÖLK

PURKERSDORF

SCHÖNBRUNN

VIENNA (Approx. 10,000)

SOULT

EBELSBERG

XXX
V LANNES

ST. PÖLTEN

PRESSBURG

HAAG

STRENGBERG

MÖDLING

DAVOUT

LINZ

AMSTETTEN

XXXX
BERNADOTTE

XXX
IV SOULT

KUTUSOV
(40,000)

WINZER

KREMSMÜNSTER

WAIDHOFEN

GAMING

DAVOUT

XXX
II MARMONT

NEUHAS

ANNABERG

NEUSTADT

MARIA ZELL

GMUNDEN

MEERFELDT
(Approx. 10,000)

HUNGARY

This brigade (4,000)
had become separated
from Meerfeldt's corps.

BRUCK

LEOBEN

Styria

NEUMARKT

GRAZ

Raab R

KÖRMEND

Carinthia

VILLACH

KLAGENFURT

MARBURG

Drave R

Mur R

Save R

ARCHD. CHARLES
(80,000)

KRAIN

LAIBACH

Carniola

TRIESTE

Istria

AUSTERLITZ CAMPAIGN

Situation 7 November 1805, and
Napoleon's Pursuit of the Allies
After the Ulm Campaign

10   0   10   20   30   40   50
SCALE OF MILES

AUSTERLITZ

CLAUDE MANCERON

AUSTERLITZ
The Story of a Battle

TRANSLATED BY GEORGE UNWIN

W · W · NORTON & COMPANY · INC ·
NEW YORK

A mon compagnon de colère,
Jean-Marie Pirot, Peintre
des temps présents, cette
fresque d'un temps révolu.

C.M.

CONTENTS

ILLUSTRATIONS

between pages 160 *and* 161

SKETCH MAPS

PART I

THE EVE OF THE BATTLE

CHAPTER I

December 1st, 2 p.m.

NAPOLEON—
OR MERELY BONAPARTE?

———

'No news from the 3rd Corps?'
'Still nothing from Marshal Davout, Sire.'

For Napoleon the battle of Austerlitz began seventeen hours before the first clashes. In spirit he was fighting it already when he set out on horseback, in the early afternoon of December 1st, on a prolonged reconnaissance of the line, stretching some seven or eight miles, along which the French troops were taking up their position. A marshy stream marked the boundary that separated for the time being the two worlds gathered there to challenge each other. Its name was hard to find. On the maps it had none, of so little importance was this swamp of rivulets. The local people finally revealed that it was called the Goldbach. So let us call it the Goldbach. On this day, since it was partly frozen over, one could cross it on horseback at dozens of places without so much as dirtying one's boots. The battle, it would seem, was to be one without a river. Yet the Emperor's order was to remain on this side of it, and on his reconnaissance he scarcely crossed it.

Beyond it, visible as far as a light grey mist would allow, only the cavalry patrols on picket duty performed their evolutions in the open field. Now and again platoons of six to twelve horsemen dashed for the clumps of bare trees or the tumbledown thatched cottages to exchange shots with the enemy patrols,

17

who could be recognized by the smallness of their horses and the greater density of their formations, sometimes as many as twenty in a tight group. These were the famous Cossacks. The same parade-ground gyrations were being executed on both sides, with more concern for elegance than effectiveness. In this no-man's-land twice the range of a cannon, which tacit eve-of-battle convention had established between the giants, the two saluted each other for the moment with the foil alone: a light crackle of shots every so often, when the riders defied each other too closely. They had no intention of wasting much powder.

Screened by this transparent curtain of skirmishing horsemen was a seething mass of humanity, like the arrival of the crowd at an open-air stadium: the mustering armies, with 3,000 officers on each side playing the part of ushers. Thanks to the slightly higher position they occupied on the brow of some long, gentle slopes, the Russian infantry as it deployed revealed nothing but its fringe, though this was enough for the French to assess its strength. And they kept on coming.

Napoleon I was setting out from his headquarters, an encampment improvised from some abandoned houses of the village of Schlapanitz. They were good for nothing but to protect the staff from the wind, though hardly from the rain, and to serve as dining quarters; so completely uninhabitable were they in fact that the Emperor preferred to sleep in his carriage. The doors and windows, and a part of the roof, had been used for fuel. As for the inhabitants, they had gone to earth further north, in the outskirts of the great Bohemian forest, and there the commissariat pursued them to recover their pigs and potatoes. Almost all that remained were a few old women in heavy skirts and some naked children in the mud. However one tried, nothing could be got out of them, for not a soul on the general staff knew a word of Czech. The Russian and Austrian staff-officers fared little better in this respect than the French, for the population loved their requisitioning parties no better, and one could count on the fingers of one hand the officers surrounding the Austrian Emperor who were able to make themselves understood to the Moravians. The two armies would be fighting each other in the dark.

'There's really still nothing from Davout?'

Napoleon's brow was furrowed. The troops of the 3rd Corps, about a sixth of the forces on which he was counting absolutely, had not yet debouched in the south, coming from Vienna.

*　　　*　　　*　　　*

This inspection of December 1st was in itself a historic occasion: it was the first time the Emperor had visited the Grand Army on the eve of battle. At Boulogne he had held dozens of reviews, but only of portions of the army, the routine duties of the Supreme Adjutant. Here, today, it was not a matter of spit and polish. Napoleon wanted to check the position of every unit, inspect its arms, and show himself to raise the men's morale. It was with this last object in mind that he took particular care in setting the scene, in the arrangement and dress of his escort: for the inspection was to be a two-way affair, and Napoleon knew that in presenting himself to the gaze of 60,000 men his image would remain with them for the rest of their lives.

Six paces behind him rode a glittering group of magnificent figures on a whole stableful of chestnuts, bays and roans, covered with the skins of tigers and leopards; the marshals in their plumed two-cornered hats and the Imperial aides-de-camp for the duration of the campaign, in buttoned top-coats the colour of bluebottles and dripping with tassels and braid, epaulettes, shoulder-knots and hat decorations all of silver. Each had selected the most elegant and well-groomed of the eight horses they were obliged to take on a campaign, just as each had to have four servants or grooms. And if it had occurred to one of them not to appear at his best on this day, he would have drawn upon himself a similar withering remark from his Master as a lady-in-waiting received from the Empress one evening at the Tuileries: 'Madame, I have already seen you in that dress.' For the marshals in particular, it was the Emperor who had drawn up the decrees determining their uniforms, loading the cuffs and lapels with as much gold as they could bear.

The troops, however, only had eyes for the one little man, the worst dressed in the whole army, in the uniform, green, white and red, of a colonel of the *chasseurs à cheval* of the Guard, as he led the rest at a lively pace. Floating on the breeze for the first time was the *redingote gris*, food for the future legend. This was to date from Austerlitz. At Marengo he had still worn a coat with a collar. Now he had found his costume, and as of old the brilliance of his entourage served, as he intended, to accentuate his own simplicity. He clung to this for two reasons, because he hated a fuss over his own clothes (it was not by intent that his redingote still bore the scorch marks of a camp fire he had approached too closely a week earlier), and because it enabled him to display a supreme contempt for honours—from the moment he had become their fountainhead.

Under his hat, which was to become as celebrated as himself, with its little tricolour cockade, a penny favour, the depth of his complexion was almost Levantine: 'A sallow little man,' said the Viennese. His body was still vigorous, though perhaps a shade less responsive. Only those who had not seen him for two or three years noticed the first signs of thickening, his chin and cheeks a little full, his gaze a trifle dulled, his thighs plump in his kerseymere breeches. Napoleon Bonaparte was thirty-six.

'Slight and low on his legs, fairly muscular and full-blooded, his body is hardy and always alert. His nerves are excellent, sensitive and tough, his reflexes awe-inspiring, his capacity for work limitless; all of which adds up to a commanding presence. See, however, the other side: a cold humidity brings on depression, a cough and dysuria; opposition provokes frightful outbursts of temper; overwork, in spite of long warm baths, extreme sobriety, and a moderate, though constant, intake of coffee and snuff, sometimes engenders brief periods of weakness which go as far as tears. His brain is one of the most perfect that has ever existed: his attention, always alert, tirelessly grasps events and ideas; his memory files them and classifies them; his imagination plays with them and, under a constant secret pressure, generates without ever wearying political and strategic ideas which reveal themselves in sudden flashes of illumination, like those of a mathematician or a poet, preferably at night, on a sudden awakening, what he himself calls "a moral spark", "the presence of the spirit of after-midnight". This spiritual ardour, when it comes, lights up through his flashing eyes the ever "sulphurous" countenance of "the lanky-haired Corsican".[1]'

[1] Georges Lefebvre: *Napoléon* (Presses Universitaires de France).

Eighteen months had passed since he became Emperor and King, five years since he won his last battle, well and truly, at Marengo, six since he became master of France, nine since he became a married man, a deceived husband and a celebrated general, eleven since he had a spell in the prisons of Thermidor, twelve since he found fleas and fame at Toulon, twenty since his father died and he took over the burden of looking after his family, and twenty-five since the cadets of Brienne made fun of a dark little boy, sad, sombre, and austere, and yet a great talker and arguer, whom they called *la paille-au-nez*: Napolioné.

He had donned his Imperial personality. His Corsican placidity helped him here, in the presentation of an almost unbroken Olympian calm and an impenetrability that gave him an authentic aura of majesty.

Today, he had assumed, on top of his calm, a certain gaiety—though it was somewhat brittle, and subject to sudden occlusions, which served to reveal the unquiet abyss within. Highly sensitive to the reticences and half-truths which he still knew how to detect amongst the flattery of his entourage, which was usually too clumsy to be sincere, he missed none of the whispered exchanges taking place a few paces from him, especially amongst the staff of Bernadotte and Murat:

'After all, it is his first battle as Emperor. Who knows, perhaps the crown has squashed his brains?'

'Besides, since Egypt we've not seen much of the great Bonaparte touch: it was Desaix who won Marengo.'

'And it was Lucien Bonaparte who carried the 18th Brumaire . . .'

'He'll need to draw damned heavily on his luck now.'

His obvious animation throughout the afternoon was above all a professional reflex: the head of an army must radiate his confidence in victory. But in addition he felt himself carried along by circumstances, and sustained by four years of mutual understanding between the great mass of the French middle classes and himself:

'With power and the means to dispose of it, with experience, even of its uncertainties, the man discovered the means most likely to be increasingly effective. It became possible for him to

21

fulfil the wishes of the nation's most influential and respectable class. It was here that the rapidity of his insight, the lucidity of his thought and the precision of his actions give cause to marvel. What a rare and remarkable coincidence between the necessities of a historical situation and the unusual qualities of the man.'[1]

The incarnation of this coincidence was Bonaparte on December 1 and 2, 1805. And from this, rather than from any kind of built-up illusion concerning events that might still elude him, came that controlled exaltation which struck his entourage so vividly.

And not only his entourage: he had 60,000 men on his mind that day.

'Look at him; how happy he is!' said one of the grenadiers of the Guard belonging to the 96th half-brigade (the term regiment had just come back into use), as the Emperor paused in front of them.

The grenadier, Sergeant Coignet, drew himself up desperately; his shortness had almost cost him his career and was the bane of his life. It was not so noticeable today, thanks to his habit on special occasions of slipping some playing cards into his boots, under his heels. And after all, the god who was just passing before them was at least four inches shorter than him—that hadn't stopped him from becoming Emperor.

'Look! Look at him talking to everyone, his hands behind his back.'

'That makes three times at least that he's taken a pinch of snuff in two minutes! Don't you think he's rather nervous?'

'Not likely! It shows that he's happy.'

'Good God! Look, he's coming towards us.'

In a flash the slight, grey silhouette was leaning over them and the questioning had begun:

'What are you doing there, eh? Instead of cleaning your muskets like the others?'

'Sire, we're eating quince jelly.'

'Where did you find it?'

'Some well-filled larders in the villages, your Majesty; we use it for all our sandwiches.'

[1] Emile Tersen: *Napoléon* (Club Français du Livre), p. 6.

The Emperor pretended to be annoyed.

'Ah, so you're eating jam! Don't move. See that you put new flints in your muskets. We shall need them tomorrow morning. Keep yourselves prepared.'

At this moment Napoleon witnessed, and then had to judge, one of the countless and often bloody squabbles over revictualling between soldiers of different units. Some grenadiers on horseback were driving before them a dozen fat pigs. The grenadiers on foot drew their sabres and intercepted them. 'The Emperor's splitting his sides,' remarked Coignet. No doubt because there was little else he could do. For after all, this quarrel right under his nose spoke volumes concerning the needy state of the Guard, the most highly-organized and well-disciplined corps in the whole Grand Army. And what a glimpse of the brotherly love within it! A thousand accounts confirmed it: this was the vanguard of a famished horde in which every morsel was disputed. 'He made the division: six pigs for us, and the other six for the horse grenadiers. The generals drew themselves a pint of good blood, and we had the makings of some fine grills.'

*   *   *   *

The Emperor moved on, and remained silent as he passed down the ranks of the next regiment. His features took on a look of profound gravity as he studied the distant horizon, swarming with enemy troops; though capable of joking one minute about pigs and jam, he never for an instant forgot that in the throw of the dice he had made, the stake, once again, was the history of the world.

He was going to fight at odds of two to three: 60,000 men against 80,000, in the middle of enemy territory, deep in the jaws of a Europe turned into a gigantic trap for the French. But he had done more than pick up the gauntlet: he had returned it. The trap had become a counter-trap. It was he who was waiting for the enemy to walk into it.

Nothing is won in advance: tomorrow all would depend on the bravery of the men, the skill of the French generals, and on how long the enemy leaders remained in the dark. Also on the mist, which might prolong the night and help to complicate matters. The Grand Army would be born—or it would die. Until this day there had been armies of France; from now on men would speak of the *French Army*. What a hazardous baptism! All the might, all the flower of French youth was to play at double or quits, further from home than they had ever been. Vienna had been taken and left behind. The scene was to unfold in Moravia, in the heart of the old Europe, which was groaning and creaking, like an iceberg in spring, under the flowering of new ideas.

Opposite, two Goliaths were now all set for the fray: Russia, drawn from her own never-ending birth-pangs by a strange fascination, and Hapsburg Austria, a fragile edifice threatening to collapse into dust under the impact. To the north Prussia was showing her teeth, preparing to cut off the French the moment they faltered. At their back, Germany, diverse and incomprehensible, was at boiling point, as likely to adore as to hate. Ten, twenty Germanies: that of the treaties of Westphalia, which was dying, along with its Margraves, Bishop-Princes and Electors, having spun out its operetta for a couple of hundred years; but also that of Fichte, Blücher, and Gneisenau, whose flashes of blue steel were beginning to swish through the fug of the beer-cellars. Bismarck would be born in ten years time, Wagner in eight.

In the background there was England, victorious at Trafalgar, where Pitt was near death, though still young, eaten up by overwork and alcohol, and yet able to maintain with a firm hand 150 ships of the line down the whole length of the French flank, like so many banderillas. Spain, ever deceitful, Portugal full of venom, a ruffled United States, Turkey in the process of decay, Sweden on the warpath to recover some greatness, and above all there was the defenceless virgin desired by everyone, even though they might not speak of her: fair Italy, rising from the water like the Venus of Botticelli. Italy, whom nobody could forgive for letting Bonaparte proclaim himself her King.

All this was ranged, tier upon tier across the world, round the Moravian plateau, which had become a setting worthy of Aeschylus, of Shakespeare, or Schiller, that great but pathetic soul who had died six months earlier. As at the time of Actium, 'the world had no more than two jaws'. The confrontation was clear-cut, between the armies of monarchical absolutism, those of the past, and the army sprung from the Revolution.

The Revolution? After five years of Bonapartist dictatorship the word roused smiles in Paris—but tremors in Vienna, Moscow, Rome and Berlin. The Revolution was sixteen years old; this was the fatal age for over-gifted children. The Jacobins were in mourning in France. But the Countess Von Friedeburg wrote to her lover:

'The time of the Apocalypse is come, my friend. Robespierre on horseback is crossing Austria.'

December 2, 1805, was still 10th Frimaire, Year XIV.[1] However ambiguous the Napoleonic experiment might be, with its profoundly reactionary aspect within France, the message it bore once her frontiers were crossed was an explosive one: that little matter of equality, which had enthroned a lieutenant of artillery. Also of centralization, of rational organization, which shamed the incoherent state of countries still medieval in structure.

'The Gordian knot is about to be cut!' proclaimed Count Apponyi in the middle of a Budapest *salon*, in front of twenty Hungarians tremulous with hope. 'The Future and the Past have each other by the throat, and they will not let go.'

And that same Bonaparte who had stifled in himself and in his country not merely the spirit of '93 but also that of '89, appeared in the eyes of the world as its propagator: 'The booted evangelist of the Revolution'.

What would he call himself on the morrow, and thereafter? Nobody could yet be sure, any more than they knew the name that day would come to bear. The Battle of the Three Emperors? The Battle of Brünn? The Battle of the Anniversary?

If it were lost one thing was certain, Bonaparte would have remained Bonaparte for all posterity, and Napoleon would never have been.

---

[1] Public enactments were still officially dated in the revolutionary manner. The calendar of Fabre d'Eglantine, adopted in 1793 by the Convention, had been abolished by a *senatus consulte*, but remained in force until January 1, 1806.

CHAPTER II

December 1st, 3 p.m.

'RIGHT IN OUR HANDS'

Barely six miles from Napoleon, further to the east, the sizable village of Krzenowitz was beginning to overflow with arrogant manhood, like an over-full sponge. The Russian Imperial Guard had been assembling there since midday, and from one end to the other the poor houses were bursting with the press of green and white soldiers within, as they stripped the doors and windows for fuel. Suddenly, at the sharp call of trumpets, they all came dashing out: the sound of acclamation, ever less distant, marked the arrival of people of importance down the length of the marching column.

The officers quickly had the ranks drawn up, arms shouldered and lines dressed.

'Hurrah! Hurrah! Hurrah!'

The great traditional Russian cry, used both for the assault and on parades, was now here, erupting three times, mechanically. Who amongst the thousands of men who uttered it dwelt on its significance, those two ancient Slav syllables: Hu-Raj, which meant 'To Paradise!', the warriors' paradise for all who fell in battle. They had eyes for nothing but the imposing squadron of horsemen in brick-red uniforms who had come from the Pratzen plateau. Two of them galloped side by side ahead of the rest. One, in a black uniform with a white plume, mounted elegantly on an English-bred chestnut; the other, perched less easily on a sable steed whose jet-black coat gleamed and shone, setting off the white uniform of its rider.

'The Emperors!'

'*The Emperor...*'

That is to say, for all the actors in this scene, the Czar. The first, the younger, the more attractive, the one who smiled and was so perfectly at one with his mount. Who cared about the second, the Emperor of Austria? Francis was not yet forty, but he looked like Alexander's father. Stiff with affected gravity, like the Habsburg monarchy personified, he turned from side to side a face already mottled by a surfeit of good living and conjugal pleasures, with its endless, pendulous chin and its large eyes, ever fearful: 'the look of the crowned conserver of the existing order'. He met with nothing but a frozen rampart of deference from the higher Russian officers, tinctured with just enough irony to remind him that in their eyes he was a defeated man, one whom they had come to extricate from this business, who without them . . .

Without Him: the Archangel. For this was what all the Russias were already calling the fair young man, a little ripe, a little effeminate, a little weary, with the haggard air of those who live in the midst of a competitive adoration: Alexander I. Shod in narrow pointed boots, he circulated among the enraptured giants who guarded his sacred person, stopping occasionally before one of them and fixing him, with an absent air, through a golden eye-glass. One noticed his pallor. He had just recovered from one of those strange indispositions, bordering on fits of epilepsy, which afflicted him periodically throughout his life. This one had kept him in bed for two days and succeeded in giving him the air of one who lacked employment. From time to time he turned his pale grey eyes towards the combined general staff who rode at a respectful distance behind the Emperors. Not to consult the most gaudy, most majestic of these men covered in decorations: the old quartermaster general Sukhtelen, or the terrible inspector-general of artillery, Arakcheev, capable of scalping his soldiers by pulling out their hair by the handful and killing them with blows from the flat of his sabre, or, again, by having them buried alive up to the neck till they died. Not even Intzov, Zakomelski, Bogdanov, or six or eight of the other survivors from the reign of Catherine II; barrels or skeletons, wrinkled Don Quixotes or chubby Sanchos, he had little to do with these 'old Russians', the murderers of his father and tomorrow, perhaps, his own murderer.

Those whom Alexander's gaze was seeking were a little further back, though ready to dash up to him at the least sign, on their well-groomed horses as frisky as themselves. His aides-de-camp. His picked men. His friends. His generation: Lieven, Gagarin, Volkonski, Wintzegerode, Czartoryski, Novosiltsov, Stroganov: a chattering flock of admirers, sure of themselves, sure of him, sure of conquering . . .

One of them sensed his mute appeal and cantered up to him all aglow. This was the favourite of favourites: Dolgoruki. His claim to distinction: he loved women as much as he hated the French, which was saying quite a lot. His slight squint and long pinched nose accentuated the infatuation he exuded from every pore:

'Your Majesty called me?'

'Oh! Not exactly, my dear fellow, but I'm surprised to find that I still don't know, even now, where Kutuzov is setting up his headquarters . . . It was supposed to be here.'

Smiles of commiseration on ten well-barbered faces: commiseration the future would condemn to decrepitude.

'Mikhail Hilarionovich has been sulking since our decision to hunt Bonaparte down. Does your Majesty believe his presence would be very diverting for us this afternoon?'

The Czar smiled too, but continued to grumble for the sake of form in his drawling French, imported from the *salons* of Versailles and affected by St Petersburg society.

'But really, my dear fellow, you must agree he's not left me much to do. Not a prisoner to interrogate! Not a corps commander to listen to! Does he think I'm good for nothing but honorary roles?'

As he spoke he threw a glance at Francis of Austria, who seemed to be dancing attendance on him patiently while talking in short, quiet phrases with the Prince of Schwarzenburg and several other Austrians, fellow-exiles in their own land in the midst of this ambulant piece of Russia: Liechtenstein, Gerhard, Kienmayer, and a handful of aides-de-camp as mournful and listless as their Russian colleagues were restless.

'I should at least like to be convinced that Bonaparte fears tomorrow's encounter as much as you say he does . . . You know, you have taken on a heavy responsibility in committing us to battle so quickly, after your interview with him the other day? Kutuzov will never forgive you, my dear fellow . . . '

'Sire, I'd stake my head on it: the usurper was green with fear and did all he could to persuade me to stop our advance. It was only when he realized that I was not going to fall into his trap that he treated me to the spectacle of one of his vulgar rages. And besides, your Majesty knows his manoeuvres of the past forty-eight hours. If Napoleon wasn't so afraid of the battle, why would he have retreated, contrary to all his methods of fighting? He's frightened, that's obvious! He's avoiding open conflict. His hour is come, I promise you. He's right in our hands . . . '

With a graceful gesture, which was also a shade fatalistic, the Czar urged his horse forward, exchanged a few friendly words with the Austrian Emperor, and for want of anything better to do, bore him off to inspect some more regiments. Behind them, the suite of high-ranking Russian and Austrian knights and the squires leading by the bridle the splendid remounts, sumptuously caparisoned by the Imperial stables, rapidly dispersed.

*   *   *   *

The two camps facing each other do not make things easy for historians, who risk forgetting their Latin when they try to co-ordinate dates. For the French, as we have seen, the date was the 9th Frimaire. The Russians, for their part, made it November 19th: faithful to the Julian calendar, introduced by Julius Caesar, they lagged ten days[1] behind the rest of the west, like all the other peoples split from Rome by the Orthodox schism, who did not accept the jump in date ordained by Pope Gregory XIII, from October 4th to 15th, which took place in one single night in 1582. Russian dates are thus duplicated for another century, and some mental gymnastics are needed to bring about agreement between the O.S. dates, the Old Style, and those the Imperial court disdainfully labelled N.S. dates, New Style.

---

[1] By 1800 the ten days had become twelve, owing to the different provisions for leap years in the two calendars.

Finally, Austerlitz did not take place on December 2nd officially except for the Austrians . . .

After four in the afternoon of this November 19th, O.S., or December 1st, N.S., the snowy greyness of the day began to give way to night, forcing the allied high command to light the night-lamps in their carriages, in which some of them were hastening towards the outposts, poring over their unrolled maps with pensive brows. An observer suddenly transported here from Napoleon's camp would have been struck above all by the difference in generation between the opposed military leaders. Not that the high-ranking allied staff consisted entirely of fossils: Alexander was twenty-eight and Francis II thirty-seven. They naturally tended to surround themselves with men of their own age and to select from amongst them their particular friends, in so far as the word meant anything for a sovereign. The aides-de-camp and certain chamberlains were thus of a youthful turbulence, which contrasted strongly with the mature scepticism of the surrounding atmosphere, the product of the traditions and memories of the century of Catherine II and Maria-Theresa, but more than anything inhibited to the very depths of the unconscious by the man who remained for these militarists the man of war *par excellence*: Frederick the Great. His shade had hovered over every army for thirty years, even when his own country had not been at war. Prussian influence determined another aspect of this dual general staff: its uniformity. A casual spectator would have had difficulty in distinguishing at first sight between Russian and Austrian officers: the same tunics, embellished mainly in white, the same profusion of medals, crosses and ribbons, the same cloaks floating on the air, lightly attached at the shoulders. The same boots—the same monocles.

And whenever these fine gentlemen came into contact with the footsloggers, the same salutations, rigid and raucous, from the exhausted battalions, the same automatic responses from the officers, with more concern for articulation than meaning: the style was German, which came more naturally to the Austrians, and needed more application amongst the Russians.

There was in fact nothing specifically Slav here at all: the language spoken by one staff or the other was usually French or

German. But if one placed these officers side by side with their opposite numbers in Napoleon's headquarters, how much better cut were the uniforms here! What ease of bearing, in dispensing salutes, to superiors and inferiors alike, in the handling of whip, two-cornered hat and gloves! The battlefield was the latest *salon*: one conversed in hints, serious matters were not discussed, 'my dear fellow' cropped up in every other sentence, and one accomplishment alone was allowed to be displayed: nonchalance. Alongside this comportment, fashioned by centuries of fine manners, the altogether raw and stilted glitter of the French general staff appeared as little assured as the pomp of the Consular Court in the eyes of the Fauburg Saint-Germain. And the marshals of the Empire cut rather parvenu figures in their brand new finery.

But tomorrow's attack would not be conducted with epigrams or acrostics. Everything would be a matter of intuition and speed both in devising and executing plans: youthful virtues *par excellence*. And it was here that in spite of the frothy simpletons who made up Alexander's entourage, the average age (physical and mental) of the two general staffs facing each other suggested a serious disadvantage for the allies. In Napoleon's camp Berthier came nearest to being a greybeard, with his fifty-five years. Murat, however, was thirty-eight, Davout thirty-five, Soult and Lannes thirty-seven, Bernadotte forty-one, and Bessières thirty-nine. Ten years earlier only three of them had been generals. At this time several of the Russian leaders who would be opposing them on the morrow appeared to be nearing the end of their careers, having been launched in the wake of Suvorov or Kutuzov by the capricious and unpredictable will of the Czarina.

Service routine would guide them in Moravia, they considered, as it had done thirty years earlier against the Turks or the Swedes. The obscure fire that still burned in the hearts of the leaders sprung from the Revolution was altogether absent in them. So too was ambition, desire, the mainspring of all else: these had long since been mortgaged. Their teeth were down to stumps: those of the French had never been longer.

As for the soldiers . . . They formed the mobile backcloth to the day's work. Sixty thousand Russians almost as exhausted as the French, half of them on bare feet, in long files of grey and dark green infantry, crushed under mountainous and ill-assorted bundles. They had been marched to death for three months, in order to arrive in time in the middle of Europe; too late, nevertheless, to save Vienna. Undernourished, rewarded with the knout, their lives at the mercy of the mood of their officers, who could, as Arakcheev had done a week before, strike off their heads with the blow of a sabre in the event of insolence, they advanced with the tenacity of ants, through the fields bordering the roads, which were left free for the convoys of wagons: three or four lines of men on either side of the procession of wood: carriages, carts, wagons, cannon, berlins, with every so often the bobbing diversion of a squadron of heavy cavalry, two hundred helmets on the crest of a whirlwind of dust. The *sotnia*, or platoons of Cossacks, wheeled about alongside the troops with the fantastic casualness of slightly savage sheep dogs.

Here and there they came upon some mournful regiments who had already been encamped for the past two days: the Austrians, if one can call them that! Hungarians, Croats, Slovenes, Italians, Poles, all of whose officers, it is true, were Germans, bound by the oath of allegiance to the Habsburgs.

They were all morally overwhelmed by the recent French victories, but a good deal less played out than their allies. They had had to do no more than retreat and about turn after a month. They felt as lost as everyone else among these Moravian people, who smiled but remained distant. And they noticed with surprise, from many an episode, the gaiety of the Russian infantry, their frank and gentle humour under the apparent fatalism: Russian morale was incomparably higher than that of the Austrians and seemed, on December 1st, to top that of the French. They greeted the least incident with ridicule, great guffaws of laughter and wide smiles, hidden in their deep wrinkles and unkempt beards.

'Eh! Little father! Move on! Are you afraid of old Jack Frost?'

'Look at those gunners round their unicorn, stuck in the mud! Just like the jackdaws on the tower of Ivan the Great.'

'Make way for His Grace, there! Can't you see how he wants to get back to his girl-friend?'

'Eh! The Pavlograd Hussars! Let's have a look at your prisoner, then; let's see if it's really true that all these good-God-ing godless French have got cloven hooves!'

Count Tolstoy, Prince Naryshkin and Serge Trubetskoy have recorded a dozen such remarks in the pages of their memoirs. Between this fabric of endless humour that underlay the wretchedness of their soldiers and the icy self-sufficiency of the officer-caste, there was an abyss that was completely absent in the opposite camp, where the French generals and men swore the same oaths, shared the same grumbles, and were faithful to the same collective impulses.

If one were tempted to sum up the main contrasts on the eve of that fateful day, one would set on the French side, youth, in men, ranks and dignities, versus ossification. Vigour versus distinction. Unity of texture in the French army versus segregation among their opponents. The bulk of the French were on the spot; most of the allies were still on the march. Finally, the essential difference emerges when one seeks to know who, on either side, was responsible for planning and direction. Among the allies one looks — and hesitates. The Czar? Francis II? Kutuzov? Weirother?

On the French side the question would have aroused smiles. Everything centred on Napoleon.

CHAPTER III

December 1st, 3 p.m.

WHY 1805?

————

The Emperor himself had stopped asking questions: he merely turned to the south every fifteen minutes, with a jerk at his horse's mouth, and received with ill grace officers despatched to him by the corps commanders.

'Ah! It's Davout he's waiting to hear from.'

It snowed, it rained; which, is not quite certain. The hard ground was powdered with moisture. One of those dreary days at the beginning of winter, under a yellow-grey sky; the last straw after six weeks of mud. Never had November so well deserved its reputation: the youth of France had gone forth to conquer in the winter with bowed heads and had come to a halt at their last gasp, half frozen, in this anteroom to the Continental climate, where they were engulfed in fiendish, gleeful winds straight from Siberia. What a hell-hole this Moravian corridor was! Where were the fields of Italy? The veterans came to regret even the burning sands of Egypt, whose horrors still haunted their camp-fire stories. Here, they were having a foretaste of fresh sufferings, those of the age of maturity. A certain military insouciance, assumed at Valmy and gaily squandered on the French campaigns from Fleurus to Marengo, began to evaporate here, under the influence of the great ordeals in preparation.

The inspection of the Guard, with which Napoleon began, was enough to relieve him of any illusions concerning the state of the troops. He passed, again and again, among men who had collapsed, over several acres, where they had not even had the energy to collect some straw. General Dorsenne, Colonel-in-Chief of the foot grenadiers, universally detested for his bark and his bulldozing manner, was everywhere, fussing and fuming: here it was, five days since he had ordered the non-commissioned officers and men 'to buy trousers of blue cloth, of a good size and without buttons down the side . . . ' and forbidden them to wear any others. They would still be laughing over this ten years later in the barracks of Courbevoie and Villers-Cotterêts: when his order was announced the Guard had already combed Brünn without discovering a single piece of material and now found themselves in a world of dry brushwood, marching towards Austerlitz. Where were the clothiers to supply them? The Emperor closed his eyes therefore to the fine collection of old clothes, threadbare, full of holes, discoloured, in which his men would be going into battle, and let Dorsenne busy himself over ensuring that at least hair would be cut according to regulations, sabre scabbards and bayonets polished, cap badges firmly fixed, collars equipped with hooks, 'and all webbing properly blancoed, God damn it!'

'D'you call that white? You can see very well it won't do. It's slovenly. You haven't used enough blue.'

But ten times, twenty times, Napoleon checked personally the cleaning of weapons, and severely reprimanded those who neglected this:

'The tips of your flints must be rounded and set as the colonel has ordered.'

Corporals, sergeants, lieutenants, captains, called upon one after the other, had to check their equipment from top to toe, as far as the colonel—and the harsh flash of invective when the Emperor discovered that a man had lost his priming-pin, the large brass needle that hung conspicuously from a ring round one of the coat buttons.

'How's this bugger here going to clear his touch-holes? I have ordered that priming-pins must be replaced by no matter what if they are lost: knitting needles if necessary! And you: what have you done with your scouring rod?'

This time Napoleon had seized on a corporal: each of them was supposed to possess one of those hooks or 'worms', attached to the ramrod, for drawing unfired charges from the barrel. This avoided useless discharges, which wasted powder and increased the wear on the bore of the gun: the scouring rod, held by the corporal, was supposed to be available for passing down the line from hand to hand, an operation that was not supposed to take longer than a round of twelve shots. (The soldier's basic weapon remained the musket of 1777, firing four balls in three minutes, with a range of about 220 yards.)

'You've lost it? Admit it then you fucker!'[1]

The giant, with a great moustache and hair drawn back in an old-fashioned pigtail, grew more and more crimson.

'You shall have a rest tomorrow. Go to the field hospital.'

A punishment worse than ten years in a fortress, on this day. It was unusual. More often the penalty was a terrible look, a shrug of the shoulders, and a brusque move away, some ten or so paces, without a word to the stricken man.

The Emperor spent nearly an hour amongst the ranks of the Guard. The commanders of the other corps reproached him with spending time which might prove wasted, for nobody knew whether they would be thrown in. Positioned as they were it was open to doubt: the strong buffer of the troops of the 4th Corps stood between them and the enemy line. Yet it was they, nevertheless, who monopolized at this moment the attention of the Supreme Chief.

There was a reason for this: the Imperial Guard, up till then, had done nothing but guard him. It had not yet been in action. True, at the time when it was still the Consular Guard it had played a significant part on June 14, 1800, by throwing all its weight into the confused melée at Marengo. One of the most majestic of French military marches commemorates this decisive intervention: 'The March of the Consular Guard at Marengo'; this is a stirring outburst of drums, fifes and trumpets against a regular, parade-ground drone. But what had become of that élan, still so Jacobin, so fresh, under the top-dressing of marble and gold of the past five years? On the 18th Brumaire of the previous year a symbolic decree had been promulgated:

'The Guard, foot and horse, is to be issued with new uniforms and buttons.'

---

[1] 'Rarely', writes Griois, 'has a general used more gross language than the Emperor to his men.'

And it was done. The 7,000 most striking and valiant men in the army had been repainted and varnished. Their vocation was to surround and protect Caesar. But he had never wished to confine them to the role of Pretorian Guard: it was his intention that they should be the finest French military unit. There was no way of knowing whether twelve months of pampering had not softened them. This, at all events, was the suspicion that could not be prevented from spreading among other units of the army, where there was much exasperation over the privileges of the Guard, sanctioned by regulations that were scarcely equalitarian:

'Wherever the troops of the Imperial Guard are stationed alongside those of the Line, they have the right, and are to be given the position of honour.

'Officers and non-commissioned officers of the Imperial Guard have seniority over equivalent officers and non-commissioned officers in units of the Line, whenever they are stationed together on the same mission.

'Whenever a corps or detachment of the Guard meets *en route* a corps or detachment of troops of the Line, the latter shall form up and shoulder arms, or draw sabres if it is a cavalry unit; flags and standards shall be dipped; drums beat a salute and trumpets sound the march, until the troops of the Imperial Guard shall have passed.'

Twelve months of this regime had opened up a gulf of profound animosity between the Guard and the rest of the army, ever obliged to give way to them. A gulf that countless brawls and duels had filled with blood. Napoleon knew it. He had decided to re-establish at least an equality under fire between the two: the Guard would fight tomorrow. But if it fought badly, it would be he who would be directly dishonoured. In that event . . .

'See to it then, Monsieur,' he said to Marshal Bessières, already overburdened with cares, 'that all knapsacks are carried at the same height.'

The commander of the Imperial Guard, who had already borne that responsibility for four years, quietly inclined his well-proportioned athletic body. His aloof and slightly bantering manner impressed everybody, even Napoleon. Bessières had never been known to lose his head, and it certainly would not happen today. He now left the cortège of staff officers and spent the next twelve hours amongst the rank and file of his men, each of whom he addressed by name, his face alert, with regular features, under hair worn long and hanging, like the ears of a dog. Of all the marshals he looked the youngest.

*   *   *   *

Bernadotte was five years older than him, and affected an air of elder wisdom. The least of his gestures proclaimed his importance and his every word, delivered in the harsh, insistent accent of the south-west, aspired to be oracular.

The Marshal, commander of the 1st Corps, also left the Imperial group, but in his own unobtrusive way: neither too much nor too little. He pulled gently on his reins, let the other riders draw ahead, and indicated that he was following, from a distance, with that mixture of reserve and irony which characterized his attitude to the army, an inspection that clearly did not concern him. His troops were encamped three miles further west. Napoleon was now on his way to visit the cavalry of Nansouty, then the infantry of Saint-Hilaire and that of Vandamme.

'This concerns Soult, not me. I'm wasting my time here,' confided Bernadotte in the dusk of the evening to two companions, whose possession of a certain intelligence and critical sense, unusual in the Emperor's entourage, qualified them to share frequently in his confidences: Colonel Jomini and General Mouton. 'It is true that if he came to me just now I should find it difficult to receive him like Soult: just look at his courtly contortions! He's trailing his hat so low he'll fall on his face, upon my word. There's a great future for such a supple spine in the Empire that lies before us. But what do you think of our strange dispositions, Colonel?'

Jomini replied with the guarded air of the Swiss, impossible to catch on the wrong foot. He was conscious of being the great master of strategy of his day, and had just published a *Treatise on High Tactics*, which had established his reputation throughout Europe.

'We have certainly covered a lot of ground without getting anywhere very much, Marshal, in order to make this inspection.'

'Why not say it bluntly: we've gone round in a circle.'

'If you wish: it was in order to take into account the circumvolutions of a military concentration of unusually thin density. In face of the allied front, which is manifestly beginning to lengthen, far from us spreading ourselves out along an extended line, the dispositions of the Emperor have contracted us into a hedgehog or a blow of the fist, according to what he wants to do. Tomorrow may equally well see us firmly entrenched or in full attack.'

'Well, Colonel, I don't understand such great matters. The enemy deploys, Napoleon concentrates. The enemy manoeuvres . . .'

'The Emperor stays where he is.'

'Do you approve or disapprove?'

The commander of a battalion of Swiss troops attached to Marshal Ney, Jomini had obtained permission, under some flimsy pretext, to leave the latter to defend the Tyrol in order to be present at the great encounter. His face, more Anglo-Saxon than Genevese, supported his reputation for infallibility in the manner of a poker player: without a wrinkle. He was well aware of the epithets each step in his strange military career had provoked, based as it was upon brains: pedant, plagiarist, armchair strategist . . . Napoleon himself had murmured some of them: he had a horror of anyone besides himself shining in the science of war, and did not use Jomini except under his immediate eye, and lost no opportunity to bully him. It was noticeable that the latter entertained a hate for him nowadays that was none the less alarming because it was so carefully suppressed. But although Jomini may well have hoped for a French defeat, he was too shrewd to predict it:

'It is tomorrow that will approve or disapprove, Marshal. But it is clear that the Emperor has a plan in mind, and that he is making a more or less final survey as he covers the ground.'

'We're now in Suchet's area,' observed Mouton, who never said anything worthwhile, though his fine square head always looked touchingly attentive. ('Mouton: head of a dog, heart of a lion, brains of a mouse,' said the malicious.)

By dint of winding amongst vast flower-beds of men assembled round stacks of muskets and pots hanging over fires, they had arrived at the division which seemed likely to be the most exposed at the start of the action, that of General Suchet. The Russians were so close that their fanfares, sharp and raucous, could be heard whenever there was a lull in the French camp.

Hat in hand, but with a dignity that shamed the servile cringing of Marshal Soult, Suchet, a general of thirty-five, did the honours of his three regiments for Napoleon, detailing the composition and effective strength of each company: it would have been impossible, even for a trained eye, to identify them by their uniforms, for these were of an abundant variety, aggravated by the hardships of the march from the Rhine: it was a seed-bed as far as the eye could see of green jackets faced with red, greatcoats of grey, breeches that looked as if they had been bleached, with here and there veritable bundles of tatters (the 59th distinguished itself greatly in this respect, for which it became known as the Royal Rag-bags), and everywhere a large number of civilian outfits: blue frock-coats, round hats.

Napoleon paid no attention to this and profited from the fact that he had in Suchet an officer full of intelligence and experience, who had already served as chief of staff in the army of Italy five years earlier, to pass from detail to the whole, to sit for a moment on a drum and trace under the eyes of Soult and Berthier the positions occupied by the principal units, as reported to him by the young general. Nothing was more important for the Emperor than the courage of his divisional commanders. There lay the essence of the organization of the Grand Army, whose main unit was a creation of the Revolution: the *division* of 6,000 to 9,000 men, made up of two or three 'half-brigades', which were called once more, definitively, by their classic name, *regiments*, each in turn made up of one to three battalions. These divisions were gathered by two, three or four into *army corps*, which became the strategic unit *par excellence*, whose command made certain names immortal. Austerlitz was thus directed, looking at the matter in broad terms, by Napoleon holding the reins of a team of four horses: the four corps of Bernadotte, Lannes, Soult and Davout, flanked by Murat with the cavalry and reinforced by the Guard. Infantry and cavalry had each come to be divided in two: infantry of the line (grenadiers) and light infantry (skirmishers, *chasseurs*); heavy cavalry (*cuirassiers*) and light cavalry. The artillery was in process of being grouped into regiments, horse and foot, but this hardly played a part here, where each division still included twelve cannon at the disposal of its general.

Bernadotte took Jomini by the arm:

'Have you noticed that the Emperor never looks Suchet in the face? He's very ready to make use of him, but he doesn't like him.'

'Do you really think so, Marshal?' The worthy Mouton was astonished.

'He's cool towards him, that's clear,' murmured Jomini, his eyes fixed on the baby-face of 'the choir boy', as his close friends called Suchet, with his rosy complexion, his finely shaped lips and rich, curly, chestnut hair. An inflexible choir boy, however, who submitted to the present Imperial coldness with eyes of steel. 'He can't forgive him for his connection with Moreau and his opinions about the trial last year . . . Suchet will have difficulty in making much of a career.'

Bernadotte drew away a little abruptly, and Jomini bit his lips. Even a Swiss can drop a brick: the Gascon marshal had been slightly implicated in the conspiracy of 1804, and if he had not married a Clary, God knows where he would have been today . . . His great nose sniffed the breeze under his shock of black, almost frizzy hair and seemed to draw him once again towards the group around the Emperor, to dance attendance on him and avoid being confused on this day with his opponents; at which moment Napoleon abruptly remounted and left Suchet standing, all the more abruptly because he had been unable to find any fault with him.

And the Emperor headed into danger, towards the enemy. Now he was almost between the two lines, his face ever turned towards the Russian side, with only a quick, telltale twitch of his mouth at the arrival of every messenger—his disquiet concerning Davout and his 10,000 men.

*　　　*　　　*　　　*

The regulation escort platoon, twenty *chasseurs à cheval* of the Guard, who up till now had kept their respectful distance, drew closer to the Emperor, round whom the aides-de-camp were bunched. From afar, the Cossacks would be led to believe that it was just a cavalry patrol, somewhat reinforced. But had one of their officers bothered to notice the plumes of the marshals round a little chap in a grey coat . . .

'We'll soon be within pistol range, I do believe . . . ' murmured the captain of the escorting *chasseurs* into the ear of an aide-de-camp, the most handsome, the finest dressed, a sort of cherub in silvery velvet, with sparkling eyes and a slightly vain smile over a receding chin: Philippe-Paul, Count of Ségur. He was always in demand amongst the general staff, where genuine aristocrats were far from numerous. The Emperor himself treated Ségur with all the indulgence of a parvenu. Many a good man risen from the ranks, and quite unaccustomed to the manners of the Court, begged the address of his tailor and bootmaker, and covertly watched when he carved a chicken.

'We're there already, my dear fellow: the destiny of the world is at the mercy of a Cossack's eye and finger.'

'I must disagree with you there, sir; we're six or eight fathoms short. I see you still lack experience of the approach.'

'I was at Grisons and Hohenlinden, you know. Not to mention Ulm just recently, Captain . . . '

'Daumesnil, monsieur le Comte, at your service . . . '

The accent of Périgueux, an honest round face, quite enormous moustaches, and a foreboding of glory. The plebeian was only three years older than the *grand seigneur*; he looked far more.

But they were both great children, like the vast majority of this crèche for heroes. Everything separated them: yet here they were, good friends. Ségur and Daumesnil, deep in discussion, unwittingly increased their pace and drew ahead of the Imperial party.

'A good way to judge the range of the Russian weapons is to keep drawing closer until . . . ' To which of the two had the thought first occurred? A couple of minutes later they were back in the midst of the group being severely told off by the chief equerry, General de Caulaincourt:

'Are you mad, gentlemen? The shots you provoked by your

rashness whistled past His Majesty's ears. He has asked me to express his displeasure . . . '

A glance in the Emperor's direction showed the two miscreants that he was not in earnest: second-lieutenant Bonaparte, comrade in mischief. He had always liked daring and peopled his entourage with spoilt children. Which was why, half an hour later, without the least compunction, the two again began to argue about the true distance of the enemy. They took advantage of the fact that the Emperor and the generals were occupied in assessing the strength of some improvised defences thrown up round a rocky knoll which the men called *le Santon*, after an Algerian hermit. This time it was Daumesnil who maintained that they were within range.

'And what's more, I'll prove it to you. Here, you!'

One of the *chasseurs* obeyed, with the alacrity of soldiers with whom the officer knew how to endear himself. Without needing to be told, he proffered his carbine and knelt down for Daumesnil to rest the gun on his shoulder.

'I can hardly see a movement amongst those savages,' murmured Ségur with half-closed eyes. 'You aren't trying to make me believe you can take aim . . .'

'Unless you're myopic you must be able to see the officer's white horse well enough?'

'You're right, and . . . Oh!. You can't have! But yes! He's down. He's hit! What a marksman you are, Captain!'

The *chasseurs* could scarce forbear to cheer.

'That's one less for tomorrow, at any rate,' said Daumesnil remounting his horse.

*　　　*　　　*　　　*

Throughout this episode Jomini and Mouton, left by Bernadotte to ride a little behind the courtiers, had not ceased to observe the enemy. Mouton ended by grumbling:

'Confound it! Tomorrow's business is going to be hot, to judge by what we've been allowed to see. Few Austrians, no doubt, but Russians . . . Phew! It's as if the earth were spewing up green uniforms.'

'You may be sure that Napoleon sees nothing but redcoats, monsieur . . . '

'I beg your pardon?'

'Haven't you heard his proclamations during the past three months? The Russians, the Austrians, are for him no more than mercenaries or soldiers of straw. The real business is between France and England, everybody knows that.'

'But there's not a single British soldier on the Continent!'

'Exactly. French flesh will be fighting English gold tomorrow. At least that is the official version that is being circulated. And we've just suffered a terrible defeat at sea, don't forget. Our fleets were almost annihilated at Trafalgar . . . The end of this memorable year may well turn out to be simply a gigantic covert duel between England and France, one making a splash at sea, the other looking for revenge in the very heart of Europe, on the interposed armies of the old monarchies.'

'But why, after all?' Mouton suddenly exclaimed, turning on Jomini the good-natured, trusting eyes of a man humble in the presence of a superior intellect. 'Why this mess, Monsieur; can you tell me that? You will recall as I do the extraordinary dawn that rose over us five years ago? Of peace—the true dawn!'

Jomini smiled, almost warmly for once, at this curious man of war who had no love for war and yet waged it so well. Mouton continued: 'You witnessed as I did the pacific invasion of English tourists who spread through France like a plague of locusts after Marengo. 1801. That was peace, the sluice-gates of disorder were closed, the Emperor . . . or rather, the First Consul, I should have said, resolutely pursuing a civilian destiny in his fine outfit of red and gold. His true greatness and true glory appeared: his harangues stupefied the councillors of the State! There were to be legal codes, road-building, urban recon-struction, the Bank of France, festivals! Well then, why 1805?'

'1792,' replied Jomini.

'What do you mean?'

'I was answering a year with a year. We have 1805 because we had 1792. The Emperor himself swears he can do nothing about it—but I'm not so sure. This will undoubtedly be disputed by history. At all events, to see clearly into the origins of this battle that is being prepared, one must go back thirteen years.'

*　　　*　　　*　　　*

Jomini was right. In 1792 the King of France, from the height of his tottering throne, had declared war against 'the King of Bohemia and Hungary', and Europe began her slow movement of mobilization against the Revolution, broken by periods of disunity and exhaustion. This was 'the First Coalition', which drew back, significantly, in the person of the old Duke of Brunswick after the brush at Valmy.

The foundation members of the huge four-cornered league who threw themselves again and again, two or three at a time, against France were England, Prussia, Austria and Russia.

A Europe of obsolete monarchies opposing a nation of progress? This would be true, and also false. It would be too facile, above all, if one pictured them as decadent countries caught in full dissolution. Of the four, the one which most nearly corresponded to this picture was, paradoxically, England, in the midst of an acute crisis, social and financial, without a valid dynasty, almost without an army, who possessed only two solid elements: her fleet and the invincible stubbornness of her aristocratic class. As for the three great Continental powers, in contrast to Spain, which was worm-eaten to the marrow, they were obviously experiencing the same drama as France under Louis XVI before 1789: an upsurge of internal vigour that could find no outlet within their *ancien régime* framework.

All three, however, had been moulded by a great sovereign, the most celebrated in their history, who had scourged them, organized them, set their faces towards the future and nourished their pride. Their great century was only yesterday, whereas that of France had begun with the advent of Louis XIV.

Compared with the disturbed kingdom of Louis XVI, the Prussia of Frederick, the Austria of Maria-Theresa, and the Russia of Catherine appeared as regenerated powers, to whom the times belonged. Each had just acquired, thanks to 'these three great men, two of whom are women', as it was said at the time, that quality which stamps its physionomy on a country for ever: its character.

But they had, if one may so describe it, worn each other out, during the strange underhand struggle lasting a quarter of a century between the bourgeois Maria-Theresa, a stay-at-home, placid, obstinate, bigoted, indomitable, and those two demonic spirits, Frederick and Catherine, sceptical and tolerant, romantic and cruel, brilliant, frivolous, deceitful, secretive; all three ceaselessly occupied in spying on each other, provoking each other's jealousy, aping each other, tearing each other to pieces, all between two embraces. The eighteenth century had consisted to a great extent of this comedy for three players, in which Poland and Turkey had paid the price in blood. And the law by which the children and servants of strong personalities are crushed ensured that for several decades after these three there was nothing. Napoleon filled the void. His adventure could never have taken the same course had he found himself opposed by one or two of these departed great rulers. A certain loneliness in the higher reaches seems to have condemned him to excess, precisely from 1805 onwards. And many, including Chateaubriand, dreamed in that year of the unprecedented page of history that might have been written, somewhere in the centre of Europe, had a meeting occurred between the four great ones who fashioned the modern west.

*   *   *   *

'In September '92,' Mouton reflected, 'Year I of the Republic, I had just put up my pips as a lieutenant in the Meurthe battalion . . . '

Jomini pointed with his chin at the bustling little outline of Napoleon in the distance, once again dismounted, who was crossing a field, his hands behind his back, indicating in person where pits should be dug to obstruct the enemy cavalry.

'And His Majesty, your colleague, was a lieutenant of artillery at Valence. But Catherine II still ruled over Russia, and the shades of Maria-Theresa and Frederick commanded the loyalty of Austria and Prussia. You see, my friend, one can make no sense of the past thirteen years of confused strife, of which we have now reached the culminating point—and from which we are unlikely to emerge for some time—if one fails to grasp that the so-called allied powers saw in the events in France above all a good opportunity to return to the attack and settle their own quarrels. That is why we overcame the first two coalitions without much difficulty. They marched against France, delighted with the chance to humiliate her, neither very quickly nor very slowly, not in order to save the Bourbon monarchy, so much detested once her docility had been secured, but with one eye on their neighbour, ready to squabble afresh over a piece of Silesia, a scrap of Balkan territory, dominion over Hanover, or the suzerainty of this or that petty princeling.'

Mouton indicated the huge reserve of soldiers of the line behind them:

'One unforeseen factor upset calculations somewhat: those hordes in clogs who sang the Marseillaise around the mills, in Champagne and Flanders. One can never foresee everything. Look how far they can go, now that they've got boots.'

'The second surprise,' Jomini went on: 'this passionate up-surge incarnated itself in a strange being, half flesh, half fish, half Jacobin, half Louis XIV, and a great strategist into the bargain. It will take years and years more of Allied conferences to integrate the Revolution and Napoleon into their universe, to weigh them at their true weight, to know their real strength and their real weakness. When that happens I'm afraid it will become easy for them to strangle them both together, by really joining forces all at the same time. The awakening will not be tomorrow.'

'You've thought a great deal about these matters, monsieur!'

Jomini straightened his shoulders, and gave free rein to his pedantic streak that had made him so many enemies. It was not every day that he had such an appreciative listener:

'I have just published a book in which I examine at length the state of Europe at the start of the Revolution. It is, if you like, the world of 1792 seen through the quizzing-glass of 1805. If we wish to understand the terrible clash that is awaiting us tomorrow in the shape of Russia, it is as well to recall that thirteen years ago, under the rule of the illustrious Catherine, she was in a state of repose resembling the sleep of a lion. The partition of Poland made it fair to assume that it would not be long before the north of Europe would erupt, and that the independence of the southern states would be threatened. The struggle with Sweden and the invasion of Turkey disclosed vast ambitions. The truce accorded to the latter power could not have been due to anything but the need to encourage by means of peace the progress of civilization, agriculture and population growth. Catherine was perceptive enough to realize that distant military expeditions were not the most certain way to increase the power of her empire, and that it was necessary first of all to bind together its huge provinces by populating the deserts that separated them and made communication almost impossible. She knew that the wealth of a nation springs from the wealth of its productivity and manpower rather than from the extension of its frontiers, and her system menaced nobody but posterity.'

'And Prussia? The Prussia of Valmy?'

'Governed by the memory of a hero, she had a ministry that was completely opportunist; but although they were still guided by the ideas of Frederick, they had inherited neither the genius nor the talent to know how to conduct themselves by the light of circumstances, rather than by the banal rules of custom. The object of her diplomacy was to be tactful towards France, to be wary of Austria, and to seize every opportunity to abase Russia in order to preserve her influence over the Germanic peoples ... And it is just this wavering course which makes it still uncertain even now against whom the Prussian cannon will thunder tomorrow or the day after.'

'Our most constant enemy has been Austria, surely—and she always will be.'

'Austria hankered after Silesia and seemed to be waiting for a favourable moment to re-establish the glory of her arms, a little tarnished in the Seven Years War. Preoccupied as she was with her Turkish ventures and her domestic quarrels, her politics were confused. Her government seems to have wanted at one and the same time to humiliate France, retake Alsace and Lorraine, dominate Italy, subjugate the German Empire, force Prussia back within her original boundaries, and partition Turkey-in-Europe as she had partitioned Poland ... '

'The result: we occupy Vienna!' concluded Mouton happily, clapping his hands all the more vigorously because he was anxious to stem the endless flow of Jomini's discourse, which had begun to be a little too much for him.

Napoleon, in the saddle again, turned towards his own camp, and the escorting *chasseurs* breathed a great sigh of relief. Since they had crossed the stream, below the village with the fiendish

name, Girziko . . . Gir-something-or-other, they had been
within reach of the Cossacks.

Jomini continued his flow:

'All this being granted, ten years of vicissitudes can then be
summed up with the aid of a few simple recollections, in order
to arrive at the year 1805.'

Mouton, wishing to show that he was no ignoramus, interrupted the flow with a schoolboy recital:

'The first coalition: Russia, Prussia, Austria, Spain, and England, unable to co-ordinate their efforts, fell to pieces after
threatening Paris. France emerged stronger and greater than
under Louis XIV; her "natural" frontiers had been reached and
passed. She forced Spain into an alliance and Prussia into
neutrality.'

'One must go to the root of matters, monsieur! Think for
a moment: by forcing the Convention into staining the Revolution with the mark of the Terror, the monarchs had succeeded in
giving the word a bloody connotation and in detaching the
middle class, Rousseau-ist and sentimental. Robespierre was defeated by this equivocation. A certain world-wide evolutionary
upsurge, or rather a certain rhythm within this upsurge, was
broken for ever at the Maison-Commune in Paris, on the 9th
Thermidor, Year II.'

'You are a philosopher in uniform. For my part I am content
to stick to a catalogue of military events. The second coalition:
in 1799, allied to Austria and England, Russia sent Suvorov as
far as Zürich. France at once had to cede Italy and part of
Switzerland. Finally, after Hohenlinden and Marengo, the coalition, undermined for a long time by the caprices of Paul I, the
mad Czar, son of Catherine, went into dissolution and capitulated. The Peace of Lunéville with Austria. The Peace of Amiens
with England.'

'But the contagion of absolutism, the virus of arbitrary power,
had filtered through the wall of arms. At the brink of the nineteenth century victorious France found herself saddled with a
regime more monarchical than if she had been conquered and
the antiquated "King in council" brought back from Coblenz.
Every stage of the war helped to prepare and then reinforce the
military dictatorship that Robespierre had predicted earlier on,

when he had so fiercely opposed the declaration of war. It turned out that instead of an obtuse general, a docile puppet in the hands of the speculators who were really ruling the country, they had a Man, half of whose virtues at least were "civilian"; it was Napoleon Bonaparte who gained from it all . . . '

The horses stumbled and panted up the little hill of Schlapanitz, behind the Man with the civilian virtues who had taken the bit between his teeth. Every minute counted now. Perhaps news of Davout awaited him at the camp.

'One word more,' said Mouton, both wearied and fascinated by Jomini's exposition. 'The Europe that faces us today is not that of '92. You would maintain, I presume, that she is in the process of developing herself in an astonishing way?'

'From a demographic point of view, it is a Europe in full expansion, and that is enough to indicate that all this belligerent commotion that disturbs it is a "malady of health". Russia has increased from fifteen million inhabitants under Peter the Great to thirty-two in 1801. Greater Austria has twenty-four. Well behind these colossi, Prussia, doubled by Frederick and now numbering six million souls, and Great Britain with ten million, have attained an equality of partnership, the one by the valour of its arms, the other by the importance of its commerce.'

'And us?'

'France numbers today twenty-five million inhabitants.'

Mouton turned round and surveyed the undulating countryside, coming increasingly into view as they climbed towards the Emperor's tent. On the Pratzen slopes, less than three miles away, the influx of Russians continued, like living lava.

'One would imagine *they* have no doubts about it all,' he said between his teeth.

'They have no doubts about it,' replied Jomini seriously. 'Their commanders haven't at any rate. The French have absolutely no idea that the whole of Europe believes they're finished. The cultivated man of the end of the eighteenth century, that's to say the well-informed man, whose customary language is our own, whether he is Bavarian, Roman or from Petersburg, saw the revolution not as the unexpected rejuvenation of France, but as the beginning of her end. And up to this year the average European has remained anchored to this view of matters.'

'What? In spite of Valmy?'

'In spite of Valmy, in spite of Fleurus, in spite of Rivoli, and in spite of Marengo.'

'In spite of Bonaparte?'

'In their eyes Bonaparte is no more than an accident. A temporary remission in the grangrene that is consuming France. A country where the street captures the palace and cuts off the head of its King is a country at the point of death. Their defeats, the warnings of their writers, or of their responsible diplomats, all this has not been enough to disturb the profound general conviction they have of French decadence.'

Sharp trumpet calls announced the arrival of the Emperor at his headquarters. The strong north wind, cold and dry, whipped the splendid standards of honour, where the eagle threatened with all his gilded claws. Mouton made haste: his presence was required near the Master. And it was only for his own benefit that Jomini concluded:

'Until this thrust right into the heart of Europe, which is awakening with an Emperor of the French stretching out his hand, after Vienna, for the universal throne: Charlemagne II. And it only took him a hundred days of campaigning to get there!'

PART II

THE HUNDRED DAYS THAT MADE
THE DAY

CHAPTER IV

BETWEEN ETERNITY, THE SEA
AND THE NIGHT

'All our troubles returned with the breaking of the Peace of Amiens . . .'

This disillusioned remark broke three months earlier from the lips of Maret, Napoleon's Secretary of State, the perfect type of Empire civil servant, with large spectacles on a pedantic face.

'You will never speak a truer word, dear fellow,' replied Talleyrand. 'One or two of these troubles, I might add, concern me directly: the Emperor, however submissive I may be to his outbursts, thinks of me as the man of the Franco-English entente and my portfolio of External Affairs hangs by a thread.'

The berlin that bore the two ministers under the burning sun of August was crossing a Holland shimmering and dressed over-all with tricolours. Sent for in haste from Paris, Maret and Talleyrand were trying to catch up with the Emperor, who was inspecting 'the extreme right of the Army of England'—the extreme left of which was in Brittany and the centre at Boulogne. The former, an extravagant admirer of Napoleon, was suspicious and shocked at the impertinence, very *grand seigneur*, with which the latter allowed himself to speak of the Master's doings. He was not exactly in the habit of seeking his company. But he was thankful enough today to profit from the exceptional comfort that Talleyrand, above all a man who knew how to live, insisted upon in his travelling carriage. Stretched indolently on cushions of brocaded damask, his left leg resting on a little bench made expressly for the purpose, his dressing-case and flagons of excellent wines within reach, in little cupboards fitted into the corners, the old Bishop of Autun provided for whoever wished to share his mobile *salon* the most rare of pleasures in that epoch of mutes: unfettered conversation.

'Ah, my friend, the Peace of Amiens was so much more than the Peace of Amiens! Several great minds sensed this, in England more than in France: Fox and Burke especially. The whole of the nineteenth century could have been shaped by it. The fate of the west lay there. Agreement between France and England would not only have been the natural meeting point of the Latin and Anglo-Saxon worlds but also of democracy, aristocracy and the constitutional monarchies. Instead of this, what remains? Each carries off between his teeth his little piece of the Declaration of Human Rights: the English liberty, we equality . . . And the Hundred Years War begins all over again.'

'Not to mention economic consequences,' breathed Maret, who dared to approve so long as nobody heard him. 'It is only with difficulty that people of quality can still get their coffee!'

'From that point of view the business is going to get worse. Individualism and competition will dominate the progress of mechanization, industrial development and scientific research.'

'What a strange man this Talleyrand is!' thought Maret. 'He holds forth with this weary elegance in every phrase and every gesture of his hand, as if exhausted by his own remarks, with the smile of a spoilt child, all powdered, all made up, all indolence, and all wit . . . And then suddenly his face takes on a look of surprising seriousness, as if shadowed by a passing cloud: a frustrated intellect behind a wall of disappointment.'

'Understand me well, Maret. Agreement between England, maritime, commercial, industrial, and France, agricultural and military, would have been, without exaggeration, the salvation of modern man.'

'Perhaps he assumed this manner on the few occasions when he had to preach from the pulpit . . . '

Already Talleyrand had once again taken refuge in irony.

'Of that great hope there remains a vast debris of dead leaves: all those twopenny souvenirs, the pipes, the scarves, the handkerchiefs, the plates stamped with Bonaparte or King George. There is enough to keep the junk shops going for a hundred years! The two peoples expressed the happiness that 1802 could have brought them. This prophetic vision was far from the minds of those who held the cards, for them as for us, and who turned the Peace of Amiens into one of the most vulgar games of poker. The French and English governments negotiated, concluded, interpreted and finally broke the treaty through limited minds, in the first rank of which one must place, well to the fore, Napoleon Bonaparte.'

'Whose agent you were, I believe!' Maret, terror-stricken, could not stop himself protesting. A silence ensued, during which the two men had time to go over in detail the circumstances that brought about the rupture of the Peace of Amiens, and thus provoked the third Coalition.

*   *   *   *

In 1802 France renounced in principle the overstepping of her natural frontiers: she gave up Switzerland, Holland, Italy. And Egypt, lost already. England relinquished Malta, Minorca, La Trinité (in Martinique), the Antilles . . . and Egypt, she too. But above all the matter was one of a double lowering of the flag. France renounced a certain insolence on land and England a certain domination at sea. However, England did not accept the fact that France kept Antwerp, and France could not tolerate that to all intents and purposes England retained her monopoly of colonial trade.

So the treaty was signed, but hearts were not in it; there was no process of pacification by which a truce such as this should be transformed rapidly into an alliance and become a co-operation under the threat of being broken. It was necessary, after 1803, to conclude a treaty of commerce, to lower customs duties, which put a mutual brake on trade, and to develop together certain colonial territories . . .

Instead, Bonaparte sent an expedition to recapture the island of San Domingo as a step towards the cruel re-establishment of slavery there; he proclaimed himself President of the cis-Alpine Republic; he intervened in Switzerland by supporting a movement among the cantons; and he instigated a complete upheaval in Germany, who by the Act of Mediation of February 25, 1803, conferred on him the suzerainty of the Confederation of the Rhine.

England kept Malta and did not evacuate Egypt except by slow degrees. The Tories were bent on war as an automatic reflex to their immediately threatened interests. In the French camp . . . Bonaparte confided in January 1803 to Thibaudeau: 'A First Consul is not like these kings by the grace of God, who regard their States as an inheritance . . . He needs renown and, as a consequence, war.'

Matters deteriorated. Positions hardened. Journalists on either side of the Channel crossed pens. Then came the public poses and the famous scene between the First Consul and the English ambassador, Whitworth, in the great *salon* of the Tuileries; this was but the outward indication of the state of war within. The struggle now was for the best position from which to force the issue, and each side manoeuvred to make the *other* appear to be the aggressor. Napoleon understood this; and England fell into the trap with surprising clumsiness: she made a brutal attack on French vessels in mid-ocean and without warning, which has given disputatious historians the chance to glut their appetite inexhaustibly concerning true responsibility for the rupture. In fact it is strictly divided. It was London who drew the sword, but Paris had piled up the provocation. Pitt maintained that he was concerned with safeguarding European equilibrium, but Bonaparte retorted with reason that that of the sea had long since been violated. Two imperialisms of ill-repute were confronting each other, when the moment was ripe for harmony between two great peoples.

Here, again, lies Napoleon's personal responsibility. No single English political figure determined the policy of his country, and it was an obscure conjunction of forces that returned Pitt to power. Bonaparte in 1802 was all powerful in France, *above all as far as peace was concerned*. It is impossible to analyze with any degree of certainty the deep reasons that made him, at the risk of his power and his glory, throw himself again into war. One can only exclude hatred of England; he was no kind of Anglophobe, and often admitted the fascination this strange nation had for all lovers of liberty. He merely did not fail, and this was quite fair, to underline the discrepancy between the façade and the reality, between the principles and the practice, which was to make it throughout the century the home of hypocrisy in the eyes of the ill-disposed. The aristocracy had just voted over the course of several years some agricultural laws that were truly radical: the redistribution and reclamation of land, the adoption of scientific methods of cultivation, and measures to increase yields. At the same time, a whole proletariat, freed by the disappearance of a certain intermediate rural class, drifted towards the towns, and this coincided with the extraordinary 'spasm' of progress, industrial and mechanical, brought about by British skill, half a century ahead of all other countries. The appearance of the flying shuttle, the multiplication of spindles, finally the adoption in 1785 of the power loom: and behold the commanding English textile industry. Already, thanks to Wilkinson and Watt, came the pressing influx of a source of energy that would completely transform human technique: that of steam.

. . . And yet electoral corruption of the most refined sort, symbolized by the system of 'Rotten Boroughs', kept effective power in the hands of a narrow, closed caste, hidebound, supercilious and uncultivated. A highly sectarian puritanism, side by side as always with an astonishing private dissoluteness, reigned at Court and in the highest circles. It engendered as a consequence the stultification of 'the lower orders', who were kept in poverty and illiteracy. And the complete absence of a middle class—a Third Estate—condemned England for a long time to a certain disequilibrium. It really was still Old England that provided an easy target for the railing, a little forced, of the Paris *Moniteur* against 'perfidious Albion'.

In every case Napoleon was not carried naturally into declarations of war. Whence came then his growing tendency to rupture which finally led him to take the most heavy responsibility for it in history? A taste for the profession of arms? A thirst to re-establish his military glory, a little tarnished—only in his own eyes and in those of his entourage—by his personal mistakes in the approaches to Marengo? A call already, by his unconscious, towards universal power?

Perhaps merely fatalism. In May 1803 he let slip a disillusioned explanation in front of Roederer:

'It is in the nature of things, the logic of events, to continue the struggle between past and present, for this firm coalition amongst our adversaries obliges us to fight them in order to avoid being annihilated.'

That, at least, was his conscious explanation for the inextinguishable war into which he was plunging, for life or for death, France and his own destiny.[1]

*   *   *   *

Maret, concerned to make a point, reopened the discussion when the two dignitaries, having failed to find the Emperor at his camp in Holland, to which he had decided not to betake himself at the last minute after having summoned half his advisers there, had resumed their travels, post-haste for the headquarters at Boulogne.

'You must admit it: for eighteen months now the English have been unable to sleep quietly in their beds! This hasn't happened since the time of the Armada! Eh? Why the sour face, Monsieur de Talleyrand?'

'Because, if we are to be frank, we must recognize that nobody on our side has taken the invasion of England seriously, although everybody has pretended remarkably well to believe in it.'

'But monsieur, you have after all heard the cheers of the men, seen them already aboard the barges, burning with impatience. . . .'

'I said that nobody believed it. I meant nobody of consequence. I did not say the soldiers. Did you believe it? You, Maret?'

'To tell the truth, I . . . I thought that . . . '

'You did not believe it any more than I did. And somebody else believed it even less than the two of us together: the Emperor.'

'There I must protest! I am well placed to know his correspondence and his intentions! Well, monsieur, scarcely a week after setting up his headquarters at Pont-de-Briques, he wrote to Marshal Brune: "I have around me here more than 120,000 men and 3,000 barges and long-boats waiting only for a favour-

---

[1] In the last analysis it is to his 'ambition' that one is forced to return. Contemporaries, however, who had before their eyes the theatrical apparatus of a wealth heavy and crude in its novelty, the gallant adventures, the quarrels of a rapacious family and the thievishness of their servants, devalued it, without denying the genius, to the level of the ordinary run of men. At this distance the picture clears and yields its secret: the heroic lure of danger, the bewitching seduction of a dream, the irresistible pressure of a temperament.' Georges Lefebvre: *Napoleon*, op. cit.

able wind to bear the imperial eagle to the Tower of London . . . "
And he has told me countless times what he wrote to Admiral
de la Touche-Tréville in the same vein: "Let us be masters of the
Straits for six hours, and we are masters of the world".'

'I have heard a hundred such remarks, and it is part of my job
to disseminate them to the four corners of Europe. But in the
end only the English have allowed themselves to be taken in.
Napoleon has thus lent substance to our dream—a spectacular
dream displayed superbly from Brest to Utrecht.'

With a wave, Talleyrand indicated the camp at Zeist, which
they were leaving behind them. Marshal Marmont had succeeded in creating there a model of organization, indeed of
recreation, for the soldier, the more remarkable since what was
virtually a military town had been set down in the midst of
swamps and fevers. The long rows of its white tents, gleaming
bright under the sun, stood out in the distance in the middle of
the plain. The two ministers had been conducted at length by
the Franco-Dutch general, Dumonceau, round the camp of three
divisions of infantry, two French and one Batavian. A little
sententious, this old citizen-soldier of the Revolution had drawn
their attention to the tall pine in front of each row of tents,
which, stripped of its lower branches and retaining only a tuft
of greenery at the top, made a fair substitute, they were told, for
the palms of Egypt, 'of which many of the corps reunited in the
camp had a glorious recollection and were pleased to find a
reminder'.

The ears of Maret and Talleyrand still rang with the long
account by the brave general, who allowed them to miss
nothing:

'You notice, gentlemen, how this long line of pointed trees
helps to break the monotonous uniformity of the encampment
and lighten its aspect, together with other decorative features,
always very ingenious, sometimes even artistic, by which the
officers' tents above all are surrounded, such as, for instance,
shady nooks with couches and chaises-longues set in greensward,
little gardens decorated with flowers, vases and statuettes, ponds
with goldfish and model ducks, boats and ships, representations
of chateaux and military fortresses, perfect copies in every
detail, in every proportion, equipped with drawbridges,

stockades, battlements and various other accessories, even down to artillery and a garrison, provided in toy form by the community of Moravian Brothers of Zeist. In short, an infinite number of creations of every kind, very interesting to see, with which the officers as well as the soldiers *occupy their leisure*. From where you stand you can see the tent of General Marmont, placed at the back in the middle of the camp, equally remarkable for its size and proportions, the whole giving a monumental impression, made up of a very high central dome, linking two wings which contain, besides sleeping quarters and a reception hall, a huge dining-room. The two great masts, set by the entrance, carry the unfurled colours of France and Batavia . . . '

'In brief . . . ', Talleyrand concluded, 'now that you have seen the camp, you have seen as I have that the picture is more pastoral than military. Eh! Months and months of practice would have to be gone through in order to achieve those "six hours of mastery of the straits", which even then would not be sufficient with any certainty to transport soldiers, cannon, horses and supplies to the English side, and granting this miracle, it would leave France without arms at the mercy of a Continent inadequately subdued. The imperial eagle on the Tower of London, but the two-headed eagle of Austria on that of Notre-Dame . . . The exchange is enough to make Napoleon hesitate!'

'Admit that he at least conceived an inspired operation at sea, to get his fleets to manoeuvre from Toulon to Guadeloupe like so many battalions over a hundred square miles. If only Villeneuve could lure Cornwallis and Nelson away to the devil, then return to join Ganteaume and appear in the Channel freed from cruising English ships . . . '

'I don't deny that at certain moments the dream has assumed splendid colours, and ended by acquiring form and substance for posterity. But Napoleon has always felt it melt away at the touch of that capricious element that has denied him all respect : the sea. And because he cannot lash at it with his riding-whip, he has sought long before now to expend his rage upon those strange beings fashioned by it, whose eyes do not please him, because they have been washed free from a certain obsequiousness: the men of the sea. You will scarcely have forgotten, any more than anyone else who was there, the famous scene with Admiral Bruix?'

A painful memory forced itself upon the two men. That abrupt voice stuttering with anger:

'Monsieur l'Amiral, why have my orders not been carried out? I insist on reviewing the fleet at once.'

'Sire, a terrible storm is rising. Your Majesty can see it, as I can. Would you wish therefore to risk needlessly the lives of many brave men?'

'Monsieur, I have given my orders. Once again, why haven't you carried them out? The consequences concern me alone. Obey!'

'Sire, I shall not obey.'

All honour to the navy! This was the only time in the whole triumphant life of Napoleon that this unbelievable phrase issued from the mouth of a man in his presence. He had advanced on the admiral, riding-crop raised:

'Monsieur, you are insubordinate.'

Bruix had recoiled, white as a sheet, his hand on the hilt of his sword:

'Sire, take care!'

'Vice-admiral Magon, you will see to the immediate execution of the movement I ordered. As for you, sir, you will leave Boulogne within twenty-four hours, and you will retire to Holland. Go!'

The review had taken place after all, in the storm. Twenty long-boats capsized. On the following day two hundred bodies were counted on the shore.

' . . . He is nevertheless the best of men, when not possessed by anger,' said Maret meekly, when they had been able to shake off the silence this terrible memory had imposed on them. 'You know that as well as I do.'

'Of course,' said Talleyrand. 'And even Napoleon is consoling himself for his intemperance in poetry: another proof that he is occupied in passing the time, that is to say, for him, in losing it. You are not unaware of the confidence with which the Empress deigns to honour me? She was unable to restrain herself from allowing me to read a passage in a letter he wrote to her recently, after another storm. I made a copy of it: it could be by Chateaubriand!

' "It was a wonderful sight! The tolling of the alarm bell, the coast a line of fires, the sea foaming and the men throughout the night in uncertainty and fear. But between eternity, the sea and the night there hovered a guardian angel. Everybody was saved and I went to bed feeling that I had lived through a dream, epic and romantic, an experience that made me feel I was alone in the world." '

'That's magnificent! What a great man!'

'Unfortunately, he is not entirely alone in the world. Nelson also exists somewhere, and we are never very sure where. Because he has just intercepted Admiral Villeneuve and kept him shut up in the roads of Ferrol first, and finally Cadiz, 120,000 men are going to perform without warning the greatest about-turn in history.'

'Are you sure of that?'

'There can be no other outcome. You know what despatches we are taking him. But the confirmation of the Austrian aggression and the stripping of our fleet are at bottom no more than a pretext for the Emperor to deliver with lightning speed a decision matured over a month ago. I would gladly have said over a year ago. Come now! Here we are, August 11, 1805, the year that was to have seen the taking of London, and Napoleon has not spent in all more than *twelve days* in camp at Boulogne! The rest of the time he has been running around getting himself crowned King of Italy, and has divided his days between Malmaison, the Tuileries, Saint-Cloud and Fontainebleau. Is this the attitude of a conqueror all set for the decisive leap? The truth is he has gone off Boulogne, as one abandons lost illusions, or as one avoids running down a blind alley.'

'It is a matter in which at this summer's end he has little choice left: for eighteen months, the English papers have been riddling him with their shafts, presenting him with his feet in the water, arms crossed, facing the cliffs of Albion. This image is invading Europe, filtering through the frontiers of the Empire and beginning to inflame public opinion. It is up to him to take the leap, at the risk of losing everything, or lose worse still: face.'

M. de Talleyrand stretched himself out comfortably on his seat, purring like a cat:

'The sword of Austria and Russia has come at just the right moment to cut the Gordian knot. The third Coalition has been formed. The whole European continent is daring to rise against France, whose fleet is bottled up at Ferrol. Don't you think we should take our afternoon nap? This heat is unbearable.'

*   *   *   *

The third Coalition consisted of first Russia, then Austria, plus English aid, plus Sweden, who never played an effective part, plus the *perhaps* of Prussia, worse at some moments for France than open hostility.

It was inaugurated after April 11, 1805, by the secret treaty of alliance, called the *Convention of St Petersburg*, between England and Russia (Napoleon never knew anything about it), which consisted of some official articles, concerning 'the restoration to Europe of the peace, independence and happiness of which she has been deprived by the unbounded ambition of the French government'. Its aim was to secure the evacuation of Hanover and north Germany by French troops, the independence of Holland and Switzerland, the restoration of the King of Sardinia to his realm, the elimination of all French influence in Italy. But the Convention also contained some secret articles designed to re-confine France within her limits of 1791, by the amputation of Savoy, the county of Nice and the territories beyond the Moselle.

England's motives are known.

What of Russia's? First and foremost a vague feeling, basically obscure, coming from the depths of the unconscious of that great people, who felt the need to test their new-found cohesion. The longing to act. To get themselves esteemed, respected and recognized by Europe. 'We are not Asiatics'—meaning 'we are not savages'. Russia had an immense desire to believe in herself, like an adolescent who rushes about, fists at the ready, to reassure himself in his own eyes more than in those of others. And this was perhaps why she identified herself so readily with her young Czar, that over-age adolescent, a mixture of shrewdness and generosity, of restlessness and timidity, Alexander I, the

Archangel whose hands were stained with his father's blood—oh, only a few drops, but still . . .

This father, Paul I, son of Catherine the Great, was undeniably unbalanced, but no less certainly a liberal, a reformer, and a convert to the *entente* with Napoleon. All that remained was for the aristocracy of Europe to declare him a dangerous lunatic, and for some of his courtiers to strangle him one fine night in 1802.

As a reaction, and by design, Alexander was a Francophobe and voluntarily undertook to be the Messiah charged with finally settling accounts with the Revolution. He resumed the policy of his grandmother Catherine, who adored him, and sought above all to play a role as supreme arbiter in Europe, faithful to that fascination of the West which had been the dominant motive of Czars since Peter the Great. It was thus he who was at the bottom of the war. In fact, of all the powers, Russia was the only one who had never agreed to make peace with 'Robespierre's' successor. The strange escapade of Suvorov, in 1799, who conquered northern Italy but was beaten by Masséna at Zürich, and retreated in as formidable manner as he had come, was still on his mind. They were convinced, at St Petersburg, that the Russian army had only to appear in full force in order to efface that dubious beginning, or rather to confirm its impressive aspects.

But, for Russia to take Bonaparte by the throat, it was necessary for her to cross Germany.

Which Germany? Broadly speaking there were three. First, along the French border, a soft cushion made up of a sprinkling of states, Swabia, Franconia, the Rhineland, swarming with needy princes hard put to preserve a few acres of vineyards and hunting rights. Beyond them, Bavaria, Württemberg, Saxony, like giants in a kingdom of dwarfs—and, in fact, their 'Elector' was to acquire a crown for a hundred years in the great prize-giving that was about to begin.

This Germany was hypnotized by Napoleon and would remain so the more powerful he became. Through fear most of all, through close proximity — but also through a certain sentimental attraction, a need to avoid becoming a purely Teutonic Germany and to 'stick to Latinity'. Through their search for a protector against those other two Germanies who, sooner or later, would establish their complete hegemony over the whole Saxon area, and who had been struggling for this, openly or surreptitiously, ever since Frederick: Prussia and Austria.

Russian diplomacy would therefore gain nothing from the states bordering France. On the other hand, she knew well that Prussia and Austria were quite prepared to join her, the principal obstacle being the profound distrust each had for the other.

The natural trend of history led Alexander to approach Prussia first. There were no problems between her and Russia, whereas with Austria the whole eastern question remained poisoned by Balkan influences, the division of bits of decaying Turkey, indeed certain Mediterranean areas. Had not Paul I had his eye on Corfu? And furthermore, there was some osmosis between the governing centres of Potsdam and St. Petersburg, exchanges of military missions, merchants, and blood by marriages. Finally, Alexander was handsome, his mysticism, still within bounds, in no way interfered with his feminine conquests, and Prussia in 1805 was an attractive, frustrated woman: Queen Louise.

The young King Frederick-William III was not a nonentity, but an erratic, meddlesome person, authoritarian by fits and starts, and in little matters. In the great ones, he was indecision itself. He was virtuous, but limited, and of a distressing ugliness. In full bloom, alluring and wilful, the Queen was driven to mild hysteria by her husband's silliness—and to the effective government of the kingdom by the homage of the courtiers and the adulation of the military party, who played on her hostility towards France. She exercised it therefore, and nobody was unaware of this, except the King. Ever since a romantic interview between the sovereigns at Memel, where the harmony of political opinion had assumed some of the character of a *ménage à trois*, a sort of amorous friendship had bound the Queen and the Czar. And on May 24, 1804, a defensive alliance was concluded between the two powers, which seemed capable of evolving quite naturally into an offensive alliance when the moment arose. Prussia would gain from the defeat of France by being able to establish herself firmly on the right bank of the Rhine, and above all by the possession of Hanover, with which she was obsessed at the opening of the century: that rich relic of England situated in the north of Germany and ensuring a decisive influence over her for whoever held it.

But that was just it: for the moment, Hanover was occupied by French troops, and this enabled Talleyrand to check the unleashing of the Prussian war-machine by laying down his ace of trumps:

'Stay neutral, and you will get it for nothing.'

The prospect of seeing her war aims fulfilled without war was enough to make any nation think, even if she did believe herself to have the best army in the world, above all when it was a matter of provoking Napoleon and of managing a tricky mobilization under the surveillance of his northern army corps, commanded by Bernadotte and Marmont, who could pounce at any moment on Berlin . . . And the 'French party', which still had some influence, even near the Queen, pointed out that it would be dangerous to pull chestnuts out of the fire for Austria . . .

Prussia therefore did not declare war on the French Empire, but remained threatening. It was quite a pantomime during the month of September in Berlin, where the court chamberlains had the greatest difficulty in avoiding an encounter in the same *salons* between the two French envoys, Duroc and de Laforest, come to offer Hanover on a plate, and the emissaries of the Czar, d'Alopeus and Dolgoruki, charged with bringing pressure to bear for the passage of a Russian army across Silesia. There followed some epic side-stepping, and the necessity for the King to play Janus to them, well supported in this by his principal minister, Hardenburg, 'the well-disposed minister', as he was called in Europe. By dint of balancing affability and half-promises, the Prussian government achieved the miracle of making each of the adversaries believe they were on the point of gaining the day.

Faced with Prussia's neutrality, Russia was obliged to appeal to Austria, who for a long time had not seemed much more hopeful. Since the Peace of Lunéville, she had been fully occupied in remarshalling her forces. It was she who had borne the brunt of the first two coalitions. For want of taxing the privileged, her finances were in a serious state of delapidation, which was only disguised for the time being by the English subsidies. Francis, whom one may label the First or the Second, according to whether he proclaimed himself Emperor of Germany still or only of Austria, was pompous, superficial and a mere cypher. But he wanted to have a finger in every pie, and his main preoccupation was to avoid whatever occurred to the outstanding ability of his brother, Archduke Charles. A large part of his policy was thus determined by the opinions of the latter, but *a contrario*. Charles recommended an overhaul of the governmental machinery? Affairs would continue to be run as in the days of Maria-Theresa. And since Charles wanted an understanding with France, Francis inclined towards renewing the war, in spite of the advice of Cobenzl, the best of his ministers. Gentz, an odd character, an intriguer up to his eyes in debt, who possessed the knack of making himself believed to be indispensible, was beginning to exercise a subterranean influence in the corridors of the Hofburg. He was in favour of the highest bidder, hence of England. But all this was not enough to bring about an Austrian act of aggression, seared as she had been by the previous campaigns, and bearing still in her flesh the claw-marks of the eagle. In spite of Russia's handsome offer of 100,000 men at the first onslaught, the prospect of a fresh encounter with the terrible soldiers of Hohenlinden and Rivoli had made Francis recoil and say as recently as January 1804: 'France has done me no harm'.

At this, Napoleon had proclaimed himself King of Italy and seized Genoa.[1]

*　　　*　　　*　　　*

Talleyrand and Maret had found here their main topic of conversation during the last hours of their journey: Napoleon was in fact at Boulogne, on August 13th, when they reached it with the despatches confirming definitely that the war party had triumphed in Austria: on June 17th, the 'Aulic Council', that is to say, the Crown Council at Vienna, had decided to join the Anglo-Russian alliance. On July 16th, Marshals Winzegerode

---

[1] It is astonishing that hostile historians always pinpoint his mistake of 1808, the seizure of Spain, and neglect this one.

and Mack had submitted to their sovereign their plan of campaign for the invasion of France through the Black Forest.

'The trouble all comes from that great cry we raised last May 26th in Milan cathedral,' said Talleyrand. 'It was still—the irony of it—the 6th Prairial, Year XIII . . . '

'We? . . . '

'I should have said He: "*Dio mi la diede! Guar à chi la toccherà!*"[1] You remember? As he helped himself so generously to the crown of the kings of Lombardy. The scene was magnificent. Better organized, more moving than the Coronation in Paris. But not one of us had the courage to reply: "Alas! Beware of yourself!" For this was, after all, a war-cry to Austria. Until he took possession of the crown of Italy, Napoleon had been able to appear as the liquidator of the quarrel between the Revolution and Europe. Nothing compelled him to endorse the cheques of the Convention and the Directory.'

'But surely,' Maret protested, 'he couldn't relinquish Antwerp, Holland, or Turin, or Milan.'

'Under what compulsion? French public opinion? It was he who made it. The army? It was in his hands. His entourage? I was not the only one to counsel moderation.'

'But he was bound to those who supported France, to Melzi and other leaders of the cis-Alpine republic. How could he abandon them to the vengeance of Austria?'

'We are alone in this carriage, Maret. Let me look you straight in the face and ask you if you really believe that it is through sensitivity to others, or a feeling of solidarity with them, that Napoleon Bonaparte has ever performed a political action.'

Having made his point, Talleyrand continued gravely:

'Nothing, moreover, prevented him from treating with Austria in order that her influence and that of France might divide between them a northern Italy neutralized on the Swiss model, thus obtaining every guarantee of security for the liberated. In any event he could have temporized, preserved the status quo and retained, although Emperor of the French, his necessarily provisional title of President of the Italian Republic. Now, by this sudden flare up of his ambition, the European

[1] 'God has given it to me! Let him beware who would lay hands on it!'

quarrel has changed its nature. The sovereigns had not been very happy about continuing an anti-revolutionary crusade against a France grown sober. But in this summer of 1805, the grounds for war, of the anti-republicans, have become anti-Bonapartist. The point of view has shifted. The fight is no longer for or against novel ideas, but for or against his dynasty. Make no mistake about it: there lies the great danger. Napoleon has given the Coalition a moral force that up till now it had lacked.'

'What's bitten him then, do you think?'

Talleyrand shrugged his shoulders:

'Some claim that he wanted at all costs to provoke a Continental aggression in order to extricate himself from the camp at Boulogne. Nothing he has said suggests that one can attribute to him such Machiavelism. But since the spring we have all heard from him fearful words that are enough to form a diagnosis concerning his mental development: it is the beginning of megalomania. You were present when he said, in front of five or six dignitaries: "There will be no peace in Europe except under a single ruler, under an emperor who would have kings as his officers, who would distribute kingdoms to his lieutenants . . . "'

Maret hung his head and admitted:

'And in the same month, alas, he let slip this little sally during a philosophical discussion: "The job of God-the-Father? I wouldn't want it. It's a dead end."'

CHAPTER V

'WE MAY FRIGHTEN THEM TOO MUCH'

'Treason! Infamous conduct!'

On August 13, 1805, Napoleon treated his entourage to the spectacle, always highly unpleasant, of one of his unbridled rages. The sea was calm outside, in the roads of Boulogne. Here, the storm was indoors; his voice shrill, his words tumbling over each other, the little man was pouring out his anger, both querulous and caustic, as he strode up and down in every direction and seemed ready to smash whatever came to hand, human or inanimate. Admiral Decrès, minister for naval affairs, silently bowed his large head, on which he carefully cultivated a rebellious lock to heighten his resemblance to the Emperor. Throughout his life, in fact, Decrès was to bow assiduously. He was a remarkable Court navigator: servile before his sovereign and harsh towards the weak. Today, Napoleon was unleashing before him and ten other witnesses two years of pent-up rancour against the sea and sailors. He had a ready-made scapegoat: Admiral Villeneuve, of whom they had just heard that he had taken refuge at Cadiz with the Franco-Spanish fleet.

'He's a miserable wretch, who should be discharged with ignominy! A coward! That man would sacrifice anything so long as he saved his skin!'

A shudder of disapproval ran through the horror-stricken group of spectators. Villeneuve was known to be a brave man: his service record under fire was one of the most honourable. It was true that he had shown himself to be pusillanimous before Nelson, but that was due to the terrible responsibility with

72

which he had been invested. And who would dare to maintain that, even with Jean-Bart or de Tourville at his disposal, Napoleon would have succeeded in holding the Channel for the six days, at least (and not the six hours that he spoke of so lightly), necessary for the passage of the 'Army of England'? The hour for taking London had failed to arrive. Hence the violence of his anger, tinged with a touch of histrionics for the gallery:

'Monsieur Decrès, I give you explicit orders to write to Villeneuve that I consider him to be the most shameful coward.' [1]

Bruix would undoubtedly have protested. He was in exile. Decrès bowed even deeper, and would obey. Napoleon discharged a few more random accusations into the audience chamber, seemed to want to have a go at Talleyrand, impassive, at Berthier, who was biting his finger-nails, at Duroc, at Caulaincourt—and surprised them all once again. He stopped short, and looked at them out of the corner of his eye, to make quite sure of the theatrical effect he was about to produce, which he had no doubt cherished for a long time. He wanted to give to his complete change of intention—and front—all the solemnity of one of the most spectacular dramatic moments of history.

There, he abruptly left them all and passed into the adjoining apartment: his map room. He merely beckoned after him one of the most inconspicuous amongst the assembled dignitaries: a somewhat pale, somewhat shrunken fifty-year-old, with the unhealthy look of the overworked and eyes that were always anxious. He made him sit down at a desk, amongst the outspread maps, took a few more paces, but quietly this time, to and fro, and finally threw out the sharp order:

'Monsieur Daru, write . . . '

Why Daru? The Intendant-General of the Grand Army was an important person in the imperial hierarchy, and the Emperor had at his disposal four secretaries better trained to catch in flight the mumbled dialogue he kept up with invisible

[1] When Villeneuve's body was discovered several months later, at Rennes, in a hotel bedroom bespattered with blood, the surgeons reported that he had transfixed himself three times with his own sword. There are words that can kill.

speakers as he marched about tirelessly, hands behind his back, and turn it into correspondence. But he needed a special witness in order, through him, to give confidence to his entourage. When Daru left the map room, utterly amazed, his hand numb from six hours of unbroken dictation and his head buzzing with the movements of all the regiments that had just been crossing it from west to east, he would be well able to testify that the decision to march into Germany was quite the opposite of an improvisation.

Stendhal has portrayed Daru in a remarkably accurate passage:

'The Emperor had had the good fortune to meet Count Daru, the former supply officer of Masséna's army, at Zürich. This remarkable man, a prodigy of method and work, was timid in everything concerning politics, and was above all a great enemy of the Jacobins, who, during the Terror, had thrown him into prison. Under the title of *Intendant-General*, the Emperor had charged Count Daru with a good many of the functions of Chief of Staff. Only troop movements were left to the latter (Berthier), who was still at the head of his forces.

'Daru dealt with: 1. Supply; 2. Army finances; 3. Conquered countries, divided into administrative regions.

'Administrators were drawn from amongst the auditors of the Council of State. It is clear that the management of supplies and the conquered countries was linked inevitably and continually with troop movements. M Daru held endless conferences with the Prince, the Chief of Staff, and dared to let him know the truth, which was often not welcome.

'The misfortunes of the army, springing from complete lack of system in its details, provoked bouts of anger in Count Daru, whose bluntness became celebrated in the army. What was unique in this epoch, he dared to stand up to the marshals. He was of strict integrity: [1] as a consequence the Emperor made

[1] Alas! Historical criticism during the past twenty years, by persistently sounding the clear waters of this mirror of honesty, has revealed there some murky depths. The remarkable network of royalist espionage, directed by Count d'Antraigues, which in these particular years passed on all information to the Czar, received a large number of reports from the Emperor's entourage. A strict process of elimination has revealed that, for the period with which

him an allowance of 66,000 francs a year; and on every New Year's Day gave him a present of 10,000 francs in cash.'

For the moment M Daru had instructions to take pen in hand, and he experienced one of the most poignant emotions of his life, so much so that he would be able to recall the scene in every detail fifteen years later.

Napoleon dictated.

Leaving on one side all that had just been exasperating him, abandoning projects contemplated for two years, to which he had devoted much care, energy and money, he entered without further ado a completely new order of ideas with the composure of someone playing chess.

'Monsieur Daru, write . . . '

One after the other, welling up from a spring, came all the necessary orders for the movements that were to transport to the heart of Germany the army strung out along the coast of France, Belgium and Holland. They included everything, they foresaw everything, the number of marches, the position of every corps and its destination, the duration of each day's march, billeting, routes, points at which waterways were to be crossed . . .

It was astounding. But it was not miraculous. If one visualizes the scene without his staff, that is to say, without the work-room so wonderfully devised by Napoleon to raise to the maximum his own efficiency, one is in the realm of pure myth, in which the imperial monster is then imagined, eyes closed, drawing from his memory the least significant battalion and the succession of the stage-post relays. In fact, what is to be admired here is system. Napoleon was able to dictate without stopping the order of march of 150,000 men from the Channel to the Rhine, and then the Danube, because he had all the materials for the job up to date and on hand. His bureaucratic side flowered visibly in the dictation to Daru. The victories of Ulm and, to a lesser extent, of Austerlitz, were victories first of all of well maintained card-indexes and registers.

we are concerned, the principal source of information came through Daru's father, ' . . . if not from Daru himself', some would add. But this is impossible to verify in the present state of research.

The whole task evolved on the basis of huge maps prepared by a sort of obscure topographical genius called Bacler d'Albe, who spent his nights sticking in pins with red and black heads to indicate the positions occupied by the troops, French and enemy. Chalks in hand he then threw into relief by coloured shading the lines of the rivers, mountains or frontiers that had most significance for the problem to be resolved. Finally, he prepared calculations of distances, indicated the scale and opened a pair of compasses near at hand.

Only then did the Emperor intervene, making great strides with the compasses and scattering the pins, all while listening to d'Albe's report summarizing the situation. The large size of the maps often forced the two men into a whole series of contortions and crawlings in order to remain masters of the conquered territory. More than once, stretched out across the huge table, they suddenly let out an exclamation scarcely in accordance with protocol when their skulls collided in an unforeseen scuffle.

So much for geography. As for the secret of the whereabouts of the army in Napoleon's mind, it lay in a pile of bound memorandum books scattered on the table, which he consulted almost every minute:

'Each compartment of his memory had its supplement in a booklet, and he excelled at making use of this resource. His office thus became a veritable keyboard where the strings of government seemed to end, and alone, with a secretary, he set in vibration whichever it pleased him to touch.

'Each minister submitted booklets drawn up according to models Napoleon himself had laid down; nothing might be altered in the framework, or in the arrangement of the contents, unless it were done by his order. It was necessary that he should know better than anyone what was to be found there and that he should be able to consult them with his eyes shut. Every fortnight, every month at the latest, these booklets were renewed: they were replaced by others that had in the meantime been brought up to date.' [1]

[1] *Mémoires du Baron Fain.*

So if we really wish to understand the facility of that memorable dictation to Daru, we must get hold of four of those little books bound in red morocco on the Emperor's desk, the thickest, the most thumbed, those of the minister for war, which represented the labours of two or three overworked clerks:

'In the booklet by numerical order, each regiment was given under its number: it had its folio, and in the columns that subdivided its strength were to be found the names of the colonel, the major and the other senior officers;

'—a summary of the encounters in which the regiment had distinguished itself;

'—in which army, in which actual division, each combat battalion had been employed;

'—the location assigned for its depot;

'—the strength of the regiment in effectives and in men at present under arms;

'—the roll of the injured and sick in hospital;

'—the number of recruits assigned to the regiment under the year's conscription;

'—finally, an indication of the departments that were to provide this recruitment.

'Another was the booklet by military divisions. Here, the point of view was local: each military division constituted a horizon; the first opened the book and the last closed it.

'Further still, the booklet by army corps represented another mirror; there, the combatants were viewed, enumerated and sub-divided as in their camps.

'In the booklet on personnel all the officers were portrayed, as in a public gallery, from the most celebrated down to the most obscure. Their service records formed the basis of the articles; one could see there by what campaigns, in which armies, by what services each had been promoted. Age, wounds, present function or place of retirement were all recorded.'

So much for his army, and for the terrain over which he was preparing to advance it. But there was still one unknown factor in the equation: the movements of the enemy. Would he risk at random the most perfect military force the world had known since Rome? Far from it: what stupefied his contemporaries most, and made them exclaim about his knack of divination, was that he foresaw the Austrian and Russian plans of campaign, knew the positions they would occupy in a week or a fortnight's time, the routes they would take, and calculated the overall economy of their forces. Miracle? Almost. But one that had nothing supernatural about it. The part played by intuition is undeniable; it merely served, however, to bind together elements already assembled and to provide support for the decision. Here again, everything was contained in a card-index placed on his desk within reach of his hand, which was born of a letter written by the Emperor to Berthier a month earlier:

'My friend, I beg you to let me know whether you have arranged for someone who knows German to follow the movements of the Austrian regiments and sort them into the compartments of a box you were to have had made for the purpose.

'The name and the number of each regiment should be written on a playing card, and the compartment changed according to changes of position. The Austrian regiments have been dispersed, into Italy, in the Tyrol, to camp at Wels and in Bohemia. Have my various ministers written to, in Vienna, München, Salzburg, Dresden, Ratisbon, and Berne, and let subscriptions be taken out for the German newspapers of these towns for the person entrusted with the job. All the German papers resound with nothing but the names and movements of Austrian regiments. This matter is very important.

'I should like you to let me have on Monday the box that I am to keep in which the distribution of regiments will be accurately made.'

The military conflagration in the autumn of 1805 had thus been prepared log by log with a research almost maniacal in its precision.

Nothing further remained but for the spark to flash out: 'Monsieur Daru, write . . . '[1]

From time to time, Napoleon stopped in front of a gigantic map (ten feet by seven!) which, hastily unrolled, covered one of the walls of the room, on top of that of the Pas-de-Calais and the south coast of England, which there had not yet been time to remove. This was the map of Europe in 1805.

The only things of significance to his scrutiny were the main physical barriers: the chains of mountains and the big rivers. It differed from the Europe that was in the making in the fluidity of its political frontiers. Until Napoleon, only the clerks at the Foreign Office knew the exact boundaries of Austria, Prussia, Turkey, Russia. Did one even know just how far France extended, who rubbed shoulders with Holland? The adventure of nationalities had scarcely begun, and the race was still open.

It was hardly frontiers that disturbed Napoleon, in his first glance over the whole 'European conspiracy'. Of little concern to him were the colours of the uniforms. He saw the whole French army stretched out along the coast of the North Sea and the Channel. He knew that two great Russian armies were assembling, one in Poland in order to bring pressure to bear on Prussia, the other further south, in Galicia, all set to move into Austria. There the Russians would join forces with two formidable Austrian armies already on a war footing, each in the region of a hundred thousand men, the one that was in the process of invading Bavaria, the other that was holding Venice. A corps of 25,000 men provided a link across the Tyrol.

He had information, besides these two colossal offensives, concerning some Swedish war preparations in Pomerania, the presence of a Russian force at Corfu, English preparations in Malta, hostile intentions by the Bourbons in Naples, and the proposed mobilization of Prussia.

---

[1] 'For the first time,' wrote Thiers, 'Napoleon was free, free as Caesar and Alexander had been. Those of his companions in arms that jealousy or reputation had rendered inconvenient had eliminated themselves from the lists by imprudent and culpable conduct (an allusion to Moreau, banished in 1804 for treason, after a sensational trial). There remained by him only those lieutenants submissive to his will and combining to the highest degree the qualities necessary for the execution of his designs. His army, wearied with long inaction, sighed for nothing but glory and combat; shaped by ten years of war and three years in camp, it was prepared for the most difficult enterprises, for the most daring marches.

'The whole of Europe was open to his schemes . . .'

Disregarding the peripheral threats, he confined his attention for the moment to central Europe, where he decided everything would take place, and proceeded to pore over another map that he had unrolled on the floor, so that he could lie across it. [1]

One thing alone counted in his eyes: the *Danube valley*. He realized at first glance that the whole campaign of 1805 would be played out around this boulevard, this great roadway that ran from Vienna in the direction of Paris, almost in a straight line—but which could also lead to Vienna armies debouching from the Black Forest.

The Austro-Russian operation, and the French counter-offensive, would run along this main axis.

Four attacks were being prepared against France. Napoleon forecast the directions they would take. The first, that of the Swedes, the Russians and the English, would come from the north, from Pomerania, and would threaten Hanover, and then Holland.

The second, by far the most menacing in the number of units it could throw in at once, that of the Russians and Austrians combined, would ascend the Danube valley in the direction of Strasburg.

The third would be mounted in Lombardy by the Austrians alone, ever avid to re-open the eternal Italian quarrel.

Finally, later on, the Russians, the English and the Neapolitans would start something based on Naples.

The first and the last threat appearing to him negligible, Napoleon only considered the two others as serious, above all the one that pointed along the Danube valley towards the flank of France herself. He drew on his spies' box for precise information concerning the allied threat and the armies on the march or in formation: 60,000 Russians in Poland commanded by Buxhouden, augmented by 12,000 picked men of the Imperial Russian Guard, of whom the Czar himself would be coming to take command. There were 60,000 others, as an advance guard, led by Kutuzov. They were late. To arrive at Ulm (the last town marked on the map if one follows the Danube up towards its source, from east to west, naturally) in order to concentrate with the Austrians in readiness for the first thrust in the invasion of

[1] See map, Plates II and III.

80

France, it would be necessary for them to cross Galicia as far as Olmütz, Moravia as far as Vienna, Austria, and finally Bavaria. There was thus a greater distance for them to cover than for Napoleon from Boulogne to Ulm.

As for the Austrians, they had not wasted time. A hundred thousand men lined the Adige, in the north of Italy, under the command of Archduke Charles; the Emperor, his brother, would be happy enough to let him retake Milan, but could never allow him the glory of entering Paris. The other tactician of the family, Archduke John, the loser, not unworthily, at Hohenlinden, was defending the Tyrol. A little less than a hundred thousand men, finally, would ascend the Danube, cross Bavaria, then Swabia, and seize the famous strong point of Ulm, where General de Kray, in 1800, had held out for a long time against Moreau. They would await the Russians there and constitute with them a terrible mass of at least 140,000 combatants, who would thrust their battering-ram straight at the flank of France.

The command of the First Austrian Army had been confided to one of the most celebrated generals, of great valour though greyed in harness: Mack. He was the author of all the plans of campaign against France and had just finished presiding with much sagacity and energy over the replacing of Austria on a war footing.

*   *   *   *

The dictation of August 13th, then, having covered the whole of Europe and surveyed all the western routes, suddenly pounced on the Danube valley and proceeded to concentrate on that. Napoleon averted the thought of Archduke Charles's army by drawing in front of him the bolt of a French contingent of only 50,000 men, but commanded by the best tactician he believed to be available, Marshal Masséna. He dismissed with a flick the secondary worries: the whole European disposition would founder when he had sawn through the main beam, that is to say when he had brought to nought the offensive along the Danube.

And there his glance spotted the enormous weakness in the enemy operation: the considerable distance, in space and time, between the Austrians over-anxious to occupy Ulm and the

Russians delayed in Galicia. The unfolding of his plan followed like a piece of mathematical reasoning:

He would wipe out the Austrian army of Ulm.

He would then hasten on to Vienna and settle his account with the Russians.

Napoleon's secret had always been as simple as that of Christopher Columbus's egg: to wring the neck of each of his adversaries separately.

But, to ensure that Mack really would be annihilated, Napoleon abandoned the classic manner of transporting a French army along the Danube valley, that which Moreau had used in 1800: the passage through the Black Forest, by ascending the Rhine from Basel to Schaffhausen. He would then have had to attack head on the Austrians firmly entrenched on the Iller, which formed an elbow with the Danube at Ulm. They would beat them without doubt, but only enough to make them retreat towards the Russians.

He would, on the contrary, surprise the Austrian First Army in the rear. From above. They would outflank it. They would cut it off from its bases. They would envelop it. They would destroy it.

It was necessary therefore that the Grand Army should descend in a general direction north-west to south-east, pass through Württemberg and Franconia, strike the Danube to the east of Ulm, between Donauwörth and Ingolstadt—and then swing round to take the Austrians by the throat.

Such was the main idea that orchestrated from beginning to end the plan of march of *my seven streams*, as the Emperor called it.

*   *   *   *

'Monsieur Daru, write . . . '

Bernadotte was to descend vertically.[1] He was at present in Hanover, where he had 30,000 men, but he would be forced to leave nearly half of them there to meet English or Prussian threats. With 17,000 soldiers he was to cross Hesse, through Fulda, and descend through Würzburg on Bavaria, where his arrival would fortify the intermittent Francophily of the Elector.

[1] See map, Plates II and III.

His left hand neighbour, Marmont, was to leave Holland, where he constituted the extreme right of the 'Army of England'. He led 20,000 men, of whom a quarter consisted of the excellent soldiers of the Batavian division confided to Dumonceau. He was to join up with Bernadotte at Würzburg by ascending the Rhine from Nijmegen to Mainz, and then crossing over by Frankfort.

The camp at Boulogne properly speaking, which assembled the main body of the army between Ambleteuse and Montreuil, on the Channel coast, provided the material for the four most dense streams:

Davout was to lead the 3rd Corps from Ambleteuse to Mannheim (on the Rhine): 26,000 men.

Soult was to march from Boulogne to Speyer with the bulk of the army, 40,000 men (the 4th Corps). When he had reached the Rhine, just above Davout, Suchet's division would be detached and would be added to Gazan's division and Oudinot's grenadiers: 18,000 men. Together they were to form the 5th Corps, which was to be entrusted to Lannes on leaving Strasburg.

Ney would have joined it by then, also at Strasburg, with the 6th Corps of 24,000 men, whom he was to lead from Montreuil through Arras, Reims, Nancy and Saverne.

Augereau, finally, was to conduct the 7th stream from west to east, from Brittany into Germany; the 14,000 men who had previously made up the extreme left of the Army of the Sea would become on the morrow the reserve of the forces for the invasion of Germany.

To these huge masses of infantry must be added the most formidable cavalry in the world, the cuirassiers of Nansouty, the carabiniers of Hautpoul, the dragoons of Klein, Walther, Beaumont, Bourcier and Baraguay-d'Hilliers. In all 22,000 horse (6,000 cuirassiers and carabiniers, 9-10,000 horse dragoons, 6,000 foot dragoons (*sic*) and a thousand horse artillery, serving the mobile batteries that added the power of shot to that of sabres). The whole was confided to the most inspiring officer who had ever lived: Murat.

This cavalry was to leave from Boulogne, four days before the line, and head for Strasburg. Then would follow the graduated departure of the infantry, by three different routes: on one day the first divisions of each corps, on the next the second divisions, and the remainder on the third day. Everything was calculated so that in twenty-four marches the army gathered by the sea should arrive along the Rhine from Mannheim to Strasburg in order then to cross it, skirt the Black Forest *from above* (whereas the Austrians would be expecting it below, at the Basel pass), cross Württemberg above Stuttgart, and reach the banks of the Danube from the north, there to take up its position upstream of Marmont and Bernadotte, who would have already arrived at Ingolstadt.

With the cavalry would march the 7,000 men of 'the finest *corps d'élite* in the world': the Imperial Guard commanded by Bessières, which would accompany 'the sacred person of the Emperor': grenadiers and *chasseurs,* mounted and on foot, plus the Italian battalion, the Mamelukes and two squadrons of the élite of the constabulary.

Such was the Grand Army that was about to make a right-about turn and unroll methodically, preceded by paymasters charged with organizing supplies at every halting-place. (Four times in five days, Napoleon stipulated in his correspondence that each man was to be issued with a greatcoat and two pairs of boots.) An extract from the 'Booklet' of effectives gives their composition with an impressive precision[1]: 226 battalions, 233 squadrons, 161 companies of artillery and engineers, all commanded by 1,108 staff officers. The number *at present under arms* had risen to 8,269 officers of the line and 202,338 non-commissioned officers and men. There were 29,474 horses for the cavalry and 6,430 horses for the artillery train. These latter drew 396 guns (58 of 12 cm., 146 of 8, and 52 of 6).

If one adds to this formidable organized horde Masséna's 50,000 men in Lombardy, Gouvion Saint Cyr's 20,000, intended to hold Naples in respect, 30,000 men from Bavaria, Baden and Württemberg, involuntary allies of France, one finally arrives at the imposing scale of the enormous masses of humanity that were going to roll against each other at this summer's end. The first to do so, Daru realized what a gigantic contest was to end with the throw of the dice at Austerlitz: with 300,000 men,

[1] About a quarter of these effectives were to remain in French garrisons or be sent on other missions.

Napoleon was going to fight 500,000 of the Coalition; 250,000 Austrians, 200,000 Russians, 50,000 English, Swedes or Neapolitans — while at Brandenburg, like gathering clouds, 200,000 Prussians were mobilizing.

When the two men left each other, they could do no more. But Daru still had time to hear the Emperor murmur:

'My one fear is that we may frighten them too much . . . '

CHAPTER VI

'HE USES OUR LEGS MORE THAN OUR BAYONETS'

After his dictation to Daru, Napoleon remained in Boulogne for twenty days, to hold numerous reviews, dispatch an astronomical number of letters, supervise in person the moving off of the regiments, and to deceive the enemy, who hypnotized themselves with his very person and believed him to be still looking towards England up to September 3rd, when he returned to Malmaison. From after August 25th, he let his ministers know what was going on by writing to Talleyrand: 'My mind is made up. My advance has begun. By September 17th I shall be in Germany with 200,000 men.'

For once, his forecast was too optimistic. He was not to get there until October 1st, which had scarcely any effect on the military course of events, the clockwork mechanism carefully wound up under his ministrations having gone off in other respects without a hitch.

It was the 'inside of the shop' that was causing him concern: Paris, France. From September 4th to 24th he cooled his heels at the chateau of Saint-Cloud trying to resolve, and perhaps to understand, the serious financial crisis of 1805. 'I am distressed', he had just written from Boulogne, in August, 'by my way of life which, by involving me in camps, in expeditions, diverts my attention from this first object of my concern, from what lies nearest to my heart: a satisfactory and solid organization of everything to do with banks, manufactures and commerce.'[1]

---

[1] A harsh blow for Bonapartists who, though compelled to admit some criticism of the Imperial period, take refuge in the bastion of the Consulate and will not admit to the least blemish in that. The Consulate, for them, is

The treasury coffers were empty, even before the start of the campaign, almost as empty as those of Louis XVI in 1789.

Each year, since its creation, the Bank of France had experienced a drop in its reserves of metal. Paradoxically, this always occurred in summer, during what were known as the 'golden months' in Fabre d'Eglantine's charming calendar: Messidor, Thermidor, and Fructidor, owing to the slackening of business and—already!—to the exodus from Paris of the affluent section of the population. In 1805, the crisis took on catastrophic proportions after the month of August. The official reasons: the prolonged absence of the Court, removed since the spring by the coronation in Milan; the late harvest; expenditure and unrest caused by the imminence of a great Continental war. The whispered reasons: the Emperor's lack of any real grip on financial questions, in which he had been blundering along, on impulse and without a view to long-term consequences; his fundamental distrust, which he undoubtedly derived from his mother, of all borrowing, even on favourable terms; the uselessness of his Treasury minister, Barbé-Marbois, whose honesty exceeded all limits, putting him as it did at the mercy of every swindle behind a virtuous façade. The very fact that the administration of public funds was divided between two ministries, that of Finance, responsible for *receipts,* and that of the Treasury, responsible for *disbursements,* was disastrous for France, whose sufferings from the maleficent effects of this economic tug-of-war were by no means ended.

Barbé-Marbois was slowly handing himself over, bound hand and foot, to an association of speculators who promised him the earth in order rapidly to refill his coffers: the *Négociants Réunis,* or Merchants Combine.

In reality, the *Négociants Réunis* was Ouvrard, one of the greatest scoundrels of the century, indispensible to no matter what regime, like all really great swindlers whose shady combinations reach the level of genius. This time he had conceived an extraordinary scheme for importing into France Mexican

---

the dogma of Napoleonic infallibility. But is it? After five years of activity, almost exclusively civil, here he is admitting nevertheless that he has been unable to organize satisfactorily the basis of every political system: a rational economy.

piastres, which were to be transported to Holland, in *English* ships. It appeared that Napoleon had not been kept informed of the details of the business—or rather that he had not wished to be, he who under the Empire would no longer allow a subaltern to be posted without his knowledge! He had always regarded money matters as a sort of Augean stables where it was normal to dirty one's hands, and preferred to leave to others this inconvenience. From this point of view, Ouvrard fascinated him with his gymnastic skill, continually leaping from one trapeze to another, and he had always refrained from having him hanged, although he had threatened him with execution several times. In this case, he let things alone until he left for Germany, and while waiting for the fabulous manipulations of the *Négociants Réunis* to succeed allowed the treasury to deplete itself further . . . by making them advances.[1]

One other matter detained Napoleon for several days: it was necessary for him to bring forward the call up under arms of 80,000 young people of over twenty, in order to have a reserve on which to draw in the event of heavy losses in effectives. The Constitution, although made to his measure, did not allow him to make this illegal levy without a convocation of the Legislative Corps, which would have taken too long. He decided to by-pass it, thanks to the docility of the 'Senat Conservateur', whose spine was of unlimited suppleness, and which passed for him on this occasion the first of the 'Senatus-Consulte', whose successors were to mark the progressive abuse of its power. So, on September 23rd, he betook himself from Saint Cloud to Paris in order to present himself before that august assembly of willing hirelings and to deliver there a speech on the objects of the war intended to inform and to excite public opinion. The senators applauded

[1] 'This was the opportunity sought and found by the returned Royalists, the English, and the financiers in their hire. Through some acknowledgements let fall, some confidences overheard, no doubt: the matter here is far from being a simple intrigue of the money men speculating for a fall, with their usual patriotism, on the possible defeat of their country; it is a formidable weapon of war, devised by England and her allies, to break the Bank of France, ruin national credit, and halt Napoleon in mid-march on Vienna. This crisis was the first manifestation of a new policy, of a method of financial war, in which the cosmopolitan bankers, consciously or not, carry out enemy orders in the interior and, with armfuls of cash, kill the soldiers from behind'. Frédéric Masson.

him but Paris sulked. In the streets followed by the imperial cortege from the Tuileries to the Luxemburg, no cheers. An almost insolent coldness. The common people were suffering: bread was dear, colonial produce lacking, the memory of the Revolution was still fresh in men's minds, they did not like the war, which took away the children of the poor, and the logic of the fauburgs was blaming it on Napoleon for having donned the crown of Italy. 'It's his fault,' they said, in gossip recorded by the police in their reports. 'Why did he have to push Austria so far?'

Annoyed, the Emperor set this down to the basic perversity of the 'weird' Parisian. He had never liked his 'fair city', and was to retain, even on the throne, the complex of an unknown provincial. On the return of the cortege, he decided that the ungrateful riff-raff of the capital was not worth the trouble he was taking over it and ordered his carriage ready for the army; he wished to leave by 4 a.m. the following morning. He had just been told that the vaults of the Bank guarded no more than 1,200,000 francs in specie, a wretched reserve at the start of a Continental war.[1] But he was tired of looking for solutions on the spot: it was for war to nourish war. In the course of his last night at Saint-Cloud, he had said to Count Mollien:

'Our finances are going badly, the Bank is becoming embarrassed; it is not here that I can put things right . . . Within a fortnight I will have defeated the Russians, the Austrians, and the bear speculators.'

For the moment, the immediate result of his departure was to precipitate the very crisis that had been smouldering for several weeks, and whose echoes had been limited up till then to the circle of the initiated. An absurd rumour went around that on leaving he had scraped the bottoms of all the drawers and carried off the cash to pay the troops. This released a flood of financial panic which was to lead the country closer to the edge of bankruptcy the nearer the French army advanced towards Vienna. Austerlitz from this angle takes on the aspect of an eleventh-hour speculative coup.

The eagle had taken his flight and left his government to face as best it could the tide of the panic-stricken who beat at the

[1] About £250,000 in our currency today.

counters for payment. On September 25th he crossed Nancy, and was in Strasbourg by the 26th. He was not to stay there more than four days, and on October 1st he plunged towards the east, to meet the sun, all his hopes and those of France with him.

Here an astonishingly bourgeois scene was enacted. In the carriage that rolled over the bridge at Kehl, Napoleon had red eyes, like the greenest of his conscripts. He had cried, in front of ten witnesses. Under the stress of the moment? No. Simply on leaving his wife. He had left Josephine in Strasburg.

* * * *

Her Majesty the Empress, the most envied of all the women of the world, was already the most unhappy, with her lovely eyes always anxious in her highly painted face, above a smile pinned up with difficulty . . . She was 'more than queen', it was true; the prediction made in her infancy had been realized. But here she was, completely taken up with devising endless plans to defend her position, beset on all sides by the bevy of superb creatures younger than herself whom Napoleon's own sisters led in the assault with abundant skill. Josephine's life, from the 18th Brumaire to the repudiation, was nothing but one long strategic campaign pursued with unflagging patience which met with nothing but failure: the proof was this autumn of 1805 when her husband's love for her undoubtedly revived.

The spring, however, had been marked by his liaison with a most attractive woman of twenty, Mme Duchatel, slim, blonde, with an aquiline nose—which Josephine knew how to make fun of, not without wit—eyes of an unusual blue and joints of ravishing delicacy. Napoleon was always sensitive to this last attraction: 'the common herd' repelled him; no woman with thick ankles was admitted to his intimacy. She sang, played the harp divinely and had known how to captivate not only the senses but also the mind of the Emperor while she diverted him. For the first time since the Italian campaign, and his late-adolescent passion for Josephine, he had been in love. Mme Duchatel had stirred in him the sentimental cord he had thought quite dead, which was to be all ready to vibrate in a year's time at the touch of Maria Walewska.

That had frightened him, as soon as he realized it, at the end of scarcely two months. A brilliant intellectual, shrewd, a bit of an adventuress, Mme Duchatel had wearied Napoleon as quickly as she had conquered him by proving too intelligent for his taste. He still submitted to a certain domination from Josephine, to whom all kinds of subtle ties bound him, memory, pity, tenderness, fear. He did not like to deceive her, took precautions in doing so that were worthy of a light comedy by Ambigu, and never found in it an unmixed pleasure—above all when his heart was involved.

And yet he had just given her, by crowning her before all the world in spite of the opposition of the indignant Bonapartes, the finest present a man had ever given a woman. Such generosity bound its author more than any possible debt of gratitude. If Napoleon was to remain faithful to Josephine for six years, officially at least, it was at first because he wanted to make an effort to be faithful to the best in himself: the only moments, perhaps, when there had been some spontaneity in his life.

One fine evening, at Malmaison, he therefore unburdened himself of everything by confessing his liaison to Josephine, who had known all about it, except for certain intimate details which Napoleon did not hesitate to fill in for her. She knew how to play to perfection her role of confidante, saved all rampaging for her rival ('She thought she was La Vallière . . . ', was all she said), and filled the role Napoleon desired of her by herself indicating to Mme Duchatel the rupture decided upon. There are thus some moments of sharp pleasure, even in the lives of the most faded.

Mme Duchatel had taken the matter with true nobility of soul: without a sigh. Did she guess, perhaps, that there would be some renewals of their intimacy? From time to time, not often, the Emperor would go to see her in the town, in a frock-coat and round hat, driven by the coachman, Caesar, in a brougham with no armorial bearings. Constant would sometimes accompany him, and even Murat, while they were still capable of camaraderie outside politics, which poisoned everything.

The Duchatel page turned, the Italian journey had been marked by a brief intimacy with a damsel called Lacoste, new reader to Josephine (who never had anyone read to her). Frail and blonde, with a pleasing figure and a delicate face, she had a certain pathetic charm that touched the Emperor, but without much to her. Soon after they had begun to attract attention, he had to endure a scene from Josephine, one evening at the chateau of Stupinigi, near Milan, and so Napoleon agreed to her dismissal. She was married off to a banker, in whose company she would be happy, a good mother, and forgotten.

After that, until Austerlitz, it was Josephine who ruled—truly. He was to write to her regularly letters so tender that love seemed to be just round the corner, in a past that had not yet frozen over and perhaps even with certain future possibilities kept open. From Paris to Strasburg, it was she who accompanied him: and this fiery conqueror suddenly felt his nerves give way, in the company of the only woman in his life to whom he was willing to reveal his weakness. With all the others, he had never been able to relax from the exhausting need to evoke admiration, even in intimacy.

There he was, embracing Josephine on this October 1st full of anguish, before the final leap into the unknown. Someone else was by her side, and had the right to a sign of favour. Who would have believed it? It was Talleyrand. And the remark the Emperor let fall makes it possible to understand, more than pages and pages of scholarly studies, why he had never had the man shot. Nothing about Talleyrand can be understood if one does not remember that he was before all else a captivating man without baseness:

'It really is painful to leave the two people one most loves . . . '

These farewells were followed by a nervous spasm, such as he had when emotionally upset. He cried and vomited. They got him to sit down and drink an infusion of orange-flowers. He regained his control, flung himself into his carriage, and left.[1]

*   *   *   *

Ettlingen, the evening of October 1st; there he received the Duke of Baden. On the 2nd, Durlach, Wilferdingen, Pforzheim, and the late arrival, at midnight, at Ludwigsburg, where a portly old man with white hair welcomed him on the steps of his

---

[1] The campaign of Austerlitz, it would seem, was to go by without a woman for him, other than 'the anonymous diversion of the soldier'. It was on his return that he was to know Eleonore Denuelle . . . and give her a child.

palace: the Elector of Württemberg. The poor Most Serene Highness was puffing with indignation because Ney had just entered Stuttgart, his capital, with scant consideration and with all his guns unlimbered. But then, Württemberg did not ask for more than to be violated, but with manners. Napoleon supported Ney on the one hand, and deployed all his powers of persuasion during forty-eight hours in order to appease his host. On October 5, the alliance was signed: 10,000 Württembergians were to augment the Grand Army, so that Württemberg might be augmented. At the Court theatre, on the evening of the 4th, Mozart's *Don Giovanni* had been presented, and Napoleon, who understood nothing about music, had been monumentally bored.

Gmünd, the evening of the 5th; he left there again at six the following morning, travelled non-stop, and was at Nordlingen by 4 p.m., mounted a horse immediately, and struck the Danube at Donauwörth — below Ulm, where the Austrian army was caught in a net without as yet having the least suspicion in the world. Marshal Mack had just established himself with arms and baggage in a position he considered formidable, and resolutely awaited the French at the opening of the Basel pass. Unperturbed, he had his back to them. Nearly two months after the conception of Napoleon's plan, the Austrians had come headlong to position themselves just there, where he had expected them. Some false reports by spies, a clever diversion by 40,000 French through the defiles of the Black Forest, and their total lack of imagination had done the rest. The greatest military march of modern times had been able to unfold in a few days as though behind a curtain. It passed into history, therefore, as a model of camouflage as much as of rapidity.

In the meantime, of course, *they* had been marching!

. . . One hundred and fifty thousand men along an eighty-mile front, the right extending to the mountains, the left converging on the plains of the Upper Palatinate, able within a few hours to form a striking force of a hundred thousand at either of its wings. It was the first example of a march by a great army that can be compared, in effectives and material, with those of modern wars. Half a century earlier, Turenne, and Marshal de Saxe too, maintained that an army of more than 50,000 men would become as 'inconvenient' to its commander as to its enemy. By passing abruptly from the marching technique of a few divisions to that of an immense army, Napoleon had posed, and resolved in exemplary fashion, one of the most difficult problems of war: to get masses moving and to keep them supplied. It was in effect vitally necessary to raise the manoeuvrability of the troops at the same time as their numbers, in order to get them to change rapidly and without confusion from the order of march to that of combat. Otherwise, what would be the use of leading a ragged troup into enemy fire? It was by the degree of precision instantly obtained in this new technique that Napoleon had here laid down at the first attempt the rules that were to serve those who came after to move all the armies of the world.

There *they* were then, marching along, gaily at first, because the weather was magnificent until the beginning of October, because they had grown bored in Boulogne, and because the prospect of ending up in the maw of a fish had not greatly attracted them. Their boots were not yet worn, and their new greatcoats were sufficient guarantee against the cool of the day. From the sea to the Rhine, the removal of the army had been carried out in exceptional conditions of good humour and of going. The march of the 2nd Corps, that of Marmont, was to become proverbial, so successful was it. It was true, he had the advantage of the splendid road Napoleon had opened up along the left bank of the Rhine, which was one of the finest constructional works of his reign. But even so, out of the 15,000 French soldiers comprising his corps, with the Batavian division, he was *nine* short on arriving in Würzburg! Whereas a loss of two or three hundred, for instance, would have been quite normal, above all at the start of a campaign when the weaklings reveal themselves immediately. As for Dupont's division, another example, it had, in crossing the department of the Aisne, left behind fifty men who came from there. They went to visit their families— and *all* rejoined on the next day but one.

In the middle of autumn, it was possible to say that the army, after having covered 450 miles, had neither sick nor stragglers.

In Davout's corps, there had just been incorporated a contingent of 197 men coming from the department of the Forests, otherwise known as the Grand-Duchy of Luxembourg. Amongst them, a quiet lad, observant, a little egotistical perhaps, for he never made any references to his compatriots in his letters: Jean-Pierre Blaise, who came from Mont, above Houffalize. He was to end up as steward of a large estate and had certainly received some elementary education in one of the numerous religious houses with which this highly clerical region abounded. His degree of culture must not be judged by his orthography, which at this time was still extremely irregular, even among the literate. His is better than Napoleon's!

A corporal in the 108th infantry regiment, Jean-Pierre Blaise took advantage of the least departure of a post to send news to his people. Hardly arrived at the bank of the Danube, here he is writing a colourful account of his march from Ambleteuse:

'My dear parents,

'We were reviewed by the Emperor on the 8th Fructidor, Year thirteen. We learnt on that day, to our joy, that we were at last to leave the coast where we had been encamped for two years[1] in order to go and make war in Germany. I can assure you that this news gave us immense pleasure, for during the long stay the army made by the sea, the troops sustained much sickness; besides we were persuaded that, led by the Emperor, we should be marching to victory.

'The first division of our army corps moved off on the ninth, and we followed them on the eleventh. I did not notice anything worthy of your attention along our way as far as the Rhine, which we crossed, without seeing the enemy, on the fifth Vendémiaire, Year fourteen. Incidentally, I must tell you that on leaving we thought we were heading for Haguenau where we would be staying for a while. We left the enemy on our right in order to proceed by crossing the Rhine at Mannheim; on the fourth, each man was issued with a cartouche and the order was given that all effects which the soldiers would not be needing were to be left at the depot at Frankenthal, so as to be as lightly loaded as possible. We did not billet with the inhabitants more than twice after crossing the Rhine. The speed of our march

[1] Sic. It should read, more probably, two months.

prevented supplies from keeping up with us, we often lacked bread, in spite of all the trouble taken by our commanding officer, Marshal Davout; and when we did get some it was so bad that one could not eat it. We were able to do without it all the better since we were then in the season of potatoes, and in a country where they are extremely good. How many times did we blight the hopes of a villager! We plundered him of the fruits of a year's work. All the same, we were more or less forced to do it. We were able to forgive ourselves for ravaging the fruit, of which there was a great quantity: I have never seen so many apples as in the country we passed through to get to Neubourg. The soldiers naturally ate a lot of them, without, however, any ill effects[1] . . . '

*   *   *   *

Watching these great disciplined hordes leaving Boulogne, Maret could not restrain a revealing exclamation:

'A roll of the drums, and ten thousand men are astir!'

It was indeed a civilian remark, but also one by a man of the eighteenth century, for whom the notion of the army was inseparable from a certain anarchy, and thus the complete opposite of what was to become the military conception of the nineteenth century: order, rigour and discipline.

There had been armies. There had never been an Army, not merely in France, but in the entire world, where ever smarter uniforms and technical progress had done no more than cover up the ancient 'system of bands of mercenaries that had presided over the whole of the middle ages. The fact that, almost everywhere, the colonel had been the proprietor of his regiment and able to impose on it the seal of his conduct, indeed of his vagaries, accentuated this feudal character, of which traces still lingered in *spirit* after the Napoleonic transformation: 'The colonel is the centre of the regiment, its living flag. It would be better for soldiers to allow their eagle to be taken than to abandon their colonel in danger,' Napoleon had said.

But, after all, the Revolution had passed that way? Yes, but

[1] Fairon and Heuse: *Lettres de Grognards.* No attempt has been made, for obvious reasons, to reproduce any of the spelling or grammatical irregularities that abound in the original (trs.).

always under the banner of a certain diversity. The great leaders of Year II had no longer been the proprietors of their corps, but they had impregnated them with their personalities. The armies of Pichegru, Marceau, Hoche, Kléber, Masséna and Joubert had each sought to fortify itself with its own spirit, traditions and memories. The gulf, especially, between the army of the Rhine and that of Italy had come close to overturning the still unsettled chariot of the Consulate. And when Bonaparte, First Consul, had carried Marengo, it was still Moreau who had won Hohenlinden. Then had come the camp at Boulogne. For the first time, all these men and all these leaders found themselves in the same mould. And the imperial crown had reinvested the supreme commander with an incontestable power. Napoleon had been able to say to Roederer: 'You know, my army is formidable! If the war had brought no other advantage than to shape it and animate it with a single spirit, it would have been useful. We have had an army of the Rhine, an army of Italy, an army of Holland: there has never been a French army. Now, it exists and we shall see it in action.'

Boulogne had been an exercise. Austerlitz was to be the real thing. One was about to see put to the test this end-product of many centuries of royal military tradition recaptured, twisted, ground up and *amalgamated,* that is the very word, in the crucible of ten years of Revolution.

The Emperor experienced a palpable incentive to travel more frequently in the midst of the Guard, whose cavalry with their splendid horses inspired complete confidence. The foot-soldiers blithely carried a knapsack bigger and heavier than that of the other regiments of the line, two pairs of boots and spare soles with studs, smock and trousers of linen, a sleeping-bag, a change of gaiters and shirt, four days' bread and biscuits. A mass of gear was stowed on top of the knapsack: the hat in its case, camping implements, greatcoat, and bearskin filled with provisions and odds and ends. All this swung to the rhythm of a firm and powerful tread, in frock-coats, black collars and grey gaiters . . . A heavy convoy of vehicles sandwiched into the column more often slowed than accelerated its progress; 35 wagons for baggage, 6 for forage, 20 for surgery and medicaments, 25 for ambulance purposes.

For the whole of the Grand Army's equipment there had not been time to procure vehicles for each division's own use. The Emperor had therefore decided that they should be provided with them from one halt to another, and a decree of the 15th Fructidor, Year XIII, had borne a requisition for '3,500 carriages yoked with four good horses and driven by two coachmen— 2,500 are to be posted for service in the parks of the Grand Army, and 1,000 as transport for the administration'.

Along mile after mile of dusty roads the men marched according to a carefully studied technique: in two parallel lines, dividing the roadway and leaving its centre free, borne along by drums distributed in threes at the head, the centre and the tail of brigades, each group of which took it in turns to beat during the march, whose rhythm was thus maintained. At the halts, of five minutes every hour, and 'of at least half an hour at the three-quarter distance of the day's march', music had to be played, complete with four clarinets, flute and horn.

The generals — in carriages — and the colonels — on horseback — were at the heads of their units. Between each battalion, a gap of a hundred paces was left. Each division of 6-7,000 men was stretched out over about two and a half miles of the way, which represented exactly the prescribed speed per hour: three miles at the maximum. The cavalry also marched in two lines, occupying a length of about eleven hundred yards per regiment. The duration of the marches imposed on each unit had never been uniform, and depended on the general plan of march. Some of them varied between seven and a half to twenty-five miles. The average oscillated between fifteen and eighteen.

The biggest headache was the halting-place, which compelled the stop to be made very early so that the whole of the afternoon could be spent looking for something to eat and to settle everybody. The start therefore usually took place at a very early hour, between 4 and 6 a.m., and the arrival somewhere between 10 and midday. The *basic unit* of the march and of the halt remained the *division*, which billeted and took up its position each evening over a depth of ten or twelve miles, one or two regiments being established in the chosen town, the rest of the troops distributed, preferably ahead.

The divisions followed each other at twenty-four hour intervals.[1]

* * * *

And then suddenly a chorus of lamentations arose from the bivouacs and gushed through the posts: the weather changed and with it the morale of the men.

Now, the Grumblers began to grumble. The army scribe who tramped alongside the conscripts from the provinces of Belgium and the Ardennes[2] caught on the wing, of an evening, at a drum in the guise of a desk, the heartrending complaints of some of these lanky lads, often still beardless. There they were, in their blue uniforms faced with black velvet and trousers of white linen, and with black gaiters, pressing round the man of learning, adept at murmuring to them the phrases they persisted in writing themselves, often distorting them in an amusing fashion, on beautiful sheets of paper decorated with multicoloured little flowers bought at the canteen:

From François-Joseph Joskin:

'I am so dreadfully bored that I can do nothing but cry every day. Oh, mother, what a great misfortune has befallen me to become a conscript! What an unhappy life it is to be a soldier!'

---

[1] It should be observed that, contrary to what one might think, the moving of huge masses of men along the roads and across the fields often presented at that time infinitely fewer difficulties than in the nineteenth century, because of the extraordinary width of some of the roads and the slight transition between them and the neighbouring ground. In some provinces of France, and in the approaches to Paris, the roads were as much as 26 yards wide, and the least of them, under the Empire, still measured from $8\frac{1}{2}$ to 15 yards between the ditches on either side, whose embankments were a great deal less pronounced than those that came later. In certain regions they did not exist at all. The land adjacent to the road was far more accessible to a troop of men than a hundred years later: the progress of industry and the rise of the working classes developed, to an extent that is hard to appreciate, walls, artificial rough-stone enclosures, metal trellis-work, drainage ditches, etc. A road in those days was a broad, ill-defined strip of land, on which the flood that rolled over it constantly overflowed to left and to right.

[2] The following testimonies are from the remarkable work by Fairon and Heuse: *Lettres de Grognards*, Liège, 1936.

From his fellow-citizen of Fize-le-Marsal, in the department of Ourthe, Joseph Florkin:

'In the night I think of you; I imagine I am by your side. I cry, but I protest in vain, it doesn't do any good. I am no longer alive at this moment, for I have nothing to amuse me in this part of the world. The hours to me seem like days and the days weeks.'

From grenadier Michel Piquet:

'I send my best regards to my sweetheart Marie-Josephe, whom I should like to see near me to bleach my shirts, to "sew" me and to fix up lots of other things. If she wishes to come, the distance is not great. There are only three hundred and fifty miles for her to cover in order to come and find me.'

From Jean-Henri Binot:

'I am beginning to be very bored, as you can see, since this is the tenth letter I have sent you. I have not yet received one letter from your hand. If, in fact, you get this letter, tell me, I beg you, if you have changed in any way, yes or no. As for me, I am just the same. Condescend to think of me as I think of you. Although I am a soldier, my heart has not changed. My dear, I hope that yours will not change either. My dear, don't be disconsolate, although I am a soldier. Be ever mine, and I will be yours always. My dear, condescend to receive this kiss as if I were placing it upon your mouth.'

From Martin Moyens:

'If ever a journey brought me grief, dear Marianne, it is without doubt this one, which has taken me far from you. It seems to me that since I left you I have lost all that could bind me to life. Nothing interests me if it does not concern you. I shall not tell you that I fear this absence, for I know that, out of your love, you have assured me to the contrary and the regard I have for you prevents me from doubting the sincerity of your promises. But the grounds I have for loving you are precisely the main causes of my torment. I regard as utterly lost the days I can never spend in the company of a person as perfect as you, mademoiselle.'

And these lamentations did not come solely from the Walloon conscripts. They permeated every post to France and provoked a serious crisis of morale in the country. Back there, it was still fine, sometimes. But it was as if the Continental climate, through the thousands of complaints, had chilled the hearts of mothers and sweethearts. There was wind. There was rain, cold, penetrating, persistent. Even snow, if one could believe one's eyes. Between October 1st and 15th the mood of the army changed drastically, and a kind of depression followed the euphoria, as always after a great effort that had succeeded too well. The men were becoming recalcitrant. 'The little corporal', they said, 'has found a new way of making war: he uses our legs more than our bayonets.' But the tone was different. Before, they had said this gaily; now they were savage. Besides the weather, the country had changed. Even friends, the Germans, were scarcely eager about revictualling—and, everything having been sacrificed to the speed of the advance, the supply convoys were awaited in vain. They were thought to be mysteriously held up at the frontier. Food was poor, scarce and irregular. Boots were holed. Their greatcoats were saturated with water. The horses were cracking up. All the accumulated fatigue suddenly descended on them. In six days the ambulances were full.

Napoleon was not unduly worried about it, even though he himself had to change three times a day. His troops lined the Danube between Ulm and Ingolstadt. They lacked not a single case of ammunition, and that alone counted in his eyes.

The time for bayonets had come.

CHAPTER VII

WHAT DOES IT MATTER TO ENGLAND!

On October 7th the curtain was torn aside; Murat, Soult, Lannes, Davout began to cross the Danube by surprising some bridges poorly held by stupefied Austrian garrisons, those of Donauwörth, Munster and Rain, over the Lech. Napoleon urged them on vigorously: at all costs Mack must be prevented from withdrawing from Ulm by the south. He therefore directed the bulk of his human tide to Augsburg, to cut the Austrians off decisively from Münich, to which, in addition, he ordered Marmont and Bernadotte to convey themselves. Only Ney remained, with 20,000 men, on the north bank of the Danube. It was too few: the first mistake of the campaign was committed here, and it could have exacted a heavy penalty.

On the 8th came the first serious encounter at Wertingen, on the road to Ulm by the south bank: the dragoons of the advance guard came upon nine Austrian battalions drawn up into a single square and were unable to sabre them. Murat himself had to come to the rescue with the main body of his cavalry, then Marshal Lannes, with Oudinot's grenadiers. Finally the French swept the field, forced the enemy into a disordered retreat and took 2,000 of them prisoner. The Emperor was brought the flags taken by the officer who had been the first to charge, almost alone, and who had had his horse killed under him: this was Cavalry-Major Exelmans, at once decorated with the Legion of Honour by Napoleon himself in front of the whole general staff, the beginning of a distinguished career.

On the following day Ulm was invested, from the south by Lannes and Murat, from the north by Ney, who made an assault, with the best regiments at his disposal, on three bridges, known as the Günzburg bridges. From them there was access to the immediate approaches to the fortress. The Marshal himself led the attack on the main bridge, at the head of Margognet's brigade. A stiff ordeal: they had to cross a multitude of islands and negotiate blow by blow some little arms of the river lined with willows and poplars, under the increasingly murderous fire of the enemy's muskets, besides their artillery. Archduke Ferdinand, having hurried out of Ulm, finally grasped the seriousness of the attack. He had the bridge blown up. The French succeeded in taking the islands well enough, but tried in vain to repair the bridge with heavy planks while the Austrian fusiliers picked them off as if at a shooting gallery, in the open on the steep gravel banks. The situation might have taken a very bad turn if in the meantime the 59th Regiment of the line had not seized the neighbouring bridge, at odds of one against three and with terrible losses, including that of their commanding officer, the brave Colonel Lacuée, the first illustrious victim of the campaign, to whom on the following day 10,000 men paid their last respects. Seeing this solitary French regiment debouching on the other side of the Danube, the Austrian cavalry charged furiously at the square at once set up. In vain. Three times the 59th broke their attack and ended by remaining in control of the bridgehead. The Austrians were therefore forced to break off the struggle for the other two bridges and retire to the shelter of the formidable stronghold of Ulm, leaving the two banks of the river to Ney.

Where was Napoleon during these battles? Further south, at Augsburg, where he wanted to establish himself for a few days between Münich and Ulm in order to be in a position to meet every possible enemy combination. Some unverifiable rumours had made him apprehensive of soon having Kutuzov's Russian army on his hands, though it was in fact still 180 miles away. On the other hand, he did not dare hope for the complete lack of will that Mack was to display, and expected to have to repulse an attempt in force by the Ulm garrison to escape towards the Tyrol.

The night of October 12th to 13th. Preceded by a squadron of

Polish light cavalry covered with splashes of dirt and mud, a furiously driven berlin pierced the murky night with its two huge lanterns, on the road from Augsburg to Ulm. Heavy snow was falling, which turned to mud as it touched the ground and made the roads impassable. All the little tributaries of the Danube were overflowing.

Who were those benumbed infantrymen, already astir, milling in confusion round reluctant fires in order to begin their march before dawn? It was Marmont's corps, the Franco-Dutch troops, overwhelmed with weariness, loaded with their arms and several days' supplies, forced repeatedly to stop and drag their artillery out of the mire.

At first the carriage overtook their endless lines without slowing. But suddenly an order from the Emperor stopped it. A few brief commands rang out, drums beat, the astonished men presented arms and shed their exhaustion like a cloak:

'Long live the Emperor!'

'Form a circle. Courage, my lads, I'll tell you what we are doing . . . '

Two or three brief phrases, no more: the men grasped a word or two: 'Encirclement . . . we shall have them . . . it will be another Marengo . . . ' And already the little silhouette, rumpled by his journey, had flung himself in a flash back into the berlin; the step was folded up, a flick of the whip, and Napoleon disappeared in a storm of cheering. By a dozen similar stops he rallied more than 10,000 men in the day.

A little further on the carriage was stopped again.

'What is it?'

'One of Marshal Ney's aides-de-camp, Sire.'

'News from Ulm? Quick tell me, monsieur.'

'Sire, I bring Your Majesty news of a very important engagement, which has just taken place at Haslach.'

Napoleon frowned: on the north bank of the Danube, abandoned over-hastily and almost denuded of French . . .

'A defeat? The Austrians broke through?'

'A victory, Sire. But almost miraculous. General Dupont, with his one division, has beaten an Austrian army!'

'Make your report.'

And Napoleon's face remained like marble while he took in the ease with which ill consequences had begun to flow from his 'family politics' by his subordinating, in front of Ulm, Ney and Lannes to Murat, although he was less of a strategist than them. But Murat was his brother-in-law . . .

'Marshal Mack seems to have understood the trap and sent out some strong detachments to probe every possible exit three days ago. Well, there was still one feasible way, on the north bank, by the Michaelsburg hills. Marshal Ney had realized this, and wanted to leave almost all his corps on that side, but Marshal Murat . . . '

'Why do you hesitate?'

'Marshal Murat didn't want to know anything about it and concentrated all the troops under him around Ulm on the south bank . . . He thus forced Marshal Ney to let him have all his men, except for the 6,000 men of Dupont's division.'

'Knowing them, there was a row?'

'It was terrible, Sire. In front of a hundred witnesses. If third parties hadn't intervened, there would have been a duel there and then, and in front of the troops.'[1]

'Go on.'

'On October 11th, General Dupont, left on the north bank of the Danube, thus found himself quite alone facing 25,000 Austrians with only three regiments of infantry, two of cavalry and a few pieces of artillery.'

'He retreated?'

'He attacked, Sire, one against five, to make believe that he was merely the advance guard of huge forces. There were five hours of terrible fighting round the village of Haslach. One of the hamlets changed hands five times. Charges, counter-charges, bayonet attacks, hand to hand fighting . . . '[2]

[1] This was the beginning of a permanent hatred between the two men, who were to perish before firing squads ten years later, both in the same year.

[2] The day was to establish beyond doubt the reputation of that excellent tactician, courageous, sensible, intelligent, General Dupont, for whom everyone now predicted a marshal's baton and the highest renown. Who could have foreseen the fearful business at Baylen, three years later, in Spain, where the fortunes of this unlucky man fell without his being responsible. To his honour, the fact would remain that with or without Dupont Napoleon could not have conquered Spain, whereas without Dupont Austerlitz would not have taken place.

'Finally, Dupont held Haslach and the Austrians went back into Ulm. Marshal Ney charged me to . . . '

'Drive on! That's enough!'

Napoleon saw how matters stood, reprimanded Murat early that morning, agreed with Lannes and Ney and decided to close as quickly as possible the gap he had left unmanned to the north of Ulm, by sending a large number of troops to lend a hand to Dupont, who was still at the mercy of a second attack by the Austrians. But to do that, it was necessary to recross the Danube under Austrian fire at the Elchingen bridge. There was no time to look for a crossing further off. The bridge in question, however, was nothing but a series of trestles without trusses. Marshal Ney was ordered to repair it, cross it, and then seize the convent and village of Elchingen, guarded by 20,000 Austrians and a formidable artillery.

A sweet revenge for him! Two days earlier, during the dispute, Murat, overwhelmed by the arguments, had told him that he understood nothing of all his plans and that he was in the habit of never making his own except in the face of the enemy. But here was Michel Ney on horseback, on the morning of October 14th, in full uniform already covered with decorations, galloping towards Murat and shaking him by the arm in front of the Emperor and all his staff officers:

'Come, my Prince, come with me and make your plans in the face of the enemy! . . . '

Half an hour later, he was in icy water up to his horse's belly, directing the work of the sappers under a hail of grapeshot. For every plank in place three men fell. But in the end the *voltigeurs* of the 6th Light Infantry and the grenadiers of the 39th made the crossing. Ney at their head, the men ascended the tortuous streets of Elchingen under plunging fire from houses crammed with sharpshooters. They cleared the houses one after the other; they took the convent that overlooked them; they debouched into the plain where Dupont had so magnificently defended himself; they unleashed some charges by the 18th Dragoons against the Austrian squares, each of 2,000 to 3,000 men. They broke them up, they sabred them, they harried them with swords towards Haslach, where Dupont came rushing up to trounce them thoroughly once again and cut off two of their regiments, who were taken prisoner. This was the first great battle of the campaign, sharp, bloody, briskly conducted. When it was over, Ney had won there the title of Duke of Elchingen, and the Austrians saw the last bolts that were to lock them up in Ulm being drawn around them.

*   *   *   *

October 14th. Marshal Mack was holding council in an operatic setting: Ulm had not yet received a single musket ball, and the whole reassuring apparatus of the Austrian armed forces was deployed in the besieged town, to culminate in this broken veteran.

'Do you think, Your Grace, that I can now still count on Kutuzov?' he asked the Prince of Schwarzenburg.

But the most capable of the generals of the Old Monarchy did not care to compromise himself. He was already sufficiently annoyed that a chance inspection mission had led him astray into this mess, where he had to content himself with the role of spectator. At least he would avoid compromising his reputation there. A handsome man, greying and affable, whose every gesture captivated anybody at any time—women, soldiers, adversaries, sovereigns—he confined himself to an evasive gesture and a silent presence.

'As for me, I can assure you, Field-Marshal, that to wait for the Russians is to ask for a miracle, and well you know it,' threw in Prince Ferdinand.

He belonged to that species of bulldog archdukes who perpetuated themselves among the Habsburgs from generation to generation. Thick-set and square under his wiry hair. Mature at twenty, old at thirty, brutal from infancy. He was made to carry a sabre and use it. His position as a relative of the Emperor allowed him to give vent to his distrust of the distinguished soldier to whom he had been subordinated—and whose somewhat plebeian extraction was displeasing to this prince, although he was himself a good deal coarser. But his vulgarity was aristocratic.

'We still have 6,000 cavalry,' he insisted. 'Two or three of the town's gates are as yet poorly watched by the French: they haven't had the necessary time to invest us completely. Outside the town, General Werneck's 10,000 men can no longer join us, but they have not yet been enveloped. This very evening, Marshal, let me take the cavalry and my infantry corps. I'll pass through the middle of the French by one of the easier outlets. I'll join up with Werneck and escape with him towards Bohemia, by the Upper Palatinate.'

Mack threw up his arms.

'You are not speaking seriously, Your Grace? By depriving me of 20,000 men, you leave me at the mercy of Bonaparte: I will have in all just 30,000 men left to defend the place until the arrival of the Russians.'

'Very well then, step into the breach yourself this evening! I will follow you as the most devoted of lieutenants, and the whole garrison of Ulm will get through behind us!'

'That makes one wonder if you have ever made war! How do you think the entire army can get through, with its artillery and material? Do you want to condemn us to capitulation in the open field?'

'Then let me take the mounted troops away.'

'Never. In our position, dispersion is the worst of solutions. We must all remain together, since we cannot all leave together. I have resolved to await the Russians.'

'You will be taken prisoner long before they get here, and the honour of Austria will be lost. You will await them without me, Marshal. I am leaving this evening with any men who wish to follow me.'

Far from setting upon and overwhelming the Archduke, Mack was even more subdued in his great velvet armchair, at the head of the oval table round which a dozen dismayed officers looked on, without saying a word, at this duel between the two men. His eyes strayed for a moment to the window, to the courtyard of the fortified chateau where the changing of the guard was taking place with clockwork precision: the white uniforms evolved slowly, their rigidity tempered by a certain musical grace. Raucous commands threw men into eyes front by the hundreds. It was still a picture of order, of calm and of power. Very faintly, far away, one could hear the French guns somewhere on the banks of the Danube.

Here, however, the maggot was in the fruit: the monarchy

had been eroded by the monarch's own relatives. Field-Marshal
Mack appeared even more frail, more emaciated, in his fine
uniform covered in medals and stars. Where were the heroic
days of the Prince of Hombourg when one of his seniors had not
hesitated to condemn to death an undisciplined Highness?
Mack contented himself with sighing:

'I have, as you know, Your Grace, received every authority
from His Majesty to exercise supreme power here in the event of
disagreement.'

He gently stirred a large envelope impressed with seals: just
enough to make him responsible, not enough to make him obey.
Archduke Ferdinand rose and clicked his heels:

'I intend to make my sortie this evening. Confine me in the
fortress if you wish to prevent me. Does your power extend to
that?'

He left the council, leaving Mack already doubly defeated:
by the French and by his lieutenants, and feeling oppressed by
the sudden burden of pitying or hostile glances. And the Archduke kept his word: that very evening he carried out his plan
and, all triumphant, carried off 20,000 survivors from out of the
net.

Not for long. Mack had been right. Napoleon launched Murat
on the heels of the escapers, with the cavalry reserve, Dupont's
indefatigable division and Oudinot's grenadiers. It was a veritable running hunt in the direction of Bohemia in which every
day the French nibbled at the Archduke's rearguard: 200 men
taken on October 16th, 8,000 surrounded and taken on the 18th,
the great park of 500 vehicles gathered the following night. The
kill was sounded on the 20th, near Nuremberg, amid the
incredible confusion of a road cluttered with the army's equipment and treasure. The greater part of the Archduke's cavalry,
scattered after some desperate charges, laid down its arms.
Prince Ferdinand himself escaped by a miracle and succeeded in
reaching Prague with 2,000 survivors.[1]

*   *   *   *

October 20th. The first part of the campaign was over. Ulm

[1] The laws of fame are strange: this hothead who sacrificed close on 20,000
men by a whim, by this adventure won the reputation of a national hero.

had capitulated. After the departure of Ferdinand, Mack knew that he could not hold out. It had been enough for Napoleon to hurl a few token shells upon the town before consenting to receive Philippe de Ségur as negotiator. The threat of a terrible assault, and of a Draconian kind for the garrison, had served to demoralize him. He had hung on grimly for three days, from the 16th to the 19th, and had pretended that he would be allowed a further week of respite:

'I will capitulate *if* between now and then the Russians are not in sight . . . '

An interview with Napoleon, blending in his usual manner persuasiveness and harshness, had relieved him of his last illusions. Lucidly, calmly, knowing that he was consigning his old age to opprobrium, Mack had signed the surrender. Ulm was thus to glow with a particular lustre always and would take a special place in the Napoleonic legend: an immense outcome had for once been obtained at the cost of little bloodshed.

Stationed at the foot of the Michaelsburg hills, Napoleon I watched the finest Austrian army file past him, the army that was to have entered Strasburg, and Paris too. Mounted on his white horse, atop a raised embankment, he had his infantry behind him ranged in a semi-circle on the side of the hill, and opposite, his cavalry, drawn up in a straight line. Between the two, the vanquished filed, crying with rage and throwing down their arms at the entry to this natural amphitheatre. The weather was so bitter that a great camp-fire had been kindled near the Emperor. It lit up pitilessly the defeated face of the powdered old man in splendid uniform of blue and white who was the first to approach and tender him his sword (immediately returned), crying:

'Sire, behold the unfortunate Mack . . . '

Whereas Mack, whose capitulation was to preserve intact for Austria 30,000 soldiers for future wars, and who lacked the ability to cause four or five thousand men to be killed to save his reputation, was to become a symbol of disgrace. It was a matter of looking for a scapegoat, Austria being quite happy to lay the disaster at the door of one man's ineptitude. In this connection Thiers lets fall a phrase very typical of a certain political mentality: 'There was in Germany (with regard to Mack) a most natural, most excusable motive for distorting the truth: that of saving their national pride by crushing a single man'.

'I don't know why we are fighting each other,' Napoleon replied, placing him at his side with the greatest respect, and speaking loudly enough for his affable words to reach the heart of Austria by the following day through the medium of the officers, whom the honourable capitulation would return there disarmed. 'I did not wish it; I did not intend to fight any but the English, when your master came along and provoked me. You see my army: I have 200,000 men in Germany; your captured soldiers will see a further 200,000 that are crossing France to come to the aid of the first. I don't need, as you know, to have so many to win. Your master should think of peace, for otherwise the fall of the House of Lorraine might well be due . . . '

He continued in this vein for five hours, while 27,000 captives filed past him. But the proclamation he addressed to his soldiers on the following day was less sparing of the vanquished. It overflowed with legitimate joy, in spite of the curious disenchantment of the allusion to England, at the end of the first paragraph. It was the triumphal cry of a Roman Emperor; here was Napoleon at the height of his arrogance:

From the General Headquarters at Elchingen,
the 29th Vendémiaire, Year XIV.

'Soldiers of the Grand Army,

'In a fortnight we have carried out a campaign; what we set ourselves to do has been done. We have driven the troops of the House of Austria from Bavaria and re-established our ally in the sovereignty of his States. The army which, with as much ostentation as rashness, had come to station itself at our frontiers has been annihilated. But what does it matter to England? Her object has been attained: we are not at Boulogne any more! . . .

'Of the hundred thousand men who made up that army sixty thousand are prisoners: they will go to replace our conscripts in the tasks of our campaigns. 200 pieces of artillery, 90 flags, all the generals are in our power. Not 15,000 men escaped.

'Soldiers, I had announced a great battle to you; but thanks to the enemy's miscalculations, I have been able to obtain the same successes without running a single risk; and, what is without parallel in the history of the nations, so great an outcome has not weakened us by more than 1,500 men out of action.

'Soldiers, this success is due to your unbounded confidence in your Emperor, to your patience in enduring fatigues and privations of every kind, to your extraordinary intrepidity.'

*   *   *   *

The 29th Vendémiaire was also October 21, 1805.

The same sun that shone down on the reading of that elated proclamation, in the euphoria of a camp abundantly moistened with brandy, which turned the whole town into something of a fairground, shone down some twelve hundred miles from there, towards six in the evening, on the end of the drama of Trafalgar. France had lost the battle at sea.

A storm was rising on the horizon that was finally to disperse the surviving French and Spanish ships, nine out of thirty-three! But in the wide bay the light of an appropriately bloody sunset still lit up the forest of broken masts, snapped off at the stumps, entangled in torn-away rigging. The pall of smoke from the fires and broadsides cleared every now and then to give the English officers, delirious with joy, sorrow, weariness and pride, a glimpse of their triumphant fleet, which devoted itself, as soon as the firing had ceased, to feverish activity during the last hour of daylight.

Admiral Villeneuve had wanted to show Napoleon that he was not a coward. And now here was the unfortunate man, of a ghastly pallor, already beyond the death he had sought in vain all afternoon, received as a captive on board the *Mars*, with all the honours of war. His flagship, the *Bucentaure*, completely demolished, floated like a cork on the waves, surrounded by the huge conquering ships of seventy-four guns, all more or less damaged: *Revenge*, *Swiftsure*, *Achilles*, *Orion*, *Ajax*, and the *Bellerophon*, whose gunners had chalked on their pieces 'Death or Glory' before the battle.

Further off was the *Agamemnon*, with a gaping side, the *Royal Sovereign*, her main-mast and mizzen-mast carried away by a ball, the *Leviathan*, which drew along, as a captive moored to her side, the Spanish vessel *San Augustin*, and the *Belleisle*, with her standard, the cross of St George, fluttering at her stump of mast.

Between these exhausted giants, the nimble patrol of little

corvettes wove a thread of salvage and restoration. *Naiad, Sirius, Phoebe, Entreprenante* and *Pickle* tacked about in search of men to rescue from the reddened waters and tirelessly transferred the injured officers and sailors.

All this activity centred on two majestic frigates, one almost unscathed, the other terribly damaged: the *Euryalus*, at whose poop shone the two lights that indicated the supreme command, to which Admiral Collingwood had just succeeded. But, next to the *Euryalus* rode the ship that had just become the most glorious of the British navy—of all the navies of the world. The *Victory* had lost her mizzen-mast and her fore-topmast. Part of her figure-head had been shot away.

Her lights of command had been extinguished for ever. Nelson was dead.

'They have done for me at last. My backbone is shot through!' he had cried when a ball fired from the fighting-top of the *Redoubtable* had penetrated to his spinal column.

But in fact, it was he who had done for them, the old wild boar, with one eye and one arm, hunted down by the whole puritan pack of England. How can an admiral-in-chief flaunt with impunity his liaison with a Lady Hamilton? He had passed beyond the reach of scandal. The return to England, covered in glory, had been denied him. To conquer or die had not been enough for Admiral Nelson. He had to conquer and die. And the *Victory* had been the first to expose herself, foolhardily, to the blows of the French fleet, her bridge transformed into a butcher's shop, forty men remaining able-bodied out of a hundred and ten —and on that bridge, Nelson, impassive in the old frock-coat he wore on days of battle, covered with decorations. 'England expects that every man will do his duty': he had just hoisted for ever at the main mast of the United Kingdom the most celebrated phrase in her history, while on every French ship there had burst out, in vain, seven times, the cry of *Vive l'Empereur*, as if to exorcise the evil. Obedient to himself, Nelson had done his duty. And this man, physically and mentally shattered, had become the hero of his country, the immortal example for her youth.

October 21, 1805. Napoleon did not know how truly he had spoken . . . 'What does Ulm matter to England?'

*　　　*　　　*　　　*

113

The Emperor was not to learn the extent of the disaster until nearly a month later and would do so without turning a hair. But while all around him were giving themselves up to the joy of the first victory, he remained from that day preoccupied, peevish, very conscious of the fact that the greater part was still to do. England, to which he had resigned himself, did not worry him so much as the still effective forces of Austria and above all, in the background, the advancing armies of Russia.

That is why, after the laurels had been distributed, the proclamation of October 21st went on:

'But we shall not stop at that. You are impatient to begin a second campaign. This Russian army that the gold of England has transported to the ends of the earth we shall cause to meet with the same fate.

'This new struggle will involve most especially the honour of the infantry. In it will be determined whether the French infantry is the second or the foremost of Europe . . .'

Nothing was settled then? Everything was about to begin. What was that sound of cannon, whose echo reverberated through the whole of Germany, from Court to Court? It was the salute on October 25th which welcomed the Czar on his state visit to Berlin. Prussia was tending irresistibly towards the Allies. Hesitant at first because of the bait of Hanover offered by Napoleon, she was prey to an irresistible swing in public opinion, from the Queen to the meanest citizen. They pretended not to forgive the French for her violation of the territory of Ansbach, which Bernadotte and Marmont had crossed in order to reach the Danube more quickly—while in fact such disrespect for territories entangled in the vagaries of treaties was quite in accord with the military morals current at that time. They realized that Napoleon, in his advance on Vienna, would find himself at the mercy of the Prussian army which would be able, by a sudden offensive from north to south, to cut his lines of communication at any moment. And they were also aware of the presence very near at hand, in Poland, of a friendship quite prepared to make itself compelling: that of the 200,000 Russians of Buxhouden. The Czar, sensing that the moment had come, proposed an interview to Frederick-William, who offered—in order not to compromise himself too quickly — to meet him clandestinely, somewhere on the frontier. Pretending to believe, on the contrary, that it was an invitation to the capital, Alexander hastened to Berlin, where they had no option but to receive him, to the knowledge of all Europe, with all the respect due to his rank. It was a somewhat forced marriage, but one of love. Embraces, acclamations, feasts, fireworks, reviews: in two days the young Czar not only convinced Queen Louise, but the whole of Prussia.

Captivating, capable, sure of himself, proclaiming the irresistible unrolling of his armies, he wrung from the last hesitations of the King his signature to the Treaty of Potsdam, by which Prussia undertook to intervene early in December (as soon as her mobilization was completed) by imposing an 'armed mediation' on the belligerent who would not accept peace on 'just conditions'. Since these conditions were naturally those of Austria and Russia, here, very poorly camouflaged by a final scrupulousness of wording, was the forthcoming entry into the war of a nation that for a further six weeks was to be prodigal of formal assurances of neutrality to France. The treaty remained secret.

At that, Alexander and Frederick descended in brotherly fashion to the little vault contrived under the Protestant church of Potsdam. Under one of the columns of the church, in a minute crypt, with bare walls dripping with saltpetre, a simple coffin of wood had been completely neglected up till now: that of Frederick the Great. Monarchical regimes, for two or three centuries, had exhibited almost unanimously—in the west at least—a distrust of dead sovereigns. It was not only in France that the bodies of monarchs, reviled by the crowd, had gone to rot without respect at Saint-Denis. Now Alexander showed that he possessed the faculty of the great politicians: the gift of tears when needed. He cried, clasped the King in his arms and swore eternal friendship on the remains of his ancestor. The two sovereigns promised each other never to differ in their interests, or in their destiny.[1]

*   *   *   *

[1] It is true that Tilsit was to come in two years time, and this oath would be betrayed by the cardboard friendship between Alexander and Napoleon.

A salvo for a salvo; on the same day, those of Münich responded to those of Berlin, but they were fired in honour of Napoleon, who was making his formal entry into the capital of Bavaria, where the people welcomed him as a liberator. A month earlier, however, matters had not been so sure, and the French ambassador, Otto, had had to play a careful game against the Electress, one of the three proud daughters of the Duke of Baden, who had ascended the thrones of Russia, Sweden and Bavaria, and from there had breathed fire and flame against France. Luckily he had been able to rely upon the principal minister, French in ancestry and in name, M. de Montgelas, who dreamed of making Bavaria the Prussia of the nineteenth century, and pursued to that end a see-saw policy between Vienna and Paris. Austria, by a too harsh pressure and the indiscreet invasion of her territory, had done the rest: Bavaria became pro-French for nearly a century.

Münich was to be no Capua for Napoleon. He spent three days of ceremonies and acclamations there, but that did not prevent him from reading despatches and taking his bearings.

The first part of his programme had been achieved—almost too well, in that the success had been sudden and complete. The main Austrian army was prisoner. Now it was the Russians' turn! They had just passed through Vienna and were ascending the Danube to their fate. It was a matter of falling upon them and encircling them in two phases: the army of Kutuzov first, then that of Buxhouden and the Czar.

But Prussia had dropped her pretence. By this October's end, too much reliable information had reached Napoleon for him to ignore the threat. Would he in spite of this launch himself 'into the very entrails of Europe', at the risk of seeing the jaws of an immense trap close on him: the Prussian army falling on his rear through Bohemia and Franconia, in order to extend a hand to Archduke Charles coming up from Italy? He was advised to

---

But something firmer than rock had been exchanged at Potsdam and would triumph in 1815: a wink. That complicity between kings of the same world, who would never agree except superficially, and under a certain constraint that released them from complete loyalty, to admit into their society a lieutenant of artillery of the La Fère regiment.

be prudent, to retreat so that he could base himself on the Rhine and wait upon events. But in that case he allowed time for the two Russian armies to unite, and form a dangerous invasive mass by joining up with the remainder of the Austrians, time also for the Prussians to furbish their arms and enter the lists. Within three months, he would have 400,000 men to cope with. What would be the good of Ulm, then?

Napoleon decided to march on Vienna: at the point he had reached temerity seemed to him the height of prudence. So he left Münich on October 28th, the very day that Masséna had a cannon fired to announce the victory of Ulm to the army of Italy, which he at once swept off, full of exuberance, to attack the Austrians beyond the Adige. He was going to pin Archduke Charles by the decisive battle of Caldiero and force him to remain on the spot, in order to prevent him from flying to the rescue of Vienna. The Austrians could not afford to leave Italy as losers. On that front Napoleon was to be undisturbed for more than a month.

*   *   *   *

Where was Corporal Jean-Pierre Blaise all this time? From Münich, where he scarcely bothered about the welcome given to the Emperor, he wrote his parents a description of his marches—without a battle so far:

' . . . We did not meet with any resistance during the crossing of the Danube, which we effected on the sixth[1] Vendémiaire. On the same day, we heard a brisk cannonade that took place between the Austrians and Marshal Bernadotte's army corps. Wherever we went, we were astonished to find not a single inhabitant: they had all fled into the woods, taking with them whatever they had of most value. This evacuation was the cause of many soldiers indulging in excesses they would not have committed if the inhabitants had stayed at home. It is true that only

[1] Read the sixteenth. The first bulletin of the Grand Army describes the march of the 3rd Army Corps commanded by Marshal Davout thus: 'This Corps crossed the Rhine on the 4th Vendémiaire, at Mannheim, and then headed towards Heidelberg, Necker-Eltz, Meckmühl, Oettingen, Donauwörth'. The second bulletin announced its arrival at Neuberg on the sixteenth Vendémiaire.

the inhabitants who were on the road and around the camps suffered much. The forced marches that we made as far as München did not permit the chief to restrain the disorder to which many soldiers were inclined in a country that we ought to respect as far as supplies allow us.

'After crossing the Danube, we did not remain in any one position, except when we were twenty-four miles from Dachau. We had a false alarm there caused by some marauders who, having ventured too far, had been charged by some Austrian hussars. Our battalion was commended for making a reconnaissance. It returned to camp in the evening, with the exception of our company which was detached out in front in order to observe the enemy. On the following day, our regiment having been assigned to form the advance guard of the army corps, we left camp at two hours after midday in order to reach Dachau, from which we were still distant by twenty-four miles. That was, in part, the day on which we suffered most during the campaign: rain and then snow not having left us for the whole march. To crown the disagreeableness, on arriving, some detachments were ordered to go and seize some enemy posts. This detachment covered a further nine miles: luckily we were billeted on the inhabitants, as were the 13th Light Infantry regiment which was on advance guard with us. It was midnight when we were settled, two sergeants, two corporals and me, who made up the company, the rest having been unable to follow. With what annoyance, at one o'clock, did we hear the sound of the drums beating the peremptory signal for the start! But luckily it was only the 13th Regiment that had to leave. On this same day, the *chasseurs* of the 2nd Regiment, who were on advance guard with us, together with the light cavalry of the King of Bavaria, charged the Austrian Hussars, whom they put to flight, after having killed many and taken a lot prisoner. We found, on the following day, along our route, the signs of the battle. In the evening, on arriving before München, we learned that Marshal Bernadotte's corps had entered. We stayed five or six days near this town, alternatively in bivouac and with the inhabitants. We received just those supplies that we had gone to München to find.

'The town is most pleasant and a great trading centre. The inhabitants there are extremely well dressed, above all the women . . . '

CHAPTER VIII

A GREAT FRIEND TO WINE
AND LOVE

———————

On October 26th, the Grand Army was given its marching
orders for the descent of the Danube, mainly by the right bank,
in the direction of Vienna. Napoleon himself set out, as always
with the Guard, in the company of the Corps of Davout, Soult
and Lannes, and the cavalry reserve. On October 29th and 30th
they crossed the Inn, left Bavaria behind, and invaded Upper
Austria, protected from a possible move by the Archdukes by
Bernadotte and Marmont, who held Salzburg, and by Ney who
shut off the Tyrol. The pace was still brisk, but it was no longer
the triumphant surge of the march of the seven streams.
Memories were dulled with the weather to a uniform grey: the
charm was broken. On All Saints day the ground was covered
by a foot of snow. In spite of the precaution of sending as many
troops as possible through Augsburg, a very well provided town,
revictualling was deplorable and the entire army had empty
stomachs. And a certain threshold of exhaustion had been
crossed: for want of being able to rest men and horses for a
fortnight, the whole of this second part of the campaign would
be conducted with overdriven troops.

Finally, it was no longer a question of a military promenade:
the ground was disputed more keenly from day to day by the
rearguard that covered the gradual withdrawal of the Austro-
Russians. One should say, rather, the Russians: it was Kutuzov
that Napoleon now had in front of him: 65,000 men, of whom
only 10,000 were Austrians, escaped with General Kienmayer
from the disaster of Ulm.

The old Prince, surly and prudent, owing his position to the favour of St. Petersburg, where he had known how to foster his reputation as the owner of a lucky star, had a horror of fighting, or rather, since his physical courage was not in doubt, a horror of sending his soldiers into battle. He was one of the most tenacious husbanders of human blood known to military history. He had already advanced, all abristle with suspicion, towards Ulm in order to join Mack there, and had grumbled against that risky offensive which to him seemed so unpromising, and now here he was suddenly in the front line, with a flood of Frenchmen twice his strength bearing down on him.

What of it? Kutuzov, delighted at heart, at once began to organize one of those stubborn retreats of which he had the secret. He set everything in motion so as to recross as quickly as possible to the left bank of the Danube and join up, somewhere in Bohemia or Moravia, with the powerful reserve his sovereign was bringing him. One small detail: this plan meant abandoning Vienna, not that this would deprive Kutuzov of his sleep. But the Austrians would not hear of it. The Emperor Francis hurried along in person to plead for his capital at the Russian headquarters. To fight for it in earnest he knew was impossible with the forces opposing them. At least, he got Kutuzov to undertake to resist every inch of the way, making use of all the tributaries to the Danube, which enter the great river at right-angles and provide natural lines of defence. At this time of year the waters were high, torrential, and full of ice-floes. The bridges could be systematically cut, and strong rear-guards could hamper the French and compel them to make their way by sheer force. The Austrians hoped that this would allow time for Archduke Charles on the one hand, and the Czar on the other, to arrive below Vienna and join up with Kutuzov for a battle that would save the city. The latter well knew that this was a vain hope, but fifty years acquaintance with princes had given him an unrivalled skill in talking away time. He shrugged his shoulders and arranged to make a show of covering Vienna. In the depths of his being an explicit resolve dictated his actions: he wanted above all to avoid the encirclement of his army. To this end he was ready to throw out as so much ballast, Vienna, the hereditary States of the Habsburgs, Poland, and even some good slices of Russia. No matter what, rather than suffer the fate of Mack.

As for Napoleon, he wanted to encircle Kutuzov. He set his army at the tributaries of the Danube and cleared them with the dash of a rider carrying his mount over a brook. Blow by blow, the Inn, the Traun, the Enns were crossed. At Linz, on November 8th, the Emperor received an envoy from the Allies, General Giulay, charged with proposing an armistice that would save Vienna and give the Russians some elbow-room. He had a good point there!

'Do you bring formal conditions of peace?' Napoleon asked him. 'If yes, I will stop at the gates of Vienna. If not, go your way: I will pursue mine.'

Giulay could only stammer and leave, bearing a letter for Francis that was a model of arrogance and insulting politeness:

'His Majesty will feel that it is right I should profit from chances that have been favourable to me and that the conditions of peace should offer me a guarantee against a fourth coalition with England . . . for I shall regard as fortunate for me all the circumstances that place me in a position to reconcile the security of my people with His friendship, to which I pray Him to allow that I may still lay claim, in spite of the number and the power of my enemies around Him.'

In the meantime, the advance went on, at the cost of hand-to-hand encounters, brief but ever more severe.

The advance proceeded amidst an impressive paraphernalia, somewhat cramped between the Danube and the Alps, from which Napoleon was haunted by the fear of seeing the Archduke Charles appear. In this progression from west to east, Marmont held the right, on the crest of the Alps. Then came Davout travelling half-way up. In the plain, along the right bank of the Danube, Soult, Lannes, Bernadotte and Murat led the bulk of the army. On the left bank, a corps had been formed under the command of Mortier with the divisions of Dupont and Gazan.

The route of the main part of the army, passable at first, became more and more uneven. It followed closely all the bends in the Danube, at the foot of high wooded mountains and precipitous rocks, amongst which the river was swallowed up in a dark gorge. Occasionally, the way was barely indicated over the slabs of granite or across the pebbly strands, leaving only a narrow path for haulage. There the infantrymen set their feet bleeding; the horses slipped and stumbled at almost every step; the artillery was dislocated by the jolts.

Jean-Pierre Blaise finally received his baptism of fire, without much apparent emotion. He told his parents of his departure from München and recounted the first episodes in the pursuit of 'some of the troops of the Emperor': that is to say, of Francis of Austria. To a lad brought up in Walloonia, 'the Emperor' meant the latter. There had been only one of them during the whole of his childhood:

'The Austrians had abandoned their positions during the night and we set off in pursuit of them. We did not come upon them again before Lambach [on the Traun], to which they had once again cut the bridge in order to have time to save themselves. We crossed the river that washes the walls of Lambach over a bridge of boats. The enemy still held a few little posts which our marksmen dispersed. We found a lot of men who, having been unable to follow the rapidity of their retreat, gave themselves up as prisoners. We noticed from that time that there were many stragglers among the Emperor's troops. That made us certain of beating them if they had wanted to wait for us. In addition, we were so cross with them for keeping us on the run that we would not have spared them in a fight.

'After Lambach, we marched as far as Steyr [on the Enns], picking up prisoners all the time, who told us of the discouragement in their army. The enemy, according to his custom, burnt the bridge over the river at Steyr. It was there that they held out the longest. Volunteers were called for in our two regiments, the 13th and the 108th, to swim across the river and to take some boats to the other side. Three men, one of whom was from the 13th and two from our own, had the courage to swim across the river. The enemy, who were lying in wait in the houses of the suburbs and who from there greatly hampered the men working on the reconstruction of the bridge, were so astonished at this excess of bravery that they gave themselves up to these men and to those who had crossed in the boats. Our division was with us on that day; along with the 13th regiment, we bivouacked in the woods that dominate the town; we crossed the river in the morning of the 14th in some boats, the bridge not yet being re-established. At midday, a reconnaissance party having reported that the enemy had evacuated completely, we set off on the march. We arrived very late in a village where we bivouacked. We left this position on the following day the fifteenth, and took the road through the gorges of Styria. We followed the enemy so closely that they were not three hours ahead of us, and we found the embers of their fires still warm. We bivouacked on the evening of the fifteenth on the great eminence that dominates the village of Undoffenne [?], in which we would have lodged if the enemy had not been so well within range. It was again one of the most wretched nights that we had spent; we could hardly remain lying down, such was the steepness of the slope and, on the other hand, there was so far to go to fetch water that we arranged matters so that we made our soup for the following day in the morning. We abandoned the position the next day at six o'clock in order to continue our march through the gorge.

'I believe I told you just now that we were following the enemy most closely. Indeed, on that day we took from them a substantial convoy of vehicles with armaments, camping equipment, clothing. What was most use to us were their sky-blue trousers like the Hungarians', their ankle boots, linen drawers, and their greatcoats. Our company of *voltigeurs* profited from the occasion to arm themselves with sabres. In this convoy there was also the equipment of a regiment of Uhlans: all their instruments and books of music were there, as well as the sacred vessels and the vestments of the chaplain. These valuable effects were not collected; we tipped the vehicles into the gorge in order not to impede the passage of the artillery. We had a most unhappy night, reduced to little organization, but we may hope that tomorrow will be more propitious.'

* * * *

To link the two banks, a numerous flotilla, made up of boats acquired after Ulm, descended well loaded with supplies, munitions and recuperating men under the direction of Captain Lostanges, a naval officer of the Guard. In one hour it could transfer 10,000 men to the left or the right.

This ingenious device was to come to an end, however, at the first serious check in the campaign, when already there occurred what was to be known as 'the miscarriage of Austerlitz'; at the moment when he was in danger of being harried too closely, Kutuzov left the Danube, the route to Vienna and the disconsolate Austrians in the lurch, so as to withdraw his army in a northerly direction.

This took place at Krems, on November 9th.

A glance at the map shows that at this town, of some importance, the Danube ends a bend to the north and resumes its direction due east. On the 5th, near Amstetten, a good deal further upstream, a fierce delaying engagement had mauled Murat's dragoons and Lannes' grenadiers, who had had to fight hand-to-hand all day in order to advance, at last, over a thousand dead. Following that, they had been somewhat astonished to tumble almost into a vacuum, because of the unexpected acceleration in the Russian retreat. Nothing on the 6th, nothing on the 7th. The French advance guard finally realized that at Amstetten they had passed through a curtain and that Kutuzov had taken a certain initiative. Spurred on by the impetuosity of Murat, whose cavalry was exhausted, and the chronic ill-humour of Lannes, the spearhead of the French army extended itself dangerously and the whole ingenious structure of the advance was thrown out of order: through the fault, mainly, of Napoleon, who remained two marches to the rear and had neglected to satisfy himself that his orders were properly carried out. He had prescribed, in theory, a close liaison between the Corps that were advancing on the two banks of the Danube. He relied too much on his lieutenants to realize it in practice.

When, on November 8th, Lannes and Murat came upon the Russians in imposing order of battle, suggesting the imminence at last of a serious encounter, no-one knew where the Danube flotilla was in tow, Mortier had no more than a corps, reduced by three days marching, on the left bank of the Danube and he was completely cut off from the rest of the army, which was itself trailing as best it could after the impetuous leaders of the advance guard. The latter were forced to contain themselves throughout the 8th, for lack of sufficient means to give battle. They cooled their heels, therefore, while waiting for reinforcements and the Emperor, at the foot of an immense conglomeration of imposing buildings, spread out under magnificent domes: the Abbey of Mölk. It extended to the impatient warriors the consolations of a rich cellar, with seemingly inexhaustible reserves, liberally distributed by the monks in exchange for respect for the premises, which they themselves prepared for the sick and wounded. The officers who imbibed there spoke of it for the rest of their lives with profound nostalgia. Ah, the wines of Mölk! Some of them drank together in groups of six or eight, from huge earthenware vessels into which they dipped drinking straws.

The next day came a dramatic surprise. The Russians withdrew without fighting, and before Murat was able to charge them, he learned that at Krems, far behind the protective curtain of troops drawn across at St Pölten, the bulk of the Russian army had crossed the river and was retreating out of reach of the encirclement that had been the supreme object laid down by Napoleon. Only one corps of Austrians remained opposite the French, and this was withdrawing along the right bank, in the direction of the bridges of Vienna, situated outside the city, to the north. The capital itself, the scouts discovered, was two days' march away by a direct route completely open to the invaders. If Murat had had an ounce of grey matter, he would have concentrated all his efforts on overtaking Kutuzov and to that end would have tried to repair the bridges that the Russians had naturally destroyed at Krems, and then hurry after him in force. There might still have been time to catch him, pin him down somewhere and resume the encircling operation. At all events, the matter was of such importance that orders from Napoleon should have been awaited before deciding what direction to take.

Murat rushed blindly on Vienna.

Nothing counted for him any more, except to be the first French leader to enter it as conqueror. For 300 years this city had defied Paris, prevented her continental expansion, threatened French frontiers and challenged her influence in the world. The captivity of Francis I had never been avenged. And now, by an odd quirk of fate, the ruler who bore that name was an Austrian! To humiliate Vienna was to provide an outlet for the repression so deeply seated in the French people, the same that had driven the Parisian crowd to look on at the execution of Marie-Antoinette. And it would be an inn-keeper's son, Joachim Murat, who would become the only man in the world to lead an army through those inviolate walls, which even the Turks had been unable to breach.

On November 10th and 11th Murat galloped towards Vienna, showering Soult and Lannes, who remained behind, with invitations to follow. He ended by stopping, as if struck with superstitious fear, six miles from his prey, in the mountainous pass of Kahlenberg. His dream shattered that evening under the terrible blow of a letter of rebuke from Napoleon, written from Mölk, where the Emperor had arrived at last.

'I cannot approve of your method of advance. You are carrying on like a lunatic, and you are taking no account of the orders I have sent you. The Russians, instead of protecting Vienna, have recrossed the Danube at Krems. This extraordinary fact should have made you realize that you ought not to move without fresh instructions . . . Without knowing what plans the enemy might have, or being aware what my intentions were in this new state of affairs, you go and set my army at Vienna . . . You have considered nothing but the petty triumph of entering Vienna. There is no glory except where there is danger. There is none in entering a defenceless capital.'

Napoleon, as usual, was all the more incensed since he wanted more than anything to seize it for himself. At the moment of writing this reprimand to Murat, he sensed the terrible danger in which Marshal Mortier found himself, completely isolated on the left bank, and with only Gazan's division at his disposal, Dupont having been left far behind. With these 5,000 men, he came upon the 40,000 Russians who had just crossed the Danube. Borne along at first by the aggressive spirit of the leap taken at Boulogne, Mortier pushed forward without really knowing what he had in front of him, and one of the best artillery officers of the Empire, Colonel Fabvier, set ten pieces to fire point-blank at the Russian squares. The carnage went on for half a day before Mortier realized that the more he battered the Russians the more they came; they threw themselves against the guns and submerged them like ants. Perceiving Mortier's weakness then, Kutuzov outflanked him, drove him to the bank of the Danube and firmly locked up his prize by taking the town of Dirnstein which the French had passed through that morning.

Mortier understood, towards evening. The thought of capitulation never crossed his mind. There remained a slender hope: Dupont's division was marching towards Dirnstein. Mortier gave orders to fall back to meet him: the fearful conflict of the day began again in reverse, but by night this time; the men slaughtered each other as best they could in the glow from torches and houses set on fire. If only the French could retake Dirnstein and barricade themselves there! But however successfully the enemy was thrust aside, wave upon wave, the way was endlessly barred. Mortier, sword in hand, fought at the head of his grenadiers, and the situation became so serious that his officers begged him to escape by boat, in order to extricate at least a Marshal of France from capture!

'No, gentlemen. One cannot part company with such brave men. One can only survive or perish with them!'

But what was that? Suddenly the sound of cannon-shots, brisk volleys of muskets, far behind, on the other side of the town . . .

'It's Dupont! We're saved!'

Realizing the threat to his chief, the brave General had hurried towards the gunfire with his division, and had surprised the Russians by a sudden attack with the same regiments that had already, at Haslach, held their own at odds of one against four: the 9th Light, the 32nd and the 96th of the Line. It was now the Russians' turn to wonder whether they had not been outflanked, and whether it was not Napoleon himself who had suddenly arrived. They disengaged themselves as quickly as they could from Dirnstein, where the two French columns met, recognized each other, and embraced in the glow from the braziers. So many bodies were recovered on the following day that it could be said that each Frenchman had killed his Russian: about 4,000. They had escaped disaster this time at odds of one against eight.

When Dumonceau's Batavian division came along it found the little town sacked abominably by the competitive pillaging of the Russian and French troops: such a scene was unusual in this campaign, for in general there was restraint towards civilians. It so impressed the honest Dutchmen that they remained distressed by it. Doors were smashed in, cupboards opened and emptied, household goods scattered, furniture, glassware, window-panes broken, pictures pierced by bayonet thrusts, hangings torn . . . Wine alone abounded. It was brought up by the bucketful from the adjacent cellars. These had all been opened, their doors forced by shots fired into the locks, and the casks had evidently been broached by a ball. The buckets had been filled at these improvised fountains, which had then been left to run; as a result the cellars were awash. One drew from them as from a pond: a few Russians were discovered there, drowned—in wine.

As soon as he was informed, Napoleon heaped rewards on the divisions of Gazan and Dupont. At one moment he had thought the former to be utterly lost: this would not have been catastrophic from the point of view of effectives, but of prestige, At a single stroke, the encirclement and destruction of a French corps would have wiped out the effect of Ulm in the whole of Europe.

The Emperor relieved his feelings—and eased his conscience—against Murat, and then set everything in motion to resume his original plan: after all, Kutuzov did not have wings, and could not be more than three days' march away at most. If the Grand Army could gain speed on him and arrive in Moravia before him, at the point where the route from Krems meets the highway to Olmütz, it would still be possible to surround him.

But between the Russians and the French the mighty Danube stretched in all its breadth and there was no time to reconstruct one of the bridges destroyed upstream of Vienna. Orders were therefore given to Murat to redeem himself, not by entering the city with impunity, but by skirting its walls and performing a miracle: he was enjoined to seize the great bridge that spanned the river beyond the suburbs. Now the Austrians, cut off from the Russian army, were holding the two ends in strength and had stuffed it with mines, ready to spring it. For want of sufficient numbers to defend their capital, they were resigned to declaring it an open city and to entrusting Count de Würbna, an able diplomat, with coming to terms with the French for a peaceful occupation. But as for letting them go further, no! All their hopes lay in preparing for the rescue of Vienna through the return in force of the large reserves coming from the north.

Vienna is situated about two-thirds of a mile from the Danube, which flows to the north of it in a number of branches that wash round wooded islands. A whole line, long and sinuous, of little bridges links the latter right up to the great bridge thrown across the main branch. On November 12th, Murat and Lannes, the two inseparables, presented themselves at this spot, accompanied by some aides-de-camp. Behind the beplumed group round the two Marshals of France, Oudinot's grenadiers advanced with the stealth of Red Indians, under cover of the luxuriant growth that fringed the Danube. On the right bank the Austrians had left only some observation posts, so as not to be enveloped there. They held chiefly the left bank with 7,000 to 8,000 men commanded by Count d'Auersberg, artillery sighted, lances burning ready to set fire to the inflammable material carefully distributed under the floor of the main bridge.

There they were, Lannes, Murat, General Bertrand, Colonel Dode, approaching the head of the bridge in the open, making vague signs, running the gauntlet of a few carbine shots. The Austrian hussars, impressed by the sudden apparition of these species of war-gods whose exploits had resounded for ten years —the great French leaders!—hesitated to shoot them down. Besides, they were shouting a magic word:

'Armistice! Armistice!'

At this very moment Napoleon was arriving almost alone at the chateau of Schönbrunn, the Versailles of Austria. He would sleep in the bed of Joseph II. Austria was stricken to the heart and full of the upheaval attendant on a great defeat, when it seems impossible that the world should continue on its way while the whole pride of a nation is tottering. Rumours of an end to hostilities, born almost spontaneously a little everywhere, ran as much through the army as through the civilian population. When therefore an N.C.O. of the Austrian artillery, at the entry to the bridge, brandished a lighted fuse in order to set fire to the faggots, he let himself be overborne by the mild violence of Dode, who seized his arms, stopped him, and pushed him firmly the whole length of the bridge towards the other bank, where the sentries saw advancing upon them a group of French officers and their own officers in some kind of discussion. One could hardly fire into that lot. So, talking casually together, Lannes, Murat and their accomplices had crossed the bridge. They gained a footing on the other side, haranguing the Austrian gunners.

'The armistice has been signed . . . or will be at any moment, my friends! How is it that you have heard nothing about it? Peace is being negotiated! Lead us to your general!'

Dode and Bertrand were taken to Count d'Auersberg. Lannes and Murat remained at the end of the bridge, quaking inwardly. Where had those dawdlers got to, those grenadiers whom they knew to be over there, on the right bank, creeping up under cover of the large trees and the reeds? Suddenly brief orders rang out: there they were! The column appeared at the double, charging towards the bridge! The bewildered Austrians gave orders to fire: Lannes and Murat threw themselves in front of the cannon roaring at the gun-crews to intimidate them, and administering a few blows:

'You're not going to break the truce, are you, you miscreants? Our soldiers over there come by agreement with your general! You'll get yourselves shot!'

The poor wretches no longer knew which way to turn. The grenadiers were upon them, taking over their pieces, disarming them and moving on. Count d'Auersberg, arriving unexpectedly at that moment, could do nothing except make a show of admitting the fiction of an armistice and order his soldiers to withdraw with him some distance from the river: if he had not, he too would have been carried away by the swelling tide of Frenchmen.

The bridges of Vienna were in Napoleon's hands.

The Emperor, delighted, completely forgave Murat, who was already away, straining his horses to cut off Kutuzov's retreat on the road to Hollabrünn, followed by the two infantry corps of Lannes and Soult. It was November 14th when Napoleon entered Vienna and received the keys from its citizens; he rode through the city calm and dignified. The inhabitants did not appear to be as friendly in French eyes as the latter would have liked to claim, but adopted a kind of impassiveness that suited the Viennese temperament: one would think that the events did not concern them. There was also, among many, relief at the sight of an army that was evidently strictly disciplined, whereas it had been represented as a horde of wolves. General Clarke, appointed governor of the city, kept a close watch over respect for persons and property, on condition that the soldiers were well lodged and amply fed.

As for the officers, they revelled, those at least to whom the urgency of the advance towards Moravia allowed the leisure. They tasted gilded ease in soft apartments, overheated by tiled stoves fed with wood from a passage outside the rooms, which enabled a fire to be kindled and maintained without disturbing the occupant. The double glazing of the windows surprised them: very few areas had them in France. They wandered without risk through the city, intimidating in its majesty, its huge open spaces, its ramparts fortified with moats, escarpment and counter-escarpment covered with turf, the glacis, or slope up to the fortress, forming a broad esplanade bounded by extensive suburbs. They flocked to the Imperial Palace of the Hofburg, 'a substantial building, of sombre aspect and slight distinction, having the appearance of a prison', to the cathedral of St Stephen, to the military arsenal 'containing sundry curiosities such as, amongst others, the great chain with which the Turks closed the Danube at the time of the siege of 1683'. Very quickly they exchanged victuals and pleasantries with the civil guard, who supported the internal police — and with a number of beauties with 'strange, gilded hair-styles'. The cultivated went to 'the Opera theatre, known as the Court, providing a most beautiful auditorium coupled with a stage of vast proportions decorated with charming scenes and often the most remarkable optical effects'. They were performing The Magic Flute. But justice requires mention of another that was much frequented, the Kasperletheater, 'a kind of variétés, situated in one of the suburbs beyond the Red Gate, and dedicated to bawdy pieces, occasionally even such as were somewhat licentious . . . '

A whole battalion was occupied for several days in listing the unprecedented riches found intact at the great arsenal: a hundred thousand muskets, two thousand artillery pieces, and virtually inexhaustible ammunition. Nothing could have been more useful to the Grand Army whose rapid march had outstripped its reserves: at a later date the Russians would remark bitterly to their allies that they had been bombarded, at Austerlitz, by projectiles presented to the French by the negligence of the Austrian government.

And so, quite astonished at finding themselves further afield than their forebears had ever been, the French contemplated their strange and agreeable enemy, Austria. And on her side, quite downcast by a rape so little painful and so very rapid, Austria raised puzzled eyes. So these were the eaters of priests![1]

*　　　*　　　*　　　*

'Dear cousin, My God, these people know how to drink!' wrote a citizen of Laybach. 'Each man would be capable of emptying a barrel on his own. I believe your cow drinks less water a day than a Frenchman does wine, and yet I am myself quite a heavy drinker; but alongside them I am really a mere shadow . . . '

And the same correspondent followed this a few days later with a striking example of this French capacity. The story also bears witness to the Draconian discipline that certain leaders imposed on their men—cruelly, in some cases. The matter here concerned the execution of a French grenadier condemned by Bernadotte to be shot because he had stolen in the open street a working-woman's ear-rings:

'My God, dear cousin, that man certainly gave proof of his courage! This comes, you know, from the fact that these people

[1] The historian Raoul Chélard, in 1893, had the good fortune to discover a series of colourful accounts by inhabitants of the invaded areas, which allow a clear idea to be formed of the image the French presented at the start of the Empire to Germany, who was seeing her for the first time: *Les Armées françaises jugées par les habitants de l'Autriche*, Plon, 1893.

have no God, no religion, and no fear of Hell, nor of purgatory, nor of death either!

'From love of death, he had got himself well and truly drunk, and when the sentence was read to him, he calmly kept his cap on his head, his pipe in his mouth, and a big bottle of brandy under his arm. He listened to the pronouncement with indifference; nevertheless, at the word *death*, he hurled his bottle from him.'

At Salzburg, an old officer of the Austrian dragoons watched the progress of a French corps with an observant eye:

'Among them one can now see a number who are dressed in peasant smocks, in coats of sheepskin or the fur of some wild animal; others are rigged out in the most strange manner and carry long sides of bacon, ham, pieces of meat hanging from their belts. They are veritable walking larders. Others march with their bodies hung all over with loaves of bread and bottles of wine . . .

' . . . Their knapsack remains, in the meantime, as lean as it was at the start of the campaign; in the matter of cash, their need is as great as their purse is empty; this doesn't prevent them from lighting their pipes with bank-notes or bills of the Bank of Vienna, of which they make great game. I know someone who, for two crowns [six francs], bought from some French hussars a bundle of bank-notes representing a value of 4,000 florins which, to their mind, were fit only for lighting their pipes. Here is the reason for this attitude: the French soldier believes that a bank-note is worth no more than the Assignats of the Revolution. He knows, moreover, of no greater enemy on earth than paper money and, if it were left to him, he would voluntarily undertake a world-wide crusade in order to destroy it.'

Canon Nicolas Trauner, a teacher at the Abbey of St Zeno, takes up the discussion:

'They were Frenchmen, that is to say people who, even in their own country, don't know how to save or live soberly; then their love of conversation makes solitude odious to them. Yet, to be frank, it must be admitted that the vivacity of their minds and the readiness of their speech animates in a singular manner our German heaviness in our conversations with them.

'Their Epicurean taste craved great variety in choice of dishes. Few things, but good ones, was their motto for the table.

'Everything they ate had to be of an agreeable flavour and of the first quality. They demanded excessive cleanliness in the kitchen and in the tableware.

'The French officers, in general, did not seem to me to like playing at cards. One could not say the same of the men. But what they loved was discussions about the high feats of arms of their leaders. They enjoyed recalling them, and I have heard them discussing matters of this kind for days on end. As for the works of Rousseau and Voltaire, they devoured them, literally; everyone possessed them; they read them and reread them; but I did not notice that besides the revolutionary books in their hands, they had also brought along any works on religious subjects.

'At every turn, they pronounce upon questions of religion and politics, and this with a freedom of opinion and an utter lack of ceremony. In the presence of others, I always heard them speak with horror of the time of Robespierre. As for the words *Liberty, Equality,* I often saw a smile on their lips as they spoke them.

' . . . It is rather difficult to discern the religion of the French today, because they have none to speak of, their religious principles being entirely negative. All the same, there are among them a lot of Christians, unfortunately also a lot of these terrible atheists . . . '

Several other accounts reveal a genuine fascination amongst the Germans, wholly shaped by a traditional Catholicism permeating every minute of life, public and private, in face of these strange men—but were they still men?—who professed not to believe in God. How could they keep their two feet on the ground? How was it they were never struck by lightning at the time of such adventures as that recounted by a completely terror-stricken Augustinian monk from the monastery of Muhlen:

'The French arrived on the 15th. Our monastery received some troops immediately. They consisted of 2 majors, 4 captains, 1 adjutant, 6 servants, 12 horses, 258 men, to which were added in the evening 102 other soldiers. One of the captains, with the name of Jardinier, took control of the monastery.

'In the evening the officers ate with very good appetite. After the meal they demanded warm wine with sugar, and the soldiers warm brandy, also sugared, which seems to be the favourite drink of the French.

'We thought we had offered them an excellent meal; it seems that it was nothing of the kind, for an officer sought out the Superior of the monastery and said to him:

' "Ah, what a dog's dinner! Filthy priests, you have no idea!" '

These, nevertheless, were the same men of whom an inhabitant of Muhldorf reported with compassion the following gesture:

'While the French were occupying our town, one of the inhabitants came to pass away in poverty, leaving a widow and four little sick children in the most extreme deprivation.

'Unexpectedly, on the evening of this sad event, the unfortunate widow had a visit from a countryman who brought her a present of money of some substance. She thanked him with tears in her eyes and asked the name of the generous donor; to which the other replied evasively, saying that he had instructions not to name him.

'Become curious, we made a little enquiry on our own account, and it was then that we discovered that he, or rather the donors, were none other than the officers of the 23rd demi-brigade, garrisoned at Muhldorf, who, at the instigation of their commander, had clubbed together in order to offer the unfortunate woman something to regain her health and supply her elementary needs.'

The synthesis is provided, with much balance and judgment, by an ecclesiastical dignitary, Joseph Philipp, the priest at Eisenerz. Napoleon's soldier springs to life in his account:

'We are far from believing that it would render a service to posterity to draw a portrait of a people who themselves were just enough to call themselves the scourge of Germany.

'But, in order to correct a large number of contradictory opinions and to enable posterity to judge for itself this strange race of men who at the end of the eighteenth century convulsed the surface of the earth, we set down here a faithful portrait, an authentic copy taken from the unforgettable original, whom we have had the misfortune to be able to study at close quarters for sixty-five days on end.

'At the moment of his entry into an inhabitant's house, the Frenchman spreads dismay and fear around him; at the same time, a disposition that knows how to preserve its composure very soon makes it clear that thunder does less harm than it makes noise!

'In the matter of contributions, requisitions, extortions, the Frenchman uses, to their full extent, the terrible rights that war and victory give him, but petty clandestine thefts, pillage and larceny in the cantonments are beneath his character.

'One would not deny him courage and resolution in battle, but he fears defence and popular uprisings.

'The Frenchman is scrupulous in the army, but hostile to every petty military restriction in what concerns the secondary exigencies of the profession of arms.

'In entering a peasant's house, he breathes forth fire and flames and there is no end to the orders he gives for the care and comfort of his person; but when he has been made welcome, when he has been shown a pleasing countenance, when an eagerness to serve him has been manifested, it is enough for several good reasons to cool his bubbling head, after which he is usually satisfied with very few things.

'He loves cleanliness above all, and this habit is indeed the cause of his robust health.

'Never does he load his stomach with over-heavy dishes or consume in too great a quantity, and there, it would seem, is the source of his great powers of mind and body.

'He is always in motion, gay, and disposed to pleasure, but even his amusements always have a certain connection with war.

'He is a great friend to wine and love. The first drives him mad and insufferable, the latter leads him to employ the most terrible means to arrive at his gallant ends.

'Even in enemy territory, he respects the local authorities and inhabitants of a superior social position, but he has no sympathy for the simple peasant.

'Frivolity and suspiciousness are his predominant weaknesses; appreciation and gratitude occupy the first rank in the list of his virtues.'

CHAPTER IX

COUNTER-TRAP IN MORAVIA

In twenty days the French army had come from the sea to the Rhine. In forty, from the Rhine to Vienna. Every capital admired, even against its will, this advance, unique in the annals of history up to that time. But it was the prowess of an acrobat, balancing in the middle of his tight-rope with victories in his arms—which were not Victory. Napoleon and the Grand Army now found themselves condemned to a decisive blow—or annihilation. The whole of Europe had turned into one vast trap, into whose depths he was plunging headlong. The remains of the Austrian forces and the Russian invasion army, which was on the point of being doubled by the addition of Buxhouden's troops to those of Kutuzov, and some day or other the Prussian army, surrounded the manifest conquerors in a terrible semi-circle.

Napoleon was fully aware of this. Despatch riders from Paris, moreover, brought him news of a frightened France, shaken by the paroxysm of the financial crisis, where sly intrigues were being hatched even in his own family to anticipate his replacement in the event of his being hit by a stray ball. He felt almost as precarious as on the eve of Marengo. The cannon of the Invalides had thundered in vain every week to announce fresh successes, the people remained inert. And the middle classes, who had hitherto been his most faithful supporters, were full of an unrest that bordered on panic.

He had in his pocket, since November 10th, despatches from Decrès telling him of Trafalgar.

Napoleon therefore concentrated all his resources, and first his mind, on this decisive victory, to secure which had been his essential aim since the dictation of August 13th. The *coup*. His *coup*. The one he had undoubtedly dreamed about ever since the school at Brienne: a battle that would supersede all battles and render them useless.

He stationed Marmont's corps in Styria, in the Alps, in order to guard the main road from Italy to Vienna and to help Masséna bar the way to Archdukes Charles and John. He left Davout at Vienna, with the two divisions of Gudin and Friant which were detached to the outskirts to watch the approaches from Hungary. And the bulk of the army, led by Soult, Lannes and Murat, set off by forced marches to intercept Kutuzov's retreat, which already had Bernadotte hard on its heels.

The Emperor himself remained in Vienna: two days too long. This might cost him dear.

. . . It was still Murat who had command of the advance guard.

*   *   *   *

November 15th. The French cavalry had won the race: thanks to the capture of the bridges of Vienna, they had arrived first at Hollabrünn and had encamped, revictualling themselves as best they could, in the fields already covered with frost around the pretty little market town with its six churches. Murat, worn out, having had no sleep for three days, arranged to defend in strength the critical point Kutuzov would have to pass in order to join the road through Moravia and head for Olmütz. He was very worried: already he had been warned of the approach of the Russian advance guard, who would undoubtedly hurl themselves upon him with the violence of those who had to open up a way at all costs. He knew that nearly 50,000 men were following them and would try to pass below the town under cover of these encounters. Now, he had at his disposal only five to six thousand cavalrymen on foundered horses, and as many infantry: Soult's corps had not yet arrived. Lannes was there, with only Oudinot's grenadiers. Even by getting themselves killed on the spot, how could they cut off the Russians effectively?

But suddenly trumpets sounded at the outposts. An emissary from Kutuzov with a flag of truce was asking to confer with the Commander-in-Chief. It was the charming general Count Winzegerode, a western German full of refined courtesy, beneath which he concealed his tenacious hatred of France. It was this that had led him into the Czar's service. He would have served the Emperor of China had it been necessary to defeat the Usurper. His distinction, and the great consideration this fine nobleman of high birth pretended to show him, impressed Murat, who moreover always tried, through a trait of his character, to cut a good figure in his enemies' eyes when he was not charging them sabre in hand. The two of them carried on a fencing bout of urbanity in front of Lannes, who looked progressively glummer the more he smelled the trap, but had to defer to Napoleon's brother-in-law.

'Prince Kutuzov sends me to inform you, my lord, of the arrival at Schönbrunn of negotiators who are to sign peace. In consequence, he proposes to you an armistice whose main condition is to halt our troops forthwith in the positions they mutually occupy. In the event of operations being resumed, the one to break the truce would give notice six hours in advance.'

Murat blossomed out into the classic role of the biter bit. Lannes made desperate signs to him in vain. Come, now! Both of them, eight days earlier, had recited almost word for word the same story to the officers defending the bridges of Vienna! The trick was being rudely returned but with such aplomb, and above all it came at such an unexpectedly opportune moment to enable them to wait for reinforcements, that Murat fell into the trap with alacrity. He accepted the armistice, subject to the approval of the Emperor, to whom he sent one of his aides-de-camp.

On the following day he was paid a visit. Kutuzov? Certainly not: he was already far away. It was Bagration, who commanded his rearguard, come to greet Murat and Lannes in order to obscure, by a screen of compliments, the veil his men were in the midst of drawing around Hollabrünn, under cover of which the whole of the rest of the Russian army was calmly marching by and taking the road through Moravia.

Bagration and Lannes felt alike: the great nobleman and the great soldier, both simple, both mistrustful and bluff in manner, too frank at heart to play out the comedy for long.

'If I had been alone,' said Lannes finally, 'we should now be engaged in fighting each other instead of exchanging civilities . . .'

'Do you believe we lose much by waiting?' answered Bagration with a smile.

He had hardly returned to his lines when a high-ranking officer on a frothing white horse, General Lemarrois, brought poor Murat an epitome in a few lines of a terrible Napoleonic rage:

'It is impossible for me to find words in which to express my displeasure to you. You have command of my advance guard only, and you do not have the right to conclude an armistice without my orders. You are causing me to lose the fruits of a campaign. Break the armistice at once and march on the enemy . . . March! Destroy the Russian army. You are in a position to take his baggage train and artillery. The Emperor of Russia's aide-de-camp is a jackass. The Austrians let themselves be taken in over the passage of the Vienna bridges; you have let yourself be taken in by an aide-de-camp of the Czar! . . .'

'At last,' said Lannes. He nevertheless took the trouble to send courteously to Bagration to inform him that it would be necessary to fight it out, while Murat, mad with humiliation, took up positions for the attack.

Kutuzov was as yet not far out of reach. Bagration had to let himself be battered in order to give him some elbow-room. It was the kind of mission he loved. On the evening of November 16th, Lannes thrust his grenadiers at him. The ground allowed no other dispositions but two lines of infantry deployed opposite each other. After an exchange of most murderous volleys, the two masses of foot-soldiers clashed resolutely at bayonet-point, without either of them giving way until they grappled. The hand-to-hand fighting, very brief, was of an unprecedented violence. Superior in numbers, Oudinot's grenadiers slashed the Russians to pieces and then carried, house by house, in the light of the flames, the fired village of Schöngraben.

By midnight Bagration had lost 3,000 men, but darkness enabled him to save the rest by a retreat in good order, and denied pursuit to Murat's cavalry.

Hollabrünn was a victory that cost the French dear: in spite of an exhausting chase, they did not catch up with Kutuzov again and had to be satisfied with collecting stragglers at every step. On November 19th they took Brünn, the capital of Moravia, which the Allies made more than a show of defending: on that day, at Olmütz, the two great Russian armies were united, as were the Emperors of Austria and Russia. An immense force was thus reconstituted to the north of Vienna, and was preparing to reverse the fortunes of war.

*   *   *   *

The general situation had therefore become extremely serious for the French. As they knew in Vienna, in Berlin, in London, in Italy—and in Paris.

Napoleon had made a success of Ulm and held Vienna. But he had then floundered, at Krems and at Hollabrünn, in his constant attempts to drive Kutuzov's army back towards the south, where it could be brought to a standstill in a region shut off by the Alps, the Danube and the Adriatic, where above all he would be able to cut its lines of communication with Prussia and Russia. After winning the first part of the gigantic game of prisoners' base, Napoleon had lost the second. The Allies, through Olmütz, held a strong line, for operations, for revictualling, and for possible retreat, either on Poland or on Silesia. A prolonged pursuit would only separate the French army from its reinforcements, already slender and remote, without providing much further opportunity for immediate battle.

Napoleon decided to halt, to allow as much breathing space as possible to his troops, who had great need of it, and chose for the whole of his army a huge waiting position that was not to vary except in detail until the Allies resumed the offensive. But that was in the hands of destiny: would they resume it? At least, would they resume it at once, on the ground where he was awaiting them, and on relatively equal terms, whereas by being patient for a few weeks they would have the whole additional weight of the Prussian army?

Napoleon had to provoke them into it, under threat of catastrophe.

The Austro-Russo-Prussian block consisted of more than

400,000 men, grouped in solid masses around the forces, half their size, which France could command. These latter were split up, moreover, dispersed by the demands of an offensive radiating deep into enemy territory. It was with fifteen to twenty little corps distributed between Brünn, Venice, Rennes and Utrecht that he would have to fight 85,000 Austro-Russians concentrated around Olmütz, 60,000 others who were coming to the rescue through Poland, 80,000 Austrians assembled in the Carnic Alps—and, at any minute, 200,000 Prussians (and Anglo-Russians) marching through lower Germany.

It is true that in the hands of a military genius as dashing as Napoleon, the dispersal of his forces becomes an advantage. He used the stratagem that had already served him by sending out rapidly in the necessary directions, and in some that were not, small forces more mobile than big armies, which would create illusion. At Vienna he retained under Davout an occupation corps of 27,000 men; there they were mid-way between the bulk of the army, with the Emperor in Moravia, and Masséna's corps in Styria. The 23,000 men whom Augereau and Ney had led into the Tyrol were themselves also twenty days' march away in two opposite directions: from the Grand Army of Austria, or from the Army of the North, near Mainz. A game of shuttlecock—or chess—limited meanwhile by the dimensions of the chess-board: Napoleon could go no further north than Brünn, all the time Masséna came no nearer to the Danube, releasing Marmont and Davout to ascend in turn to back up and support the Emperor who, without them, would be ridiculously exposed. All the more so since the danger was in the north, and growing the further they went. For the moment Kutuzov, who had just taken over an army stronger than that of Napoleon, by the addition of Buxhouden's corps, would not accept the contest, because his troops were exhausted. If he were pressed, he would retreat a little further, towards fresh reinforcements—and towards the Prussians.

So Napoleon stopped, just where he was, in order to draw his adversary towards him by showing himself to be at the same time both bold and cautious. It has been the supreme art of the great tacticians to turn entire countries into a stage for comedy: the preparations for Austerlitz were first and foremost the work of a very good actor. Everything depended on the farce being rapidly staged and on the Allies 'nibbling' within a month. During this period the Prussians would not stir in the north: they would not be ready to threaten French territory and the communications of the Grand Army for a good month. At the moment they had 18,000 men at Münster, 35,000 at Erfurt and 40,000 at Hanover. The Prussian general staff had just ordered the latter to move towards the Upper Danube: a march of 250 miles. Napoleon was unaware of this, and had reason to fear that they might on the contrary move on the Rhine in order to threaten France. But they would still have had to cover 190 miles. The cavalry demonstrations they were currently making on their western frontier were not sufficient to alarm the Emperor, who was satisfied with his decree of November 8th, elevating pompously into the 'Army of the North' several battalions grouped on the Rhine and in the Low Countries. This phantom of an army, which would obviously have been incapable of resisting a Prussian invasion, would have quite enough to do in the event of a landing by English troops on the coasts.

But after all Prussia was still, officially, at peace with France.

The only plan to which Napoleon gave all his attention, all his efforts, all his means, was the one he himself called 'the plan of campaign in Moravia'.[1]

There were therefore, in the movements of the Grand Army from that moment on, some themes, some constant lines that would lead up to the lightning action of Austerlitz, just as the vital motif emerges suddenly and epitomizes a whole symphony after stuttering from instrument to instrument. Even a certain melancholy was not lacking: that of having missed the main aim of the plan, which had been to cut off the Allies from their retreat to the north. After Krems and Hollabrünn, it was no use thinking about that any more: at least the battle that was preparing would settle all outstanding accounts and recapture a part of the operation that had miscarried.

*　　　*　　　*　　　*

[1] He was to write in 1806: 'The Battle of Austerlitz was nothing but the outcome of the plan of campaign in Moravia. In an art as difficult as that of war, it is often in the scheme of the campaign that one conceives the scheme of the battle; only highly experienced military minds will grasp this.'

Here then was the decisive hour, striking in a country prepared for it: between the south-eastern edge of the Bohemian massif, made up of featureless hills, and the wooded brow of the Carpathians, the dry and fertile plains of the Moravian corridor had been one of the most ancient areas of settlement of prehistoric man. They still held beneath the surface invaluable paleontological riches. Next, they had witnessed the migrations of peoples, and countless battles there had already decided the fate of empires and changed the face of Europe. For several centuries Moravia had been a 'margravate', hence a state still medieval in structure, governed by the little court of a princeling dependant on the crown of Austria, and its capital had been at Brünn. Always united with Bohemia, it had shared in her economic development. The predominant language was Czech, but a strong Teutonic minority mitigated the sense of foreignness a traveller coming from Germany experienced among the Slav population, which gave a foretaste of Poland and Russia.

Situated thus between two broken and mountainous regions, it was above all a zone of transition and passage to the European scale, from the physical point of view as much as from the human, worthy of this battle that was to provide a link between war in the old style and that of modern times. Geological evolution had created a depression there, sheltered from the winds of the west, with a climate distinctly Continental in character. Rain was infrequent. The winters colder and the summers hotter than in Bohemia. Before the great influx of the Magyars, Moravia had even had her own hour of glory: it had been the starting point for the great Slav empire of Prince Svatophlek, which united Bohemia and the Carpathians for a few years.[1]

The inhabitants were gathered in villages with long rows of thatched roofs, on either side of a single street, and in two peaceful old towns enclosed by ramparts: Brünn and Olmütz in German, Brno and Olomouc in Czech. Important European centres of agriculture, they were the scene of magnificent fairs.

To the right of Olmütz, the restriction known as the Moravian Gap narrowed to only a few miles between the forests of the Carpathians and of Jesenicy. It gave access to 'the other Europe',

[1] It provided a curious analogy, geographically at least, with the future Czechoslovakia.

mysterious, unpredictable. Here was the call of the boundless plain. Over the centuries, the crossing had been made from east to west: it had been the outlet for the inexhaustible Asiatic migration. Was it now time to reverse the trend of history? Would it at last begin to travel towards the sun? France, newly arrived at this threshold, felt for the first time the lure of Moscow.

Finally, Moravia had constituted, half a century earlier, the lists for important battles between Frederick the Great and the Austrians, during the Seven Years War. All the military academies utilized them, and the young Bonaparte had noted them down at length and in detail in the exercise books of Brienne. He knew, for example, that Olmütz was a fortress of the first order, very easy to defend and to fortify, and the risk of coming up against a sort of new St John of Acre gave him an additional reason for not pursuing Kutuzov. He knew too that Moravia, more open than Bohemia, was less liable than the latter to turn into a trap for an army in retreat, and that subsistence was more plentiful in that relatively fertile region. And he had brought along in his little campaign library a handsome, brand-new book bound in red morocco and still smelling of it: *Treatise on High Tactics*, by Colonel Jomini. It had appeared a few months earlier and had established the reputation of that enigmatic man. The passage in his book devoted to the region where the French army was engaged was almost prophetic:

'Between Olmütz and Brünn there are several little rivers tucked away among the mountains which provide very favourable camps. On the whole, Moravia can be defended against a superior army. The war of succession of Charles VI proved it. The able Kevenhuller, with inferior forces, drove his enemies from it, by manoeuvres which the nature of the terrain allowed him to carry out.'

Such were the newly-written lines that haunted Napoleon's mind as he dictated the main dispositions of the plan of campaign in Moravia.

*   *   *   *

He began by advancing on Brünn with a bare third of his

army, in order principally to encourage his adversary and induce him to take the offensive. The latter had, exposed to his gaze, no more than the corps of Lannes and Soult, the Guard, and three divisions of cavalry, that is, about 50,000 combatants, whereas there were already 80,000 Russians at Olmütz, soon to be joined by other reinforcements. Round about December 1st the Allies would thus have reason to think themselves at odds of two to one. Napoleon intended to do all he could to persuade them of that. In fact, the effectives of the two main armies were still evenly balanced towards the beginning of November, and the Allies would be augmented in the proportion of only three to two.

Napoleon gambled basically on persuading them that they would be 100,000 against 50,000 on the decisive day. At first, he set only some cavalry posts opposite them. On the road to Olmütz, about eighteen or so miles from Brünn, he stationed at Wischau an almost isolated brigade of hussars. An observation post? Also a bait, which the Russians would study, fascinated and distrustful at first, would taste on November 25th, and swallow on the 28th: 'If I had really wanted to hold Wischau,' Napoleon said later, contemptuously, 'it would not have been with cavalry, but a good division of infantry protected to left and right by redoubts.'

There was certainly no question of really confronting Kutuzov with scarcely 50,000 men. In Napoleon's mind, the Grand Army numbered more than 70,000: he considered that it was *united*— and on this point it is necessary to have a knowledge of his vocabulary—when its various corps were in a position to *concentrate* within a few days for a joint action, as they were in the present case, the foremost at Brünn and Wischau, Bernadotte's near Iglau, thirty-eight miles from there, and Davout's at Vienna: more than sixty-two miles away as the crow flies. This would be one of the great differences between the two military blocks facing each other in Moravia: on November 20th Kutuzov's army was already *concentrated* round Olmütz. Napoleon's was not, except in spirit. When he fought the decisive battle in his imagination, he counted on Bernadotte and Davout. Once again, he was running an enormous risk in relying on the wonderful mobility of his troops and in calculating it so finely: this was to cause the terrible suspense during the whole of December 1st, when the French army would so nearly find herself quite simply amputated of her right.

Sure of equipping these two distant corps, at the first sign, with seven-league boots, and of having them on hand at the desired moment, Napoleon concerned himself mainly with arranging his cantonments in Moravia in such a manner as to conceal from the enemy the sudden influx of reinforcements that might cause him to reflect. Lannes, Murat and Soult occupying both Brünn and that little town whose name had begun to appear in correspondence from headquarters, Austerlitz, screened the main roads from Vienna and Iglau with a curtain of cavalry. They denied the Allies exact knowledge of the movements of the great masses of French infantry, the divisions of Cafarelli, Beaumont, Bourcier, Klein. Certainly, there was always the danger of spies, but Napoleon doubted whether they would have the intelligence and above all the necessary flexibility of movement to keep enemy headquarters informed of the very rapid concentrating marches by which Bernadotte and Davout would come along at the last minute.

*   *   *   *

Napoleon's aim was thus to transform into a counter-trap this Moravia where all Europe believed him to be trapped. And his Moravian plan can be reduced to two arrows.[1] He would march from Vienna to Brünn, and then from Brünn to Olmütz, without going quite that far, hence in a direction from S.W. to N.E., if one takes no account of bends and retracings in his march.

He would halt on a huge quadrilateral chosen by him, at the foot of the mountains of Moravia, and seek to provoke a 'descent' by Kutuzov, in an exactly contrary direction, from Olmütz towards Vienna.

The positions taken up, and the lines of retreat arranged by Napoleon show that he counted on bringing the two armies into contact along this diagonal on ground he had studied carefully.

The French operation, mounted during the next ten days with Draconian thoroughness, would stretch out to make the Allies pass below the French. Why? Because Napoleon was

[1] See diagram, p. 150

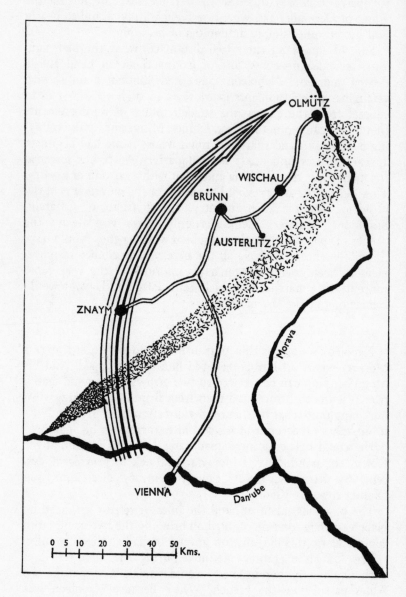

OLMÜTZ

WISCHAU

BRÜNN

AUSTERLITZ

ZNAYM

Morava

VIENNA

Dan'ube

0 5 10   20   30   40   50 Kms.

I. Counter-trap in Moravia

looking for a decisive battle. He could not afford the luxury of a drawn game, and still less a defeat. It was therefore necessary for Kutuzov to commit himself completely to the attack, and Russia would not do that unless, for her part, she thought she had Napoleon entirely at her mercy. For this, the Allies had to believe they could cut the French off from their retreat on Vienna by attacking their right.

After November 21st, Napoleon knew that Soult would command his centre, Lannes his left, and that he would make up his right with Davout's corps, coming from Vienna.

And it was evidently Davout who was to bear the weight of the attack: the Allies, if they wanted to cut the Grand Army off from its base and drive it back towards Bohemia, where it would find retreat almost impossible, would have no other course but to go at him with their battering ram. No less logically, Napoleon would try to seize them by their own right, in order to cut the road to Olmütz. The only thing he could not yet foresee with any precision was the part the centres would play in this Graeco-Roman wrestling hold. A battle of the wings only, round unshakable pivots? A confrontation of four blocks launched one against the other: the French left and centre against the Russian right and centre, simultaneously with the struggle between the Russian left and the French right? That remained to be seen. In the expectation of last-minute improvisations, Napoleon systematically prepared the trap. He exposed his communications with Vienna, and closed up the main part of the army (the Guard, Soult and Lannes) into the least possible space to increase the temptation to envelop him. According to a memorandum inspired by him, 'he wanted the Russians to make some false moves and mistakes, all springing from his plan of campaign in Moravia, a plan the enemy was unable to fathom. In addition, the Emperor remarked two days before the battle, while surveying the Pratzen hills and the villages of Sokolnitz, Telnitz and Mönitz: "If I wanted to prevent the enemy from passing, it is here that I would station myself; but I would have only an ordinary battle. If, on the other hand, I refuse my right by withdrawing it towards Brünn, and if the Russians abandon these hills, were they

300,000 men, they would be caught red-handed and lost with no way to turn." '

When the Allies should begin their movement, Napoleon would close up all his troops at the foot of the mountains, into an area of nine square miles. He would render almost impossible any attempt to move against his left by basing it on some hills easy to defend. He would discourage a frontal attack by presenting an imposing centre. On the other hand, the temptation to outflank him to the south would be so natural and so strong that one could not see how his adversary would be able to resist it. [1]

*　　　*　　　*　　　*

Olmütz, November 27th. After eight days of confusion the harassed Russian officers managed to establish a little order in the immense throng of men and materials that submerged the old fortified town and overflowed the too-narrow corset of its ramparts in every direction. The brutal confluence of the forces coming from Galicia with those flowing back from Austria, each as exhausted as the other, had submerged the neighbouring area for miles around, under a flood of pillage and marauding at least as merciless as that of the French. Loose discipline,

[1] And yet, supposing the Allies had not attacked? This question (sacrilege to Bonapartists) reveals an appalling void. The conscientious Colonel Colin, who has worked out an incomparable analysis of the days in question, allows his integrity to get the better of his veneration for the great man by revealing that the Emperor played at double or quits and had not provided for any other line of retreat except towards the south, towards Vienna or Znaim; but the latter would have been equally cut off in the event of the French right being outflanked. Apart from these two directions, no route had been organized, or even explored, and nothing had therefore been arranged to provide for a change in the line of operations.

'Napoleon staked all for all,' adds the military historian, and he goes on to heave a heavy brick of admiration at the Emperor:

'He always attached the greatest importance to demonstrating (and perhaps to persuading himself as much as posterity) the conformity of his actions to absolute principles, whose precision he maintained and whose rigorous observance he recommended without ceasing; this is what he did here in particular, though it is necessary to play with words slightly in order to sustain their demonstration. In reality, he was inspired only by a feeling of his personal superiority, a feeling that proceeded, moreover, to add to this actual superiority one of its most powerful forces. He awaited the battle and waged it under the conditions we know of *because he did not think he could not be the victor.*'

grumbling and low morale, ill-treatment of the few inhabitants who ventured out of their barricaded houses: everything at first had been a whirlwind of uncertainty. And then the granite wall of the Russian military hierarchy, cast in Prussian mould, had stemmed the tide, had sorted, canalized, invigorated it, and held it ready to launch again. But why hurry?

In the lofty rooms of Olmütz Castle there was also a whirl-wind: one of contrary opinions and discussions between the counsellors of the sovereigns. Of the sovereign, rather, the only one that counted having at that moment been given the report of forces overwhelmingly in his favour: the Czar. Francis of Austria, who could only put into the line, immediately, 14,000 men, held himself in reserve. His position, moreover, was known: on the advice of his chief of staff, Weirother, and in spite of counsels of prudence from the Prince of Schwarzenburg, coming from Ulm quite scorched by his contact with the Grand Army, he inclined towards the immediate resumption of an offensive that would lead to the liberation of Vienna.

Opposite him, Kutuzov. He was strictly for temporizing, and had no reason to hide it. From November 17th he had set down his reservations in writing:

'I dare not conceal from you, Sire, that it is impossible to sacrifice at random and to confide the fate of the war to a single battle. It is all the more difficult for me to expose myself to the possibility of a fight since our troops, in spite of their zeal and their impatience to distinguish themselves, are bereft of physical strength. Exhausted by the forced marches and the constant bivouacs, they can scarcely drag themselves along; they often go twenty-four hours without nourishment, for lack of time to prepare their meals, constantly harried as they are by the enemy. When we have been further reinforced, the enemy, who will be overawed by our numbers, will undoubtedly leave us a few days rest. We would then be able to resume the offensive again.'

But the old Commander-in-Chief was almost alone in his opinion. Five or six braggarts succeeded each other in their Sovereign's closet to preach the immediate resumption of hostilities. There was not, strictly speaking, any conclusive advice at Olmütz around the Czar. That would not have been his way: he had a horror of feeling several pairs of eyes bent upon him waiting for the decision. He therefore received them one after the other, with his customary affability, and listened to them, leaning slightly towards them with his good ear: he was afflicted with a certain deafness. Each returned sure of having convinced: all the advice was drowned in his myopic air.

Between November 20th and 25th, therefore, no course decided upon, but ten, twenty courses proposed . . .

Sukhtelen, a bearded giant of Dutch extraction, Quarter-master-General (in other words attached to the Supreme Command) of the Russian army:

'Let us march into Hungary, where mobilization is being effected. Let Archduke Charles join us, who tells us he has 60,000 men. And then attack Napoleon from the south.'

Count de Langeron, spokesman for the émigré Frenchmen, who commanded a Russian division with great military skill:

'Let us march to our right. Concentrate ourselves in Bohemia with the troops of Benningsen and Archduke Ferdinand. We would then form a mass of 120,000 men capable of moving against the left flank of the French and even against the areas to the rear of their lines of communication. And if the Prussians finally made up their minds, we should be able to extend them a hand from there quite naturally.'

Prince Adam Czartoryski — that curious phenomenon, a cautious Pole! Honest, serious, of strong feelings under a cold exterior, the Minister for External Affairs lost his master's favour for ever by supporting Kutuzov:

'If we march on Bonaparte at the beginning of December, we would be able to line up against him, in the final count, only 100,000 men. But by withdrawing into Upper Silesia and by waiting a little, we should have 140,000 combatants by the 15th and 170,000 by Christmas, at a moment when the Prussians, at least as numerous, would cut off his retreat! Finally, Sire, I have the audacity to think that Your Majesty's place is not with the army on the eve of a decisive encounter, since you have never yet exercised supreme command. Your presence at head-quarters would annul the authority of the generals and, at the same time, their responsibility. In this campaign which they are all fighting with more or less apprehension, they would ask nothing better than to unload their burden on to the young nobles of your entourage, who are often foolhardy . . . and, in the event of defeat, on to you through them.'

But Cobenzl, who arrived hell for leather from St. Petersburg:

'All Russia is quivering with joy, Sire, at the thought of their beloved leader taking into his own hands the fate of the army. In this way, you escape the gloomy morass of politics and become, at a single blow, the new St George of Europe crushing the dragon.'

But Dolgoruki, ever present at the side of the Czar, on whom he exercised an almost hypnotic influence in those days:

'We have only a few days left in which to secure *our* victory. Will you let the Prussians rob us of the glory and the fruit of it? War is not an art for the old, Sire, and Bonaparte has just proved it brilliantly. One thing alone can break the impetus of a young conqueror: the spirit of an Emperor equally young—and every bit as valiant as he. Finally, Sire, you were present on the 18th, at Wischau, when I had the honour of taking prisoner before your eyes more than a hundred French hussars! Your Majesty saw, with your own eyes, the retreat of these fire-eaters who are so terrorizing our unfortunate allies.'

Dolgoruki was one of the few men in whom Alexander confided:

'You could have added, *mon cher*, that Bonaparte showed his fear by sending me just now General Savary, his aide-de-camp, bearer of an obscure message. I listened at length to this worthy man, with very strict manners. I asked him finally whether he was the bearer of definite peace conditions. Nothing. Hot air. Empty phrases. It seems clear to me that they want above all to persuade us to stay where we are and that they fear our offensive . . . '

*   *   *   *

Night fell. At the same hour the regulation trumpet calls were exchanged between the outposts and the French lines opened a little to receive General Savary. He dismissed politely the strong Russian escort that had just accompanied him from Olmütz, and set off in search of Napoleon. He found him under the thatched roof of the staging-house of Posoritz, little more than three-quarters of a mile from the furthest observation posts, still within range of enemy guns. He had spent the whole day going over the ground on horseback.

'Well, Savary, how is it they have allowed you to return at this hour?'

'I do not know, Sire. I found the Czar full of courtesy and, it seemed to me, of good will . . . He listened to me very attentively and appeared most anxious to conclude peace as soon as possible. He handed me this letter for Your Majesty.'

Napoleon broke the seals and looked through the parchment rapidly, shrugging his shoulders:

'You are all the same. Do you wonder when it is said all over Europe that my Court is peopled with upstarts? Because a legitimate sovereign receives you pleasantly, there you are, all smiles. He has lulled you with words. This young man is as wily as a Greek of the Roman Empire, I always thought as much. Do you know what this letter contains? Nothing less than a call to evacuate Italy! Now, when I am almost in Poland! And you should never have accepted it under this infamous superscription: "*To the head of the French Government*". Am I Emperor, anointed by the Pope, yes or no?'

'Sire, I thought . . . '

'Since when have you thought, Savary?'

The worthy man bowed his head and held his tongue. Completely straightforward and without malice, he had decided once for all to worship Napoleon and would never change. The Emperor found this at the same time extremely pleasant and also exasperating, and was not sparing in his rebuffs. But Savary now found himself the ideal man for such a delicate mission. In order to dupe the Czar, he had himself to be the dupe of his master.

Napoleon paced up and down a few times, lost in thought. The darkness punctuated by the fiery glow of torches made his waxen face even more impenetrable than ever. He felt the hook had struck home, that the Russians were ready to resume the offensive, but something was missing still, some little device . . .

He went up to Savary abruptly, took him on one side and said:

'Take a trumpeter. Make your way back to the Emperor of Russia. You will tell him that I propose an interview tomorrow, at an hour convenient to him, between the two armies, and that naturally there would be during that time a suspension of hostilities for twenty-four hours.'

'An interview? But then, Sire, is it . . . is it Peace?'

Napoleon smiled, and waved his hand: 'Go!'

Savary went off again, intoxicated with his important mission, into the night criss-crossed with calls and signals: simultaneously, Napoleon proceeded to order a general withdrawal of his troops from the far side of the Goldbach, the evacuation of Pratzen and Austerlitz, a whole series of movements that gave the enemy an impression of a frightened army timorously huddling together . . . But at the same time officers set out hell for leather to summon up Bernadotte and Davout with their corps.

There had not yet been time to relieve the sentinels at the Russian outposts when Savary presented himself there, two hours after passing them in the opposite direction. He was recognized. He was received — and conducted all night from bivouac to bivouac through units under the command of Bagration, who finally treated him in princely fashion, but invented all sorts of pretexts for not sending him to the Czar until late in the morning. Amongst them too, a chain of orders was being set irresistibly in motion, though nobody knew who had given them the first impetus: their tide of troops was beginning to flow south-westwards. Their case had been heard: they were sure that Napoleon feared an immediate battle more than anything.

In the morning, Dolgoruki woke Alexander. The young

Czar, in silken night-shirt, lay beneath furs of a bluish sheen. Between the two young men a scene of friendly intimacy was enacted without protocol, while the servants revived a great wood fire. Everything was gaiety, revenge, laughter that morning.

'Sire, Savary has come back!'

'Already! What does he want now?'

'Bonaparte requests you for an immediate interview. His poltroonery begins to assume indecent forms!'

Alexander always withdrew a little from his interlocutors, even from his favourites, even from those most devoted to him. He let Dolgoruki exclaim and exult, while he reflected, his eyes half-closed. He was, after all, a sensitive man, with a horror of spilt blood. This meeting could save thirty or forty thousand men. Who knew whether this thought had not occurred to Napoleon too. Finally, Alexander was too shrewd not to test an obscure bit of information . . .

'I am not inclined, *mon cher*, to raise too harsh an objection. I will given General Savary a hearing. Why not oblige these people to unburden themselves?'

'But, Your Majesty will not accept the interview? The Czar of all the Russias will not treat on equal terms with a crowned blackguard trembling with fear?'

'I shall accept it, *mon cher*. But I shall not go. I shall have myself represented by someone who has my complete confidence. And that will not halt for an instant the offensive movement of our troops.'

Dolgoruki understood; transported with joy and pride, he knelt by the bed and kissed the Czar's hand, adorned with a diamond as big as a Patriarch's.

*　　　　*　　　　*　　　　*

The last scene before the battle, but almost unreal, a kind of wild dream unrelated to the immense forces in motion. All the cogs in the machine of war had been set turning. Between the lines of sentinels, now so close that they could shout insults at each other like the warriors at the battle of Troy, Prince Dolgoruki took the necessary few steps. Savary had conducted him back, had left him on neutral ground, and hurried to inform

Napoleon, whom he found amongst the infantry bivouacs. He had slept that night on straw. The Emperor listened to his messenger's first words only, jumped on a horse and himself galloped away to the outlying sentinels, so quickly that the escorting picket had difficulty in following him. Prince Dolgoruki awaited him in the majestic pose of a conquering Tartar. He suddenly saw, he recounted later, appearing round a bend in the road 'a little figure, extremely dirty and ill-dressed'. The Emperor dismounted, sent everyone away, and began to walk alone with him along the highway.

Peace? War? One butchery the less in the history of the world? Those present held their breath, without the least illusion: the two men very quickly became animated, made brisk gestures, and the conversation would not last five minutes. Dolgoruki was bursting with vainglory. He held at his mercy the man who had made the world tremble—and he considered the world extremely stupid.

'Peace at once if you give up Italy immediately'—he avoided addressing Napoleon by any name whatsoever in order not to acknowledge his royalty—'but if France goes on with the war, it will be Belgium, Savoy, Piedmont that the Allies will see themselves forced to exact from the treaty of peace . . . '

He stopped short. Whence came that unexpected note, that impressive firmness behind the flat voice that answered him dryly? Napoleon made prodigious efforts to control himself. He had no wish to bring down his whole structure of deception by suddenly appearing too sure of himself. But he had been sent a booby too insolent by far! 'A veritable trumpeter of England,' he called him later.

'If that is what you had to tell me, go and report to the Emperor Alexander that our conversation has been quite useless. Belgium? You dare speak of it to me when my army occupies Vienna? Even if you were encamped on the very heights of Montmartre, *monsieur*, you would never get me to abandon Antwerp! Your master wants us to fight. I wash my hands of it.'

Dolgoruki did not insist. Savary conducted him back and returned to find Napoleon fuming with a rage he could at last unleash. His suite all heard him storm:

'Those people must be mad to expect me to evacuate Italy, when they find it impossible to get me out of Vienna! What were their plans then, and what would they have done to France if I had been beaten? Upon my soul, whatever it may please God to let happen, within forty-eight hours I shall have given it them well and truly!'

Still speaking, he returned on foot as far as the first infantry post of the army. These were the carbiniers of the 17th Light. The Emperor, at the height of his rage, continued to growl as he passed them, slashing with his riding-crop at the clods of earth strewn in his path. Suddenly, he became aware of a look fixed upon him. Overtopping him by eight inches, an old soldier was listening to him and, quite unimpressed, went on filling his pipe as he gave his leader his opinion. Napoleon smiled and called out to him:

'Those buggers think they can just gobble us up!'

'Oh! Oh!' the brave fellow replied, 'It won't be like that! We'll f . . . k ourselves sideways! . . . '

Napoleon and all his followers then returned, laughing, to their headquarters, at the same hour as Dolgoruki, surrounded by a throng of young admirers, was going towards the Czar's carriage, which he met bowling along in the direction of Austerlitz, and called out to whoever wished to hear:

'He wanted to dictate to me! But I saw through him fast enough: he would do anything to secure a delay!'

* * * *

The die was cast at that moment. The powerful Allied army was going to advance against the French in order to encircle them, and proceeded to take up the following positions for the final march:

Bagration led the advance guard, with 12,000 men, including 15 squadrons of Cossacks.

Buxhouden had command of the right wing, divided into two columns:

Wimfen with 8,320 men;

Langeron with 11,420.

Kutuzov, while remaining General-in-Chief, led in particular the centre, made up of Prszbyzewski's column: 13,800 men.

Napoleon 1   [enlarged section from a painting by David]

The surrender of Ulm, October 1805, by Thévenin

Marshal Bessières

[*Mansell Collection*]

Marshal Soult

[*Mansell Collection*]

The Prince of Schwarzenberg, Austrian Field Marshal
[Mansell Collection]

Baron Henri Jomini   [Mansell Collection]

Marshal Lannes by Perrin

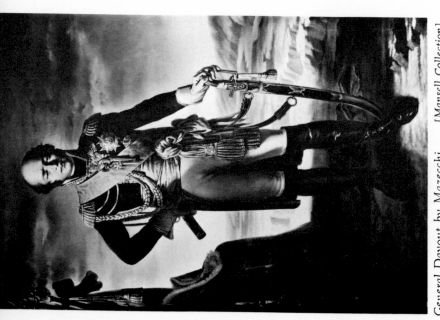

General Davout by Mazecchi [Mansell Collection]

Prince Mikhail Illarionovich Kutuzov.
General-in-Chief of the Russian Armies
[Radio Times]

Prince Bagration   [Mansell Collection]

Prince Mikhail Petrovich Dolgoruki
[Radio Times]

Alexander I   [Mansell Collection]

Francis I of Austria after Lawrence

Napoleon's bivouac on the eve of Austerlitz by Lejeune

Austerlitz

[Mansell Collection

Napoleon's bivouac on the night preceding the memorable
battle of Austerlitz, engraved by George Cruikshank

[Radio Time

Battle of Austerlitz by Gérard

Meeting of Napoleon and Francis II after the battle of Austerlitz, from a painting by Gros

The left wing, under the command of the Prince of Liechtenstein, was also in two columns:

Kollowrath and Miloradovitch with 22,400 men, including 20 battalions of Austrians;

Hohenlohe and Ouvarov with 4,600 men, including 40 squadrons of Austrian cavalry.

Finally, Grand-Duke Constantine came in reserve, with the 10 battalions and 18 squadrons of the Russian Guard.

PART III

THE BATTLE

CHAPTER X

December 1st, 4 p.m.

THE FIELD OF BATTLE

Napoleon had just made an about turn, with his usual impulsiveness, and was hurrying his suite along towards the spot he had selected as his headquarters for the afternoon, about five or six hundred yards higher than the place where he had spent the night. The Emperor rode all the more quickly since he hoped to find news there at last of the 3rd Corps.

At about four o'clock, then, soaked, chilled and weary, but calm in spite of the continued silence from Davout, the Emperor arrived back at his bivouac, set up on the right of the general disposition of the troops since their regrouping, rather than at the centre, a short distance from the main road from Brünn to Olmütz, in front of the hamlet of Bellowitz, near the Ricka of Girzikowitz. The sappers had only just finished their work: they had constructed for him a sort of woodman's hut on a relatively high mound from which part of the surrounding plain could be surveyed. It was a vast round hut, lit from the top, with a fire in the middle, very like that of an Indian chief. Drawn up nearby was the unharnessed berlin in which he had spent the previous nights. To one side of the mound, less than fifty yards away, the kitchen department had set up its canteen after a fashion in a miserable, thatched peasant's cottage, of which only the walls and a part of the roof remained. It consisted of just one low room in which, by some hefty work with an axe, the men had contrived to make a single long table and some benches out of the debris of doors and windows. In front, facing the enemy, Oudinot's grenadiers; on either side and to the rear, the Guard.

The entourage relaxed. The high-ranking officers handed over their reins to the grooms: each went in search of a crust of bread and a bottle. Napoleon was thought to be in the hands of Constant, his valet-de-chambre, when a sudden resurgence occurred: there he was, after scarcely ten minutes, reappearing at the threshold of his hut, a spy-glass in his hand. A messenger, sent from the advance guard by Murat, had just given him information so important that he had not even slipped on his grey redingote. Every available person rushed up for his orders. Would he be leaving again already? He merely took a few paces and requisitioned a page's shoulder as a telescope-rest. His face revealed something most unusual for him: palpable hope of good news. Without hesitating, he pointed the glass to the east, to where a regularity in the pattern of the hills disclosed a sort of plateau, which most of those present did not as yet know was called the Pratzen plateau. Thirty pairs of eyes followed his and discerned nothing but a fleecy greyness, a mile and a half away, above the muted colours of winter, further subdued by the gloomy weather.

How could those who were not in the secret understand his surge of hope? The countryside was inscrutable. It had none of those clear-cut positions where the movements of armies are written in advance. To the north, in clear weather, one could glimpse the edge of the Bohemian massif, bleak and haughty like a huge feudal keep. But it was grey. One found oneself lost in a heavily undulated region where indecisive and occasionally peaty slopes broke in every direction, overlapped, and ran into each other, with scarcely discernible variations of altitude: the bottom of the slight depressions which one hardly dared call valleys, settled down at about 650 feet. The highest of the 'peaks' three or four hillocks that would play an important role on the following day, reached 1,000 feet. There was thus at the very most, here and there, a difference in level of 350 feet, which was often spread over a wide area by way of compensation, across ploughed or bushy land and a few vineyards troublesome for cavalry.

But Napoleon turned towards the few initiates; one could count them on the fingers of one hand:

'No doubt about it! It's a great flanking movement by the

centre of the Russian army that is taking shape on the Pratzen. Have a look, Berthier.'

. . . The Russians! For the first time in large numbers before Napoleon's eyes, this new enemy, this mystery, this living forest on the march towards the west, like the one that foretold the death of Macbeth. He had beaten the Austrians, the Piedmontese, the Turks, even the English at Toulon, and ten or fifteen lesser nationalities. But all who had come near him since the start of this campaign knew that he regarded with particular seriousness this conflict with the army that he insisted on calling the advance guard of Asia. The Emperor of the West, he turned his face towards the Golden Horde, Genghis Khan, Tamerlane.

'The enemy's front line seems stationary, Sire.'

'Of course: that is to allow enemy columns to spread out behind it to their left, towards Augezd and the two lakes . . . '

The general staff all gave a start: a bomb would have surprised these formal men less than the sudden explosion of joy that made Napoleon jump in the air and clap his hands:

'It's a shocking movement! They're walking into the trap! They're exposing themselves! Before tomorrow evening, this army will be mine!'

And as if everything was tending at the same time to turn out favourably, along came an officer covered with dust, climbing the hill with rapid strides, followed by a handful of men.

'Sire, Marshal Davout sends me to inform you that he is arriving with the advance guard of his troops. They are completing a march of ninety miles. Friant's division is in process of regrouping at Gross-Raygern.'

*   *   *   *

Napoleon went back into his 'house' at last for good—that is to say, for an hour, into the corner of the hut where maps of the territory were spread out, zebra-striped with fierce strokes of coloured chalks. He sat down on a drum, allowed his face and hair to be massaged by Constant with his favourite eau-de-cologne, drank a cup of orange-water for his digestive troubles (which forced those officers present to be somewhat discreet in their acceptance of the mulled wine that Caulaincourt was distributing), but all as in a dream. He was not there.

His chin resting on his hand, leaning with an elbow on his knee, his brow furrowed, he was soaring in spirit over the field of battle, his eye fixed on the map where he would now at last be able to put all his forces into the field.

It was on November 21st that Napoleon had chosen his ground. For four or five days, he had gone over Moravia, here, there and everywhere, sniffing the breeze with an absent air, his thoughts far away. He had been searching. The unimportant skirmishes towards Olmütz that had been reported to him had served as a pretext for his hunt: he had gone there in person, listened vaguely to the reports, shrugged his shoulders, and come back finally towards Brünn by a roundabout way. Whenever he had this slightly heavy air of being utterly withdrawn into himself, he was in fact all attention, all memory. Every fold in the ground came to life in his prodigious imagination and was classified in the archives of his memory: square mile upon square mile was covered with troops, stationary or in movement; each hectare became a square in the chessboard. As soon as he spied a hill, a peak, a plateau, he galloped to it and scanned the horizon. Was this it? He would shake his head and come down again: something had failed to satisfy him in the landscape he had studied: hedges too thick, which would break the cavalry charges, streams too wide, a slope too gentle, where the enemy would be able to manoeuvre at leisure. More than ten times, he had rejected this or that position, before his choice finally lighted on a certain locality, incomprehensible at first to those who accompanied him. To the majority of them, it was the living geometry of the opposing forces that would give meaning to the selected terrain. Until December 1st they had not distinguished between the soft undulations they had traversed uphill and down since Vienna. There lay one of Napoleon's great superiorities over them all: his military genius was first and foremost prophetic.

'Reconnoitre all these hills thoroughly: it is here that you will be fighting.'

'*Messieurs*, study the ground well: you will have a role to play there.'

'Study this ground well: it will be a field of battle.'

The memorialists fall over each other to report his exact

words, which matter little. They are all in agreement on the essential: November 21st was the day of presentiment. More, of resolution.

It was bitterly cold, more unpleasant than ten days later, when the battle was fought. The Emperor had come back from Wischau, where Murat had been too full of himself at having dealt with the enemy cavalry. It had only been a matter of the advance guard, and a minor verbal lashing from the master had reduced it to its true proportions: he never lost and never would lose an opportunity to humiliate Murat, whose braggadocio exasperated him. 'Learning that the enemy had fallen back on his reinforcements as far as Olmütz,' wrote Ségur, 'he returned to Brünn. On his way back, he stopped on the highway, at about seven and a half miles from Brünn, near a knoll by the road, a kind of fairly steep truncated cone.'[1]

It was thus 'the Santon' above all that had attracted him. This peak of sorts was not to be christened until the eve of battle, by the soldiers who had been in Egypt: it reminded them of the tombs of the Moslem saints, standing on end like menhirs, that had so intrigued them over there. This name therefore had nothing to do with the santons of Provence.[2]

'He ordered the foot of it on the enemy side to be dug in order to strengthen the escarpment. Then turning towards the south, he entered a high plain, enclosed between two containing streams running from the north to the south-west . . . The Emperor went over this open plain slowly and in silence. He stopped repeatedly on the most elevated points, above all towards Pratzen. He studied all the irregularities attentively. Several times, during this reconnaissance, he turned to us and said: "*Messieurs . . .*" '

How did he himself see this high plain? [3]

[1] It can be seen in the picture by Lejeune (Plate II).

[2] Little coloured clay figures used to group round the crib at Christmas.

[3] From now on, original maps are provided in order to facilitate a complete view of the different phases of the day. They are diagrammatic, and by reducing the battle to its essential elements, geographic or tactical, they will endeavour to convey to the reader the view Napoleon himself had of it. It is for this reason that the road from Brünn to Olmütz, for example, has been reduced here to a straight line, and that the course of the Goldbach has been simplified. For greater accuracy, these diagrams should be compared with the

II. Main features of the battlefield of Austerlitz

If Napoleon had not scorned captive balloons, an observer stationed directly above the Santon would have overlooked an area twelve to fifteen miles across: it was less than sixteen miles from Brünn to Austerlitz. And neither of the two towns would be touched by the battle that was to take place between them.

The whole of the top of the rectangle, the north, was bounded

---

map of the area, taken from Thiers' album, reproduced in the end-papers.

Above, first, is a simplified map of the battlefield of Austerlitz, such as the Emperor had made after a hasty survey by his topographical department, so that his plan might be able to unfold there freely. It enables the description of the terrain to be understood.

by a continuous straight line of wooded heights: these were as yet only large hills, but they were already known as the mountains of Moravia. They were sufficient to limit the envisaged manoeuvres: one could not fight a battle there. Napoleon knew that they would therefore provide an anchor for his extreme left.

Parallel to them, and running at about two miles from where they begin, a straight line: the main road from Vienna to Olmütz, a regularly paved causeway, bordered by trees in some places, which forms a right-angle at Brünn. It runs from south to north, as far as this town, bends there, and runs due east until, just as it is passing out of our field of interest, it turns north-east in the direction of Olmütz.

A little before this turn, a road of minor importance branches off to connect with Austerlitz, just over three miles to the southeast.

What was Austerlitz? A rectangle of gardens and dwellings around the little chateau of the counts of Kaunitz. Strategically a position of no value, but a suitable enough locality for setting up a headquarters.

Brünn was a large star, a city bulging out all over with ramparts in points and redans, where a corps of troops could withstand a siege. In the background, therefore, there would at least be this possible hedgehog as a last resort, in the event of catastrophe.

Crossing the field from top to bottom, a Y divides it in two: a stream, a river if one likes—and Napoleon did like. It was through the importance that he gave to it and the manner in which he made use of it to delimit the two camps that the Goldbach was to assume such great importance, out of proportion to its actual appearance: a few marshy rivulets of water. It is formed by the union of two water-courses that run down the mountains and cross the main road: the Ricka, each of which bears the name of a village it waters before their confluence. To the left, the Ricka of Schlapanitz, to the right the Ricka of Girzikowitz. They merge at a third village: Puntowitz. Next, the Goldbach runs southwards, always very scanty and fordable without difficulty. It dawdles through increasingly spongy ground where unhealthy pools develop in summer, because of their slight depth, but which, with the first of the great frosts, are more or less covered by ice.

The essential interest of the Goldbach, in what concerns the battle of Austerlitz, is that it delimited with precision the two aspects of the terrain.

To the left, a plain with hardly a valley, crossed by convenient roads, favourable to the evolutions of all the army corps, which would enable them to retreat in haste on Brünn. It was almost uninhabited; only the large village of Turas occupied its centre and gave it its name.

To the right of the Goldbach, the Pratzen plateau, which was by no means a mountainous plateau.[1]

To those who approach it coming from the west, after crossing the Goldbach, it offers at first only a slight modification in the ground. The bottom of the valley is at an altitude of 650 to 700 feet. The plateau reaches just under 1,000 feet at one of its dominant points, the Stahré Vinobrady. The difference in height is therefore about 350 feet, and this is built up slowly on the side of the Goldbach. However, the opposite edge of the plateau, to the east, dominates the continuation of the plain with a more abrupt drop—and the south of the Pratzen ends in lakes, which provide more difficult access to it from this side. In other respects, the plateau strictly speaking is the southern part, around the village of Pratzen and the Stahré Vinobrady, the Czech name for a little eminence not unlike the Santon. The Pratzen forms a triangle there, the lower point of which falls between the Goldbach and the lakes and rests on the village of Telnitz. Higher up, to the right of the fork of the Y formed by the confluence of the two Rickas, there is a rectangular plain, whose surface, almost level, was to become the quite natural theatre of cavalry engagements. Everywhere else, the latter would be restricted.

Finally, there were the villages. If one sees the ground through Napoleon's eyes, as if it consisted of two connected pieces—the

[1] 'The most widespread plans, those most often reproduced,' writes Colonel Colin, 'give a rather false idea of the field of battle: the ground is made to appear very broken; in them, escarpments, topographical details of every sort are multiplied. In reality, the terrain where the battle of Austerlitz was fought is very largely undulating. It rises *in gentle slopes* from the Goldbach to the Pratzen plateau . . . '

one, the plain of Turas, to the left, where he was already considering concentrating his army, the other, the Pratzen plateau and the cavalry plain, to the right, where he reckoned to leave the field more or less open to the enemy—it was the Y of the Goldbach that marked the frontier, and the Moravian villages strung out along its course were so many stitches through which the two pieces of material were held together and communicated. From the top downwards, one meets first the most important: Schlapanitz, on the left Ricka, and opposite it Girzikowitz, which taps a little horizontal valley serving to some extent as a division between the Pratzen plateau and 'the cavalry plain'.

Puntowitz unites the two Rickas and sends the Goldbach on its way. Below it, spaced at regular intervals of under two miles, one finds Kobelnitz, Sokolnitz, Telnitz and Mönitz. These last four villages, all of very slight importance—some thirty chimneys each—are inseparable from the lakes fed by the sluggishness of the Goldbach, some of which bear their names. But the most important of all the lakes, the one situated below the village of Telnitz, at the foot of the Pratzen, is called Lake Satschan.

Such, then, was the setting. The ingredients of Austerlitz amounted essentially to these few facts, which one must try to bear in mind *all together*, since they contributed, *all together*, to the manoeuvre conceived by Napoleon: the Pratzen plateau, the lakes, the Goldbach, the mountains of Moravia, the road parallel to them, the villages, the Santon like a corner-stone to the whole and, facing each other, crouching on either side beyond immediate events, those guardians, the two passive towns: Brünn and Austerlitz—if one dare call Austerlitz a town.

CHAPTER XI

December 1st, 6 p.m. to 10 p.m.
'HE'S RIGHT IN OUR HANDS'

It was as if Napoleon had been waiting to see the enemy movement declare itself before his own eyes, for then, and only then,
did he give the order to read to the troops the customary
proclamation before every battle.

Dictated towards the end of the night, it had been printed
during the morning in a hundred or so copies on the little mobile
press that followed his headquarters. The placards, all fresh, in
large smudged letters, fixed to the top of a menacing eagle, were
carried to the colonels, who distributed them to their company
commanders: the nature of the terrain and tactical necessity
prevented the gathering together into a single mass of the two
or three thousand men of each regiment, as would have been
done in open country or in garrison. The drums beat, and it was
as though a sudden impact had coagulated the huge layer of
men spread over a hundred square miles into a patchwork of
soldiers crystallized into groups of two or three hundreds: the
companies, through whom there ran the sparkling word:

'Soldiers!

'The Russian army is presenting itself before you in order to
avenge the Austrian army of Ulm. These are the same battalions
which you defeated at Hollabrünn, and which since then you
have pursued steadily to this point.

'The positions we occupy are strong, and as they advance to
turn my right, they will expose their flank to me.

'Soldiers, I shall direct your battalions myself. I will hold

174

myself far from the firing if, with your accustomed bravery, you carry disorder and confusion into the ranks of the enemy. But, if victory should for a moment be uncertain, you will see your Emperor expose himself to the first blows; for victory shall know no hesitation during this day, when the honour of the French infantry is at stake, which means so much to the honour of the whole nation.

'Lest, under pretext of bearing away the wounded, the ranks shall be thinned, let every man be well imbued with this thought: that we must defeat these hirelings of England, who are animated by so great a hatred for our nation.

'This victory will end the campaign and we shall be able to resume our winter quarters, where we shall be joined by the new armies that are forming in France, and then the peace I shall make will be worthy of my people, of you and of me.

NAPOLEON

Every echo reverberated the cheers wrung from the men by the studied progression, phrase on phrase, of this well-turned piece of warlike rhetoric, up to the final pause. It was 'Vive l'Empereur!' right down the line, from the most recent ensign to the Marshals of the Empire. The army was going to fight without reserve: true, the limits of bearable fatigue having been passed, it had lived for the past week in a sort of torpor. Yet, here it was, revived, as if by a distribution of brandy, and intent on action. Unanimous reports speak, from this moment, of a genuine emotion among the bivouacs.[1]

[1] Who would think of dwelling on any points in this text, so richly revealing, however, when one comes to analyze it?? One would have to pass over hundreds of miles of exalted brains to arrive at the despised Circles of the Vallée-aux-loups or of Coppet, at Chateaubriand's, at Germaine de Staël's or Benjamin Constant's. These, all veils torn aside, were to point out that the definition—and the condemnation to failure—of the Napoleonic Empire are contained in the final phrase: 'the peace I shall make will be worthy of MY people, of you and of ME'. It marks a rupture of the fundamental unity, the creation of a hierarchy, the erection of an arbitrary and artificial division between the people (MY people!), you, that is to say, the army, and ME, that is to say Me alone. The Empire becomes an Adventure by this single phrase.

There are other points to consider, notably the promise of the third paragraph: 'I will hold myself far from the firing, if . . .'

'Never before had History recorded such a promise,' writes Emil Ludwig. 'All the generals maintained, on the contrary, that they would brave death at

But certain defeatist or timorous circles, in the French general staff itself, were dumbfounded at the enormous risk taken in the second paragraph of the proclamation:

'The positions we occupy are strong, and as they advance to turn my right, they will expose their flank to me.'

Ever the pedant, Jomini pointed out to his audience:

'Never in the history of the world, has the leader of an army revealed his plan in this way to the whole of his forces. One might ask oneself whether, at the last minute, he isn't hoping the enemy will draw back! Is it a last idiotic appeal to the Czar for a negotiated peace? We have here the very first battle in the world in which at least half the performers will be aware of the scheme! The map of the day has been thrust into the hands of the last illiterate . . . '

It would have been enough indeed for this proclamation, issued on the eve of the battle, to fall into the hands of the enemy for success to be seriously compromised: until nine o'clock the next morning the Allied dispositions could have been halted. The partition that separated two opposing armies was still so watertight in those days that Napoleon coolly ran this enormous risk; and to what end? One is at a loss to conjecture. Would the soldiers have been less enthusiastic if they had not received this disclosure? One could say, perhaps, that he quite simply yielded to the pleasure of a communion without precedent between command and army by setting a seal of style and extravagance on the day.

It was moreover a fact that neither the Russians nor the Austrians knew anything about the proclamation. No copy of it fell into enemy hands. It would have been sufficient, however, for them to have questioned a captured French soldier. But one

---

the head of their men. Napoleon, whose grenadiers had seen him in twenty battles and whom they considered to be protected by Fortune, can only offer his soldiers, as the price of their bravery, the assurance that he would not expose himself to danger.'

This too was Austerlitz. And no one will be able to understand that day who fails to understand what the soldiers of the Grand Army were feeling: a hunger for Napoleon's safety as imperious as that for bread and wine. They identified themselves so closely, in their dreams, with the unprecedented trajectory of his destiny that his death would have been that of their hopes. The Napoleon of 1805 was a general whose soldiers demanded that he take care of himself . . . and who knew it.

can find no record anywhere of a man being carried off in the course of the night, as was often done on the eve of great encounters. Not on either side, moreover: Napoleon would capture no enemy outpost. His glance had satisfied him so well that he was almost afraid of seeing it invalidated by more accurate verification. As for the Allies, one is inclined to ask whether they experienced the least desire to know what Napoleon was up to: they were bursting with vainglory.

Towards six o'clock, at the precise moment when 300 stentorian voices were shouting out the intended manoeuvre in the French camp, where Napoleon's secret was becoming an open one, Count Tolstoy, Grand Marshal of the Imperial Russian Court, heard Dolgoruki exclaim, as he held forth glibly in the midst of a group of gaudy young goslings:

'If Napoleon wasn't so afraid of the battle, why would he have retreated, contrary to all his methods of fighting? He's frightened, that's obvious! He's avoiding open conflict. His hour is come, I promise you. He's right in our hands!'

'They will expose their flank to me . . . '

'He's right in our hands!'

As evening fell on December 1st, the crime in both the camps was over-confidence.

* * * *

Each was sure of his plan. But the fundamental difference was that the Allies knew nothing of Napoleon's, whereas he had set up his own only because he had ascertained theirs.[1] More precisely: the Allied plan formed a part of his. Austerlitz was a model of the successful strategic battle, that is to say, half-won before it had started, because the conditions for it had been established in advance by the victor.

In the depths of the night, where was the Allied master-mind?

[1] They may be seen facing each other in the following pages: the one that Napoleon's 'plan of campaign in Moravia' had finally dictated to, or imposed on the Austro-Russian army: the outflanking of the French army by its right, with the help of terrain that seemed to lend itself to it miraculously, and the crushing counter-trap conceived by Napoleon: the brutal smashing of the Allied centre at the moment when the Austro-Russian manoeuvre had irrevocably begun. The shaded arrow shows a last-minute modification which will be discussed later.

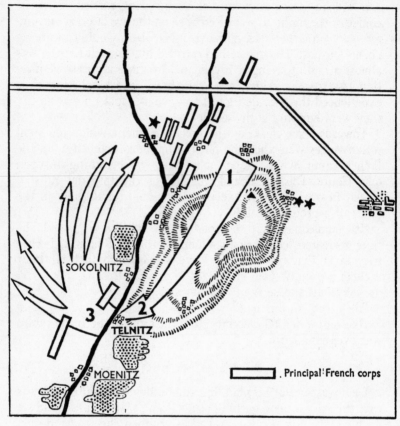

III. *The Allied plan of battle*

1. *Direction of the Allied attack*
2. *Planned point of breakthrough: Telnitz*
3. *Proposed exploitation of break to encircle the French Army*

And, first of all, who had conceived this 'Austro-Russian plan'?
Who was seeing to its execution?

Neither one Emperor nor the other was really in control.
There was indeed a commander-in-chief: Prince Kutuzov. But
he was on strike. The old leader of the old wars was fed up with
the job since at Olmütz, a week earlier, the 'party of youth' had
prevailed over his counsels of prudence.

178

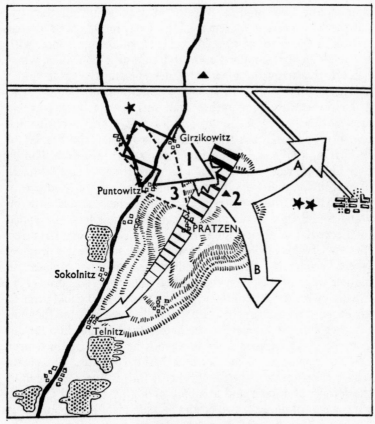

IV. *Napoleon's plan of battle*

1. *Breaching of the Allied front by the flank*
2. *Proposed exploitation of the breakthrough by a double encircling movement:*
   (a) Of the Russian right driven back on the mountains of Moravia
   (b) Of the Russian left driven back on the lakes
3. *Modification of the plan, interposed at midnight, by the inclination towards Pratzen*

'Very well,' Kutuzov had said.

And it had been no more than that: a massive 'very well', quite as fatalistic as the meanest moujik rolled up in his sheepskin on the bare ground. By dint of shaking up all the staff officers, a persistent searcher might have found, towards ten o'clock in the evening, the old, one-eyed, puffed-up Prince, with his noble Bourbonesque figure and carefully powdered white hair: in Kutuzov the greatest refinement and the most vulgar coarseness were evenly balanced. A peasant-prince.

There he was, lying rather than sitting in a huge portable armchair, hollowed out by his heavy frame, which accompanied him everywhere. In a little country seat near the hamlet of Birnbaum, a mile and a half from his Czar, from whom, had he been able, he would have been a hundred times as far. A village so lost, in the midst of advancing troops, and a house so poorly indicated that the couriers wasted hours looking for him by going round in a circle, and the corps commanders summoned to the final conference suffered astronomical delays in routing him out. To his left, despatches were piled on a great oak table, where he tolerated only one candlestick with three candles. He did not want it to be seen that he was asleep. He was drunk. He usually overcame his annoyance with some girls: he had three in his baggage-train and would undoubtedly have sent for them all together, in accordance with the habits attributed to him for ten years on great occasions, if his wagons had not remained near Olmütz. Fortunately, his personal berlin contained immediate relief: the armchair, the fur-lined coat for his knees, the icon of the Virgin of Kazan and a supply of highly fortified Crimean wine, a sort of liqueur, two bottles of which had been poured out for him before supper. He reacted by giving sketchy salutes to the messengers who came to bring him news, and smiled and grunted without anyone knowing why or what he was trying to say. If an importunate visitor persisted he sent him to his aides-de-camp, all equally disabled, but who could at least acquit themselves with a few conventional phrases. 'You see how it is, *mon cher!* . . . Mikhail Illarionovich is exhausted, don't you understand? . . .'

Mikhail Illarionovich, for that was how one addressed him in the Russian manner, Michael, son of Hilarion, was silent.

If one looked further into the machinery of the Allied general staff, one found everyone occupied in shifting responsibility on to his neighbour. In these hours loaded with tension, a sort of cleavage developed between the personalities and burst open the triangular antagonism that was to poison the Austro-Russian alliance: on the part of Petersburg, hostility between the *old Russians*, of the Kutuzov type, and the *foreigners* (Germans, Poles, or . . . Frenchmen!) who had invaded the Court of Catherine II, often by passing through the imperial alcove; on the Austrian side, a mixture of distrust and necessity in their attitude towards their enormous, cumbersome ally, who had come along full of bluster announcing that all would be lost without them. The Austrians were eaten up with the 'Ulm complex', which had just added to the series of defeats and humiliations they had suffered over ten years in the business with France. They were all the more aggressive.

Only after exercising much patience could one have finally discovered the man who was really responsible for the Allied plan for the following day, the man who proclaimed himself by his self-assurance and a rather courageous way of shouldering his responsibilities: Weirother, chief of staff to the Emperor of Austria.

*   *   *   *

Weirother enters history in the darkest hour of the night, at the house of Mikhail Illarionovich, Prince Kutuzov. The latter was in such a state of debility that he never officially opened the proceedings and was content with the exhausting effort of opening from time to time the sole eye the Turks had left him. Summoned during the afternoon, the corps commanders arrived whenever they could, leaving caps and coats in the hands of the valets, and did justice to the venison and chicken-breasts laid out on a vast sideboard covered with plate bearing the arms of the commander-in-chief. They greeted the latter, exchanged views with each other, immediately revised the co-ordination of their movements, went out again in order to go to greet their sovereigns (the Emperor of Austria had just rejoined the Czar at Krzenowitz), came back again, fretting at the time they were wasting there, enquired of their aides-de-camp the latest news of their forces, stamped about, fuming, and drank hard by way of consolation.

The calmest among them, who was also the most lucid, and hence utterly disconsolate, observed the scene with keen irony.

This was a Frenchman: Count de Langeron, a general in the service of the Czar, would command on the morrow the second column of attack. Upright in a dark corner of the room, where he had found a place for his long, thin body, he wet his lips with a tall glass of Tokay and screwed up his eyes a little, which were extremely short-sighted, above an aquiline nose and a thin mouth, set in humorous lines. One would have thought he was in Marie-Antoinette's *salon*, where twenty years earlier he had made some fashionable debuts fatal to a few reputations. And the world had remained a *salon* for him, war a ball and the whole of life, his own and that of others, a pretext for a *bon mot*. He belonged to the brilliant little group of *émigrés*, likeable because perfectly sincere and true to themselves: not for a moment did it occur to them to come to terms with the Revolution, or whatever might have come out of it, the Consulate, the Empire.

Remaining faithful to the rhythm of the waltz that had carried them away at sixteen, they were condemned to a wandering existence in order to defend their conception of life. Three of them had made successful careers in Russia, where Alexander appreciated their refreshing imagination compared with the German heaviness that had been until then the only outside contribution to St Petersburg society: Langeron, Rochechouart and Richelieu, the latter having become Governor of the Crimea. The idea of patriotism was rightly incomprehensible to them and loyalty to Louis XVIII, whom they distrusted and detested, played only an insignificant part in their decisions: they belonged to the pleasure-loving International, which makes brothers of an Englishman and a Russian out of nothing but the way they have in common of raising a glass or drawing on the reins of a horse. This kind of frivolousness, of internal freedom, gave them the easy bearing of forerunners of a world without frontiers, even while they appeared as vestigial figures from the past in a Europe of nationalisms in process of congealing. Men of the future or of the past, the present rejected them—but they confronted it with remarkable dignity. Like the knights of chivalry they were all for the allegiance of the moment: the Czar welcomed them, he was fighting the revolutionary hydra, and he was the most charming monarch of the century. Good for the Czar, then. Langeron, of all his generals, would be the one to display the most sagacity during the day of Austerlitz.

As for the Austrian chief of staff, he was a veteran of the war office at Vienna, obsessed with blackboard tactics. Brave, but unlucky on the battlefield, he had been running around for twenty years in search of a revenge that would impress his fellows. His moment seemed to have come: the previous year, he had conducted the extensive manoeuvres of the Austrian army over the very ground which the French were now offering him. He had drawn up a minute survey of it containing the least undulation in the terrain, and he had become indispensible at Olmütz through the favour of Francis I, who had appreciated his fussy side, as the man for the situation. Since then, the young Russian bantams, supporters of the offensive, had been inexhaustible in their encomiums on his knowledge of the area, his foresight over every possibility, his expertise in detail. Not much more was needed for Kutuzov to hate him. And, since he was unable to be rid of him, he ignored him.

Mikhail Illarionovich appeared therefore to plunge into unsuspected depths of slumber, advertised by a sonorous snoring, when General Weirother at last gave direction and life to the conference by spreading out on a large table a huge and very accurate map of the area around Brünn and Austerlitz. Another twelve candles were lighted, which underlined pitilessly the puffiness of fatigue and the ill-kempt beards of these commanders nearing the end of their strength. Weirother was tottering with exhaustion and giving off as much moisture as badly rinsed washing: he had spent the day in the field and had just been again, twice, in the course of the evening to reconnoitre in person the enemy's outposts. He had probably not slept for a fortnight. But he was at the height of his self-conceit. His face, somewhat like a weasel, surmounted by a thick brush of grey hair and barred with a brief moustache, was bursting with satisfaction. He liked the sound of his own voice. He was the only one.[1]

[1] 'He read his dispositions to us,' writes Langeron, 'in an elevated tone and with an air of boastfulness that proclaimed his intimate conviction of his merit and our incapacity. He resembled a form-master in a high-school reading a lesson to the young pupils. We were perhaps indeed pupils; but he was far from being a good teacher.'

M. de Langeron had to experience there—and overcome in the same instant, with a light tap of his riding-crop against his chest —one of those lost moments far away, in the midst of a life, when a man stretches out his hands gropingly and asks himself what he is doing there. Where was his gilded youth within the desiccated stones of the manor-house in Provence, the olive trees, the ten villages gathered together each year for the 'feast' of the seneschalship round his father the Bailiff? Here he was, in a smoky room, among these old sharks drunk with tiredness, living a nightmare that lacked not even the snores of the Most Serene Commander-in-chief above the ground-swell of grating German.

'*Da der Feind mit seinem linken Flügel an die mit Wald bedeckten Berge . . .*'

'In that the enemy rests his left wing on the wooded hills and extends his right wing along Kobelnitz and Sokolnitz to the rear of some marshes that are to be found there . . .'

The generals suffered these circumlocutory phrases like submissive schoolboys. General Buxhouden, large and fair-haired, was upright against the wall, his eyes fixed on a wax-candle, visibly pretending not to be listening. Sitting in martial pose, hands on knees and elbows turned out, directly opposite Weirother, on whom he trained his watery eyes, General Miloradovitch, ruddy-faced, with handlebar moustaches and jutting shoulders, was doggedly silent. A polite smile fixed on his face, Count Langeron, immediately next to Weirother, contemplated his slender fingers which toyed with a golden snuff-box bearing a miniature.

'A geography lesson,' he murmured at length, loud enough to be heard.

Prszbyzewski,[1] with respectful politeness, but dignity, was trying hard to look like someone completely absorbed by what he was hearing. Leaning over the map, the little Doctorov, with a modest and diligent air, studied the dispositions and terrain conscientiously. He even carried his zeal so far as to beg his Austrian colleague to repeat passages he had failed to hear well, and some difficult names of villages . . .

Weirother's scheme consisted in turning the French right by crossing the Goldbach between Telnitz and Sokolnitz in order

[1] A Russian general of Polish origin, pronounced Pribichevski.

then to wheel round and attack in a south-to-north direction. The attack on the Goldbach was to begin at break of day. The first column (Doctorov) was to take Telnitz and swing to the right, dressing on the second (Langeron), which was to cross the stream higher up, between the two hamlets. At the head of the third column, Prszbyzewski was to cross the Goldbach at Sokolnitz itself. The three columns of attack were then to make their wheeling movement, and ascend, parallel to the Goldbach, as far as the Kobelnitz lakes. There, Weirother imagined, they would meet the French army, hastily withdrawn along a front Turas-Puntowitz, in order to cover its retreat on Brünn.

Smash it? A mere bagatelle: a fourth column, led by Kollowrath (an Austrian) and Miloradovitch, was at this moment to come to the rescue of the other three, by descending from Pratzen on to Puntowitz. At the other end of the line of attack, Kienmayer's little corps of Austrian cavalry was to provide constant cover for Doctorov's left flank. He was to be in a position to rush towards Turas ahead of the rest in order to take possession of the town and sabre the French fugitives at the moment of their inevitable rout.

During this time, Prince Bagration's corps and Liechtenstein's cavalry were to seize the Santon (known here as 'the Tvarosna hill'). From there, it was to submit the French army to the grip of an intolerable angle-iron which was to be tightened round it to the point of total defeat.

Weirother's voice rose to a screech for the last lines of his lecture, as if he were already reading the victorious order of the day:

'The whole army is to join up before the village of Latein, near Losch, and Prince Liechtenstein's cavalry, as soon as the passes of Schlapanitz and Bellowitz have been abandoned by the enemy, is to take advantage of this moment to move forward and destroy them in their flight towards Brünn.'

It was ended. The good pupils turned their heads from side to side hopefully: 'Can one go now? . . . ' But a sharp click made them start: Count Langeron closed his snuff-box and spoke:

'*Mon Général*, all this is extremely fine. But if the enemy forestalls us and attacks us near Pratzen, what would we do? The possibility has not been provided for.'

Weirother shrugged his shoulders indulgently.

'You know Bonaparte's audacity. If he had been able to attack us, he would have done so today.'

'You really believe him to be weak, then?'

'If he has 40,000 men, that's putting it too high.'

Such lack of awareness exasperated Langeron, who for once raised his voice so much that Kutuzov could no longer decently remain asleep, and had to look up:

'Surely, *mon Général*, in that event he is courting disaster by awaiting our attack! I believe he is too clever to be so imprudent. If, as you say, we cut him off from Vienna, he has no other retreat than the mountains of Bohemia. But I credit him with another idea: he has put out his fires and one can hear a lot of noise in his camp . . . '

At once, Weirother was exultant:

'It's because he's withdrawing! He's changing position! See how well it falls in with my predictions. Even if we admit that he is retreating on Turas, well then, he is saving us a lot of trouble . . . and our dispositions remain the same . . . '

Langeron raised his arms to the ceiling and prepared to let loose his southern spirit, but His Most Serene Highness Prince Kutuzov at last intervened, with all the weight of his three hours of silence:

'Gentlemen, the dispositions for tomorrow, or rather for today, since midnight is past, will not be altered. You have heard them read out and we shall all do our duty. But before a battle, there is nothing more important that to sleep well. Gentlemen, let us take some rest.'

CHAPTER XII

December 1st, 10 p.m.

'WISH TO LIVE AND KNOW HOW TO DIE'

Six miles away, on the other side of the world, the counterpart to that scene was astonishing in its serenity and magnificence. Even if Napoleon had wanted to conceive it as a dramatist he would not have gone about it in any other way. And the contrast between the leaders of the two camps, at that moment, marked him out with such a poetic advantage, one might say, that it was there that he began to gain the day.

Philippe de Ségur has recorded the evening vividly. 'Now . . . [that is to say, well after nightfall, towards seven or eight o'clock] entering with us the thatched cottage near by, he sat down gaily at table'.

It was the Emperor's bivouac ritual, one of those moments of relaxation and freedom that he was always to delight in, and nostalgia for which, perhaps, would make him cherish the idea of war in the midst of his palaces. 'It was a feast for all of us,' a chamberlain recalled. 'The foodstuffs were displayed before him, and everybody, from the pages to the highest officers, could find here and there whatever he required.' 'On these occasions,' adds Savary, 'the Emperor was not an egoist, as one has been led to believe. He did not know what it was to think of tomorrow, when that was all that mattered; he shared his supper and his hearth with all who had been able to follow him; he went so far as to urge food on those whom he saw, who were held back by discretion.'

A large number of candlesticks set the plaster walls of the

cottage shimmering and gave a rosy glow to the provisions spread over the long tablecloth amidst the silver and the baskets: cutlets, legs of mutton, hams, fresh butter, white bread, chicken. The kitchen department had succeeded, just in time, in surpassing itself on this occasion: the first since Brünn when it was possible for the Imperial table to be furnished in profusion. At other moments in the campaign, Napoleon had had to fast, because of the extreme rapidity of their marches. But here, even 'the Emperor's Chambertin' had arrived and the pages poured liberally into all the silver goblets this richness of a Burgundy at fifty-five degrees, a little too shaken up to be truly mellow. 'He made me drink a real "loser-of-friends",' an ill-disposed person would one day say. For those who tasted it there and then, it was the finest wine of their life. Physically and nervously racked by three months of fatigue, carried along by the wild winds of enormous risk, they were all beside themselves, in that state of deprivation that allowed them suddenly to throw themselves on the meat or the wine as if they had completely forgotten the taste of them. Above all, they devoured Napoleon.

He, scorning the meats, allowed himself one of his rare indulgences: a plate of potatoes and onions fried in oil, his treat. He would devour it in ten minutes, but at the moment when everybody was expecting to see him rise, he threw himself back in his folding arm-chair, unbent at last, and turned with his winning smile towards the screen of men standing by the entrance who were pressing in to see him, the orderly staff officers, the duty officers, the constabulary, the paymasters of the Imperial household, the quarter-master-sergeants of the palace, the topographers. He sensed the watching centuries behind them. 'What did he talk about, on that evening, the great Napoleon?'

Ségur kept his eyes wide open, for he had been persuaded 'that the great issue whose fate was about to be decided would provide the main topic of conversation.' He listened attentively; but what happened was quite the reverse!

Of course. It was nothing to do with service matters. The springs had been wound up, orders given, the die cast. True, less than fifty yards away, in his large yellow and blue tent, Marshal Berthier, chief of the general staff, worn down with overwork, had not even had time to come and sit at his master's table: he dictated more than a hundred letters, carefully noted in the register of operations, and politely tormented an army of secretaries by gnawing his finger-nails more than ever. But the execution of orders, that was his affair. Here, the one who had given them had a longing for an hour off duty.

Napoleon's eye passed fondly over the privileged ones, insane in their pride: those whom he had invited to sit round the table. Only one marshal, Murat. Ségur, next to the surgeon Yvan. The master of the horse, Caulaincourt, frozen into conventional respect. And a band of men still young, but each already wounded two or three times, whom he preferred to any other audience because they existed only through him: his aides-de-camp. Generals, colonels or captains, Junot, Mouton, Rapp, Lemarrois, Lebrun (son of the worthy man who had just been made Duke of Plaisance and head of the treasury, to console him for not being third Consul any more), Macon and Thiard, who also kept his diary. If he was capable of love, these were the ones he loved: these great uncomplicated boys. He never encountered in the depths of their gaze the ineradicable reserve of a Bernadotte, a Masséna or an Augereau: 'After all, I too could have done it . . . '

'What did the courier from Paris have to tell you, Junot?'

With his round head, large lips, and brow unfurrowed but already inflamed with alcohol, Junot that evening became once more the comrade of the lean years, the brave, the handsome Andoche, who had brushed himself down laughingly at Toulon, under the bombardment.

'They are talking of nothing but the porpoise, Sire.'

Was that not a sign of the same order as a comet? On the 15th Brumaire, nearly 50,000 Parisians had crowded the banks of the Seine to watch a porpoise swim upstream between the Pont-Neuf and the Pont des Arts, before disappearing in the Port-au-Blé.

'I should not have thought such trivial matters would have interested you, *monsieur*, and I expected you to tell me about the arts.'

Junot prided himself on his literary interests, no doubt in emulation of his wife, the garrulous and vinegary Laure Permon.

'There is much comment concerning the poetry prize awarded on the 8th Brumaire to M. Millevoye in the first class of the Institute for a poem on the *Independence of Men of Letters*.'

A quick glance by the Emperor confirmed that nobody around him had smiled. All military men with no sense of irony, they had missed a nice moment there. He alone remained capable of humour, even in camp. It was his incorrigibly civilian side. But if Junot was little given to pleasantry, he was not lacking in prudence and carefully avoided all mention of the real literary event of the year: the publication of *René*. It was known that Napoleon already detested M. de Chateaubriand, all the more because he recognized his worth.

'And the theatrical season?'

Tongues were loosened. They had all received on the previous day a great bag of delayed mail and wanted to show that Junot was not the only one to know what was going on. The Moravian cottage vanished, they no longer heard the crackling of the huge wood fire, the stamping of the horses tied up near by, the clatter of arms and the muffled cries of the sentries in the bitter mist, exchanging carefully selected passwords:

'Arcole!'

'Rivoli!'

They were in Paris, at the Opéra, which had been known for the past year as the Imperial Academy of Music, where *Don Juan* had just had a lively success, not because of its Austrian composer, who had died so young thirteen years earlier, Wolfgang Amadeus Mozart, but thanks to a M. Kalkbrenner, who had had the happy thought of *arranging* this 'daring' music by adding some bits of his own composition. It was these that had been applauded. They were at the Vaudeville, with *Harlequin, Domestic Tyrant*, at the Montasier with *Monsieur Vautour, or the Proprietor under Lock and Key*. And when Napoleon frowned, because he detested comedy, they moved on quickly to the Théâtre Français:

'The public is still flocking as much as ever to the *Templars* by M. Raynouard.'

Five indigestible acts full of political allusion, which had carried its author into the Academy. The son a Templar, the father a minister of Philip-the-Handsome, the latter ending up, not without anguish, by having the former shot, sacrificed for reasons of State. A sublime soporific in the worst tradition of Voltaire's tragedies. Everybody was outdoing his neighbour in rhapsodizing over it, until the Emperor's voice rose, ever louder and more inspired, for one of his celebrated monologues. He had made it clear that he wished to be given the opportunity for it.

'This piece is a failure, gentlemen. I have said as much to Raynouard, and I am well aware that the poet will never forgive me. One has to praise these gentlemen in order to be praised by them! But never mind about that: no author of our day has understood the new principle that must provide the basis of our modern tragedies. Come now! In this *Templars*, there is only one well-drawn character: that of a man who wants to die! That is not true to life, that is useless. Gentlemen, one must wish to live and know how to die.'

'Wish to live and know how to die.' The phrase struck powerful chords in those imperious hearts. It could have been the motto of their generation, the inscription on the Austerlitz medal. They lived it with no illusions. And the Emperor went on with his dissertation; he had occasion, within an hour, to bring in Corneille:

'Look at Corneille! What creative force! He could have been a statesman! . . . Now that pagan religion no longer has the same prestige, our tragic theatre needs a different source of power. It is politics that should be the great spring of modern tragedy! That is what should replace, on our stage, the fatalism of antiquity: that fatalism that makes Oedipus a criminal without his being guilty . . . It is a mistake to think that tragic subjects are exhausted; there are plenty of them in the necessities of politics. One must know how to sense and touch this chord . . . It is only a matter of placing one's characters, in opposition to other passions or inclinations, under the absolute sway of this powerful necessity! In this manner, all that one calls a *coup d'État* or a political crime, would become a subject for a tragedy in which, horror being tempered by necessity, a new and sustained interest would be developed.'

All eyes avoided each other, and Napoleon changed the subject rather abruptly, as if he had become aware that the shadow of a body riddled with bullets in the still-fresh tomb at

191

Vincennes — eighteen months before — had snuffed out his tirade: that of the Duke d'Enghien.

A few examples summoned to the rescue came hurrying from afar. From Egypt, especially, 'which allowed him,' thought Ségur, 'to pass on to a subject more in keeping with our present situation and to the habits of those who surrounded him.' It is astonishing that on the eve of his most brilliant success his mind should select, out of a tally already so rich in heartening successes, his only undeniable defeat up to that time: the lifting of the seige of St John of Acre. That mound of ochre earth stuffed with English cannon and crowned with half-naked fanatics against whom his oriental venture had broken six years earlier.

'If I had captured Acre, I should have taken the turban! I should have put my army into baggy trousers, I should not have exposed it any more except in the last extreme; I should have made them my sacred battalions, my immortals! It would have been with Arabs, Greeks, Armenians, that I should have finished the war against the Turks. [And the context of the phrase shows that, as far as this cannon-fodder recruited on the spot was concerned, it would not have occurred to him to be economical.] Instead of a battle in Moravia, I should have won a battle of Issus, I should have made myself Emperor of the East, and I should have returned to Paris via Constantinople.' [1]

But a strange smile crossed his lips at that moment, like an invitation to leap from the past to the future, from the memory to the project . . .

Ségur murmured, tentatively:

'If it's a question of Constantinople, we are on the way to it again . . .'

[1] 'Was this scene itself not a dream?' writes Emil Ludwig. 'Would one not think oneself in the days of Homer when the princes, in single combat, settled the fate of whole generations? Here he was, as in the epic poems, sitting in a mud-hut, in the middle of an unknown plain. He was thirty-five years old. While conveying to his mouth a few potatoes and onions, on the eve of the day on which he wished by a single victory to revive the Empire of Charlemagne, he was dreaming of the deserts of Asia where long before a pile of stones had barred his way. He relived his schemes of yesteryear and in thought followed Alexander the Great as far as the banks of the Ganges . . . '

Unfortunately, the criticism of the most recent and objective historians has dispersed this colourful dream, and has revealed above all that it was made *a posteriori*. First, even if we skip the obstacle of St John of Acre, it would

Junot took up the idea in full cry.

'The road to Constantinople . . . '

The Emperor pretended to resist:

'No, I know the French: they only consider themselves well off wherever they are not. With them, long expeditions are never easy. And consider: if at this moment you gathered together the voices of the army, you would hear them all calling on France! Such are the French, it is their character. France is too beautiful; they never like to go far from her and remain separated from her for too long! . . . '

He stopped, and would have been disappointed if nobody had contradicted him. But they were bursting to speak, half-risen to their feet. One could almost see them for a moment draw sabre and cry *Dieu-le-veut*.

'Sire! The enthusiasm of the soldiers! . . . '

'All the fervent demonstrations Your Majesty has received today! . . . '

'They would even march to China!'

'In all ranks, the same spirit . . . '

But the stern and unbending voice of General Mouton was now raised for the first time:

'You are mistaken, gentlemen. And you are misleading His Majesty. The cheers you speak of prove the contrary. The army is tired. It is a rapid peace they are clamouring for by hailing the one who alone can give it to us.'

They made signs to him. They glared at him. The idiot! The blundering ass! But he was in full spate:

'I well know that what I say is painful to you, but my conscience obliges me to tell you that the army can do no more. If it were led still further, it would obey, but against its will. It is

---

have been unrealizable: Napoleon could not have advanced freely except with the support of the revolted Hindus. But that is the point; on May 4, 1799, the English defeated Tippoo-Sahib at Seringapatam, and the Sepoys came to occupy the shores of the Red Sea. Secondly, at that time, still republican, and at the head of an army all of whose higher officers were getting out of hand, General Bonaparte could have conceived the project of proclaiming himself Emperor of the East only under the influence of quartan fever. In fact, there was really no question of it. And what some devotees of his legend have called 'Napoleon's great design' was born of the vagaries of his imagination, that evening of December 1, 1805, at the foot of the Pratzen.

showing such fervour on the eve of battle only because it is reckoning on finishing tomorrow and returning home.'

They were unable to silence this man with his six wounds. His bravery was already legendary. Slim, cold, cutting in civilian life, as he was that evening, he became transformed into a pillar of fire in battle, as he would be on the morrow. He was the same age as these braggarts he had just put in their place, but seemed ten years older. He was the Cassandra of the service, whom Napoleon not only tolerated but elevated into his entourage—free to curtail his career ruthlessly when the incumbent of the post fulfilled it too well. Mouton would never be a duke, or a marshal.

Of them all, he was the most sincerely devoted to the Emperor. The latter as he listened to him grimaced as if he were taking medicine. And since this clumsy fellow had broken the spell, Napoleon broke off the conversation. How far away Constantinople seemed all of a sudden! It was eleven o'clock in the evening, and tomorrow would see them perhaps cut off from Vienna, wandering in the bogs.

'In the meantime, gentlemen, let us fight.'

*   *   *   *

To inspect was the very least they could do. Five minutes later, the whole general staff made their way, horses stepping hesitantly in the black night, towards the artillery park and the field hospital. Mouton was scarcely wanted there, and would remain alone until the next day: one does not risk being seen with a courter of disgrace. However, he did not feel himself to be alone: he spent some hours going from bivouac to bivouac listening to the men. It was their voice that had intervened through his own to break the dream of conquest as it passed all bounds. A son of the people, he disowned nothing of his origins and remained on a level with those whose suffering was to be painted in the colours of martyrdom by calling them 'Grumblers'. Their true nobility was much higher: they marched, yes, but in the constant hope of peace and home. Towards their family, the further they went from it.

Had Mouton passed by the bivouac of the poor boys torn from the department of the Forests? Was that him, that tall

phantom-officer wrapped up in his cloak, who listened, straight
as a statue of shadows, to the interminable dictation by Gérard
Jacquot of Liège of a letter to his sweetheart—whom he would
never see again? The hands of a child of nineteen reached out
desperately into the night:

'Alas, where is the time when I was able to talk with you and
taste the pleasure of your presence? We spent some happy
moments when our hearts were filled by the most tender
exchanges. But when shall we see each other again? Shall the
fruits of our love come to nothing? Will the war last for ever?
Alas, I cannot tell. In the meantime, if peace were able to
resume its rights, it would give me back what it took from me;
this tender hope is ever in my heart and consoles me now more
than ever. You are destined to make my happiness. My fate is in
your hands, I deliver myself up completely; never will there be
a woman for me, except it be you, or unless I am told of your
death. All that I have suffered and all that I shall perhaps still
suffer has already cost me much pain, but I count all that as
nothing if I have the good fortune to be able to reach what I
desire every day . . . If I were on the way back to you . . . oh,
what shears love has! What ravages has it not made in my
heart since I have had the honour to know you? No, I had
never really understood what love was before loving you . . .'

There were pages and pages like this, until the final heartrending laments:

'I cannot finish my letter without shedding some tears, with
which my eyes are quite filled. Farewell, my dear one, whom I
miss so much. Farewell. Farewell, touch my hand and receive
my tender embraces. Do not let my grief be the cause of yours.
Take heart, away with sorrow. Enjoy yourself with your friends,
while awaiting that most happy and most lucky day when we
can be united and can comfort each other with our embraces
and tell each other by mouth what we dare not say in our
letters.'

There they were then, those braggarts ready to take the

turban, those adventurers of the Ganges and the desert! This glimpse into their heart does not diminish the victors of December 2nd. For such they were, in the depths of their homesickness, who tomorrow would be fighting. And winning. By marching first towards themselves, as they did for three months, but in the truth of war, beyond the mirage.

'It is repugnant to me to obey every order I am given, and at the first word spoken to me, and by men indifferent to my existence . . . ' (infantryman Jean-Simon Banneux).

'If I had thirty-six brothers, I should not recommend one of them to serve, for in truth it is a poor state' (Pierre-Joseph Leclercq).

A strange silence had reigned for a minute or two in Gérard Jacquot's bivouac, at the end of his dictation, and even the army scribe, who had heard however many others, had not at once found the sallies he needed to rouse the tall lad, quite overcome, with his shaking shoulders. It was another youth, a fellow-countryman of his, who had left the circle and shamed him out of it by pressing his arm—with a word of comfort in itself far sadder than all the other's outpourings:

'Come, now, we've just got to put up with it,' Urbain-Joseph Dispa had said to him. 'Why, a dog when you strangle him, he's just got to put up with it . . . After all, *they* do just what they like with us: *they* are the masters . . . '

CHAPTER XIII

December 2nd, midnight

'THE FINEST EVENING OF
MY LIFE'

The booths of the field hospital of the Guard, which Napoleon went to visit, had been set up a few hours before and unpacked in the positions where on the following day the surgeons would be operating without stopping, up to their elbows in blood, mainly on officers, since they were forbidden to attend to wounded soldiers. They had chosen as usual hollow positions sheltered from stray cannon-balls and musket-shots, which the vagaries of ballistics often caused to ricochet well beyond their normal range. The tents had been laid out in a circle, in order to provide as much protection as possible for the bodies set down in the middle of them on the straw scattered by the armful, while they awaited their turn. The attendants, in long, blue-grey tunics, busied themselves without much enthusiasm in setting out the rudimentary materials already depleted by three months marching and fighting. They consisted for the most part of those sad figures likened by Stendhal and Paul-Louis Courier to Calabrian brigands. The servants of healing belonged to a despised race: of those who did not fight. They were aware of it, and were spared no insults. It was true, moreover, that the majority of these disreputable apothecaries, without the least idea of medicine or even hygiene, had got themselves relegated to the hospitals through cowardice or incapacity.

The testimony of the wounded describes in no uncertain terms their brutality, their coarseness, their indifference, their drunkenness. This last tendency was, alas, shared by most of the surgeons, forced to harden themselves and stimulate themselves artificially in order to cut up bodies twenty hours at a stretch in a mire of pus and foetid odours—and having to resign themselves to ten losses for one life saved. The majority of them followed their calling by accident, often because they lacked sufficient skill or qualifications to exercise it in civilian life—and they were scarcely distinguishable from the hospital orderlies in their manner of expressing themselves or in their behaviour. The soldiers had no love for them on the whole, and were always ready to exchange the mordant memories they owed to them.

Except when it concerned 'the gentlemen of the Grand Field-hospital' . . . Ah, as for them, woe to anybody who ventured to show disrespect! Ten indignant veterans would call them to order. This little group of men, honest, generous, energetic, and of a gallantry eclipsing Murat's, saved the honour of the Imperial health services, whose blemishes they concealed under the brilliance of their reputation: Desgenettes, Percy, and above all the Chief, the master of them all, Baron Larrey.

There he was cap in hand in front of the Emperor, whose present inspection would be confined to putting a series of questions to him mechanically, as if he were thinking of something else. The torches threw into relief the pallor of exhaustion on his smooth face, between the two grizzly side-whiskers, above a six-inch red gorget. A surgeon-major of the first class, responsible for the hospitals of the Guard, but at the same time inspector of all the hospitals of the Grand Army, he had just shaved himself carefully, for he knew he would be unable to do so again until God alone knew when. He wore a sabre, white breeches, the boots of a senior officer, and carried himself well. Very agreeable under his icy manner, he saved the lives of thousands of seriously wounded by his invariable composure and his Draconian method: amputate, amputate quickly, amputate high and without appeal, even if many of the injured limbs had a chance of preservation. It was the only method of warding off gangrene which, during the wars of that time, caused the death of seven out of ten wounded. Larrey spoke little, wrote badly, lived prudently, and worked to the point of wrecking his health. He was one of the Emperor's best choices.

They did not like each other, however. The conflict between

their natures and their functions—the one constantly occupied in patching up as best he could the splendid men the other squandered — was apparent this evening, when Napoleon endured with ill-grace the precise and dry answers by which his surgeon-major, without useless complaints, compelled him to face the wretched state of the hospitals.

They had never been in good order, even at Boulogne. So painstaking when it was a matter of authorizing payment for the movement of the least detachment and of prescribing, regulation on regulation, the composition of the 'records kit' (300 deserter's certificates and 100 death certificates to be issued at the departure of each regiment), Napoleon never seemed to have conceived and still less followed a rational plan for the organization and provisioning of his sanitary services. Without Larrey's ant-like industry these would have been destitute of vital supplies within a month.

'What is the average distribution by hospital of surgical materials?'

'Sire, the only articles complete are the 30 splints and 12 supports for the reduction of fracture, which can always be cut out of any kind of wood. But there are no more than 45 rolls of bandage instead of 72, 3 kilogrammes of large surgical squares instead of 12, 10 of small instead of 22, and 5 kilogrammes of lint when there should be 12.'

'Pins?'

'They are almost completely lacking.'

'Well, you will make do as at Genoa! Give orders to use two where there should be six. And thread? Wax? Twine? Sponges?'

'They will have to be economized in the same proportion, Sire.'

'How about your medicine chests properly speaking?'

'One would think they had already been depleted by a hecatomb. All I have, by the chest, is 120 grammes of lead extract instead of 240, 50 grammes of Hoffmann's fluid instead of 180, 300 grammes of tincture of camphor instead of . . . '

Napoleon thought to extricate himself by breaking in:

'Ammonia?'

'Completely lacking. So too is laudanum, which is the most

serious. I shall be forced to operate tomorrow almost without sedatives . . . as usual,' Larrey added under his breath.

'Come now, you always see everything in a bad light! Didn't you receive brandy this morning, supplied from Vienna by the barrelful?'

'Yes, Sire. I have issued triple quantities to each hospital, that is, six litres.'

'Monsieur Larrey, you will do your best,' said Napoleon giving rein and leaving him, bowing, resigned, abandoned, between his two excellent assistants, chosen by him, who discharged the secondary duties admirably: the tall Sue, chief physician, and Sureau, the pharmacist, a gangly man of bone.

*   *   *   *

Near at hand, though further back still, the sight of the artillery park of the Guard had something to comfort the Emperor.

The artillery pieces had enjoyed complete priority over all other convoys. Brigadier-General Couin, Major Doguereau, and Cavalry-Majors Digeon, Greiner and Chauveau had been occupied since morning in distributing the cannons over a vast area, harnessed to horses or drawn by gunners 'on the ropes', and in scattering as widely as possible from each other the artillery ammunition wagons, many of which were still made from open vehicles which the least spark would explode.

In 1805, the general park of the French artillery, massively enlarged since the Consulate, consisted of 4,506 pieces of large calibre, 7,366 of small calibre, 8,320 howitzers, and 1,746 mortars. To convey about a hundredth of them into the heart of Moravia, endless foresight and ingenuity had been necessary. Each piece had been followed through from its departure from La Fère or Toulon in order to lead it, as if to a family reunion, to the assembly over an acre or two of firing-pieces whose barrels gleamed dully in the faint light from the shrouded lamps: torches were strictly forbidden here. But the moon shone clear in this middle of the night and favoured the gunners: lovingly cleaned and polished all day long, the pieces would be going into battle like the soldiers of the Guard, in full dress, on their two-wheeled wooden gun-carriages.

Napoleon stopped in front of one of the largest monsters, a twelve-centimetre, capable, that is to say, of hurling a cannonball weighing some thirteen pounds a distance of over 1,000 yards. It was surrounded by no less than fifteen men, who were necessary to serve it; eight of them had had to be specially trained for several months.

'How many shots are there for tomorrow?'

'One hundred and forty solid balls, Sire, and ninety of grape-shot.'

'What kind are they?'

'The large, Sire, each filled with forty-two lead balls.'

The Emperor gave a satisfied tap on the cross-piece of the gun-carriage, a caress of his whip, and moved on, leaving an astonished witness, Captain Reizet, who would attribute him with unusually disturbed feelings to account for his having asked such an unprecedented question in the mouth of an old artillery captain, since every artilleryman knew that the twelve-centimetre guns could fire only the large grape-shot; the smaller ones, filled according to calibre with sixty to a hundred tiny pieces of metal, were suitable only for the eight- or four-centimetre pieces.

Napoleon went round the park rapidly and as if at random, coming back to the same spot several times, with an absent air. He had rediscovered his preoccupation of the afternoon: his right was slow in taking up its position, in spite of the arrival of Davout with the advance guard. How many men would he have at his disposal at dawn the next day at the exposed nerve-point of his dispositions? And in what state would these breath-less men be? This obsession did not prevent him from pouring his flood of questions in fits and starts over the shoulders of the thirteen servers of an eight-centimetre gun, or the eight of a four-centimetre, nor from reckoning for himself that a mortar had at most under 200 rounds left to fire (350 in normal practice) by looking for them one by one in the battery's ammunition wagons, and in the narrow casket fitted into the cheeks of the gun-carriage. He insisted on himself opening a cartridge case and in splitting the serge bag containing the charge of powder, packed in by hand, on top of which the 'spiked ball' was introduced: he tested the powder, sniffed it, and placed a few grains on the tip of his tongue to gauge its dryness and quality.

'Where are your firing lances? Your powder pouches? What length of fuse have you left?'

He interrupted himself, paid no attention to replies, sawed at the mouth of his horse, whose sudden about-turns more than once came near to unseating its clumsy rider, and galloped off ahead of his group, who followed him by the light of the moon.

Davout! The tireless Marshal, 'the man of wood with the gait of a man-of-the-woods', [1] had arrived at last in person after establishing his column commanders in the odd, incomprehensible positions designated by the Emperor as the locality for his right: the woods and fens of Gross-Raygern, more than six miles further to the south-east, without a break, from the other units. Lost men in a lost spot.

Had they at least got there? Napoleon had such a jubilant expression that those present expected to see him embrace Davout.

'Sire, I left General Friant's division in process of establishing its bivouac at Gross-Raygern. The men are exhausted, they are very cold, there are not more than 6,000 of them, but they are there.'

A memorable march: never before had a foot unit performed the like. They had covered forty-five miles on the previous day and forty-five on that day: ninety miles in two days. Some hundreds of men, that afternoon, had dropped from exhaustion along the side of the road. In order to rally them, Friant had hit upon a clever stratagem: he had a few cannon fired at the head of the column. The brave men, thinking the battle had begun, got up, covered in shame, to hurry along on their bleeding feet.

That evening, they were strewn about like corpses, in the woods and fens around an abbey tucked cosily under its Gothic roofs. The officers had to kick them to their feet in order to collect them round the fires. One of them, however, found the energy to write a few lines to his parents, on large sheets which he was confident of finishing the next day, when the battle was ended. It was our friend Jean-Pierre Blaise:

[1] *Orang-outang*, in French.

'We left the village where we had billeted between eight and nine o'clock in the evening. We marched until two in the morning, when we made a halt in a wood. We lit fires there, and then we rested until five o'clock, when we set off again. We marched all day and we bivouacked in a wood; at six o'clock in the evening we did not prepare a meal, since we had been warned that we should be leaving at nine. We preferred to use the time for resting. We had received bread for three days at Vienna before leaving; we were therefore not short of it: it provided our sole nourishment. On leaving this position, we marched until five o'clock, when the regiment made a halt. I can assure you that that was the hour, for there was nobody left in the companies. The Colonel, whose kindness towards us never flagged throughout the campaign, had wine issued to us in abundance. This restored our energies and put us into a state to continue our march. When it was judged that the majority of the men had returned to their companies, we were marched off; the Colonel left an officer to collect the stragglers. We arrived at last this evening, at seven o'clock in the evening, in a village where we bivouacked with a division of dragoons. We had a false alarm there, caused by the cries of a woman, but we were sent back one after the other to our fires. I leave you to imagine whether we made good use of the night to rest ourselves, after such a long march!'

*   *   *   *

On returning to his bivouac, Napoleon refused the collapsible bed that Constant would have been able to set up for him meantime in ten minutes. He did not want to take off his boots and threw himself on to a few bundles of straw, where he at once went to sleep for less than an hour. He had given explicit orders to wake him at the least abnormal event, and the sustained fusillade that could be heard a little after midnight crackling, barely audibly, a long way to the south, where everybody now knew the French weak-point to lie, disturbed his aides-de-camp sufficiently for them to drag the Emperor from his sleep. Not without difficulty. He had to be shaken.

'Has anyone been sent for news?'

'Two officers, Sire. One of them was to turn back as soon as he had located the position of the affray. He will be here any minute.'

'There is fairly violent firing on either side of the village of Telnitz, Sire, near the lakes.'

This was therefore clearly in one of the last villages to their extreme right. Where Napoleon knew that a ridiculously weak screen of men would crack at the slightest thrust.

'Lebrun, go and find out for yourself. Let me know if the Russians are really executing their manoeuvre already.'

He left the hut, came to warm himself at the fire of the picket of grenadiers, walked up and down in the midst of his familiars, who strained their ears and all more or less shivered: it was the hour of suspense when a soldier felt himself uprooted between sleep and combat, between dream and reality. One no longer knew whether it was December 1st or 2nd. But the keen breeze and the temperature bordering on nine below freezing (Fahrenheit) was sufficient reminder that one was in Frimaire. They stopped, they kept quiet, they strained their ears to the continued crackling of the fusillade, more than four miles away. At that distance, it was often overlaid by the thousand muffled sounds of the two huge armies encamped opposite each other. But it persisted enough to impose itself on the hearing. Lebrun not having come back, the Emperor sent another messenger, who was also held up, as in the song. It was the next one's turn!

'Savary!'

'At your orders, Sire.'

'Go at once as far as the communication between General Legrand's division and the first detachments of the 3rd Corps. You will no doubt find Friant at their head. Come back immediately. But not without being in a position to inform me fully about what the Russians are doing. The persistent firing must be covering some advance.'

General Savary hurried off, with that quite extraordinary rapture he showed each time his god honoured him with a mission, even if it had been a legal assassination. An obtuse man, but a good soldier, he lost no time going down the Goldbach, passed rapidly through the line of posts in echelon and arrived at Legrand's division, where the young general who had the task of commanding the right of the French centre, very calm, very sure of himself, informed him that 400 hussars (Austrian, not Russian) had in fact presented themselves an hour earlier before Telnitz and had driven away the weak post placed there by the sharpshooters of the Po. The nature of the ground had favoured their advance by allowing them to gather momentum down a sloping plain that dominated the village. But Legrand had at once taken the head of a battalion of the 111th regiment of the Line, which was encamped nearby, and had plunged bayonet first down the single street of the village, whose hovels the enemy hussars, scarcely dismounted from their horses, had not yet occupied. The very clear moon which had helped their charge began to cloud over just at that moment, allowing the French infantrymen to advance along the walls without being seen, until they were able to discharge murderous volleys at pointblank range. The Austrians, expecting at any moment the arrival of their infantry, which was already firing away, at a guess above the Goldbach, withdrew only slowly, in good order and not without losses. But the progressive clouding over had ended by settling the engagement in favour of the French, reinstated without great security in a position where they felt themselves somewhat 'in the air'.

'It was certainly a warm attack, Sire, but on a reduced scale, and one that did not suggest more extensive fighting, at least until daybreak.'

Savary, back in less than an hour, was making his report to Napoleon, whom he found asleep once again on the straw in his hut, and whom he too had to shake respectfully: nature had resumed its rights. Everybody was stretched out at headquarters, and disappointment at this sleepless night was sharp for all the commanders, who had counted on it to restore their vigour. Stretched out at full length on his bearskin thrown over the bundles of straw, Napoleon listened attentively, his hands clasped behind his heavy Roman head raising it a little.

'I noticed on the other hand that on the far side of the Goldbach, opposite Telnitz and Sokolnitz, a considerable enemy force is being gathered.'

Napoleon raised himself on one elbow.

'So far down already? You did say opposite Telnitz?'

He clicked his finger impatiently, and a page rushed up with an unrolled map which he presented, one knee on the ground. Savary's finger did not hestitate:

'Above the great lake, yes, Sire, at this sort of tip where the Pratzen plateau ends. More exactly, between Telnitz and Augezd. That is where many reports, and my own observation of the noise and the lights, have convinced me of the presence of an extremely strong concentration in process of taking place.'

'How substantial?'

'An army corps, I should say.'

'Infantry? Cavalry?'

'A corps of every arm.'

'How is it that nobody reported this to me during the day?'

'The movement cannot have taken place until after dark, Sire. And this part of the terrain is concealed from Your Majesty's view by the last detached outcrops of the hills towards the Goldbach.'

'Is Friant in touch with Legrand?'

'No, Sire, not at all. I had dealings with some elements of the 5th Corps only. Marshal Davout's troops are still nearly three miles from there.'

So, in the middle of the night, a significant hiatus between the French centre and right just opposite what was perhaps the enemy's spearhead. Napoleon's face became very sombre. If he had tried to compose his features his head would have burst. Trap and counter-trap were so confounding each other at that moment that vertigo was not far from seizing the chief engineer.

The fusillade had ended, away towards Telnitz. There was nothing more to do but go back to sleep. His entourage began to calculate the possible hours of rest . . . But this man who had so often been described as sure of himself, this self-styled gambler confident of his chessboard, rose with a rapid movement and shook his people:

'To horse. Find Soult for me. I have decided to set out on a personal reconnaissance by approaching the enemy camps as closely as possible. Nobody has cared a damn about giving me the exact boundaries.'

There followed a pantomime of looks and stifled yawns. But Caulaincourt bowed. Braced up in his gilded uniform, the master of the horse, whose *raison d'etre* was to cling like a shadow three paces behind the Emperor, had no right to know fatigue. His complexion was fresh. Whenever had he found the time to shave?

'Who will accompany Your Majesty?'

'Five officers.'

More, that was certain, the surgeon who always had to be ready to tend Napoleon instantly in the event of injury, and the escort picket of twelve *chasseurs*. Soult, who had not gone to bed any more than the other corps commanders, arrived with red eyes and a startled air, followed by two aides-de-camp equipped with large note-books, in which the meticulous commander required a record to be made of the least detail of the moment. The little Imperial group quickly descended the hillock at Girzikowitz and set off on a fresh reconnaissance in a pre-figuration of the field of battle: the ground was strewn as far as one could see with sleeping men, who resembled so many cadavers in the darkness that grew increasingly damp.

It was two o'clock in the morning.

*   *   *   *

The Emperor headed boldly towards the east, and in descending the gentle slope of his observation hill had been sufficiently struck by the grandiose beauty of the night scene for a trace of it to be discernible in what he wrote two days later: 'the immense number of fires of the two armies encompassed the atmosphere.'

More than 1,500 glowing in two parallel lines, from 400 to 1,000 yards apart, made a sparkling river that Napoleon gave the impression of wanting to cross. The fires of the French were better supplied, higher, more regular than those of the Allies. The testimony of Austrian civilians noted, with slightly apprehensive astonishment, that the invaders 'love huge, blazing fires'. This observation was made by a gentleman called Bacher, a teacher at Siegdorf, who added: 'For their bivouac fires, not only was wood necessary but also enormous quantities of straw; even in front of the house occupied by the general-in-chief at the time of his passing through our midst, they had lit a formidable camp fire. I have noticed the same tastes amongst the cooks concerning their braziers . . . There is good reason to believe that large fires are among the national customs of the French.' Certainly, the encampment that evening had nothing in common with the one at Neumark, where Hautpoul's cuirassiers had beaten all records in temporary comfort: 'They requisitioned some beds, carried them to the camp and lay down in them in the open air. It was a most curious sight to see them. To the right of each group, there was the horse attached to a stake, to the left blazed a magnificient bivouac fire, and the centre was occupied by the cavalryman lying thus in the open field in a good bed, smoking his pipe, the bedclothes pulled up to his chin. Multiply this sight a few hundred times, add some piles of baggage, stacks of arms, ammunition wagons, cannons, carriages, and you will have a faithful idea of a French camp like the one I saw not far from us, which was nearly two miles long.'

There was no question of beds that night. Straw itself was scarce, and frequently reserved for the hospitals. The men lay in their coats, next to the frozen ground. The arrival of Napoleon produced the effect of a bomb at the village of Girzikowitz, when he crossed the Ricka separating him from the advance posts. A regiment of dragoons was on picket duty in the street, in the middle of a hamlet turned into a veritable sponge of men ready to run to arms. The colonel gave him the latest reports from the sentinels:

'The sound of the enemy army has just stopped, Sire. But until two o'clock in the morning, we heard the regular commotion of their march.'

'In what direction?'

'Always to their left.'

The Emperor was already spurring away, advancing yet further in the direction of the first slopes of the Pratzen plateau. He had left behind him the Guard, Nansouty's cavalry, the infantrymen of Oudinot and Vandamme, and was crossing General Boyé's cavalry division. The commanders of the outposts were all in agreement in saying that the enemy army was carrying out a big movement in order to shift itself to its left against the French right. He became annoyed, swore under his breath, consigned to oblivion that imbecile colonel, just now at

Girzikowitz. Had the Russian movement not stopped after all? In the great silence he now ordained, everybody could indeed discern the sound of artillery vehicles and the step of horses on the march from the north to the south, behind the near-by fires close to which one could imagine the look-out man on the watch.

The destiny of the world depended on the exact location of this movement that obsessed the Emperor. As if hypnotised, to the great consternation of Caulaincourt, he ventured between the two lines. He was riding along them when, in spite of several warnings, having turned in the darkness towards Pratzen, he stumbled unawares upon a Cossack post! They threw themselves so promptly at him that they only just failed to capture or kill him. But a violent charge by the *chasseurs* of the escort enabled Napoleon to get back to his own fires at full speed. This return was so precipitate that, forced to recross, with no option, the marshy Ricka, several of the men and horses that were following him remained there stuck in the mire (proof of the thinness of the film of ice reported by other witnesses) 'amongst others Yvan, his surgeon since 1796, whose responsibility it was never to be separated from his person.'

The excitement had been fierce. Very pale, the Emperor felt the silent reproach of his companions and endured Marshal Soult's coldness, whose reports, if he had deigned to listen to them, would have spared him this affront, in which all his fortunes so nearly came to grief. Soult had himself just made, and far more prudently, the same reconnaissance, and had reached the same conclusions.

No-one knows why Napoleon got off his horse and handed the reins to a page. The need to recover himself by walking a few paces? To reflect before dictating his final orders? Anxiety concerning the fate of those stuck in the mire, whom he wanted to wait for? Everybody jumped to the ground behind him. They re-ascended on foot, without hurrying, towards the Imperial bivouac, via some digressions that went from fire to fire across the encampments of the 13th regiment of the Line, in Vandamme's division. The moon was quite overcast. The intense darkness hampered their progress. It was now that an amazing scene would arise from a false step. Napoleon, who was advancing almost blindfold, collided with the trunk of an overturned tree.

*   *   *   *

Violent and sudden alarm among the Austro-Russians:
'Can you hear it?'
'What is it?'
'It's coming from the French camp.'
'At least a hundred of them are shouting at once.'
'What on earth's got into them?'
'It's spreading. There must be more than a thousand men yelling together.'
'Can you hear what they're shouting?'
'It's the cry they've stolen from us: *Vive l'Empereur*. Their new rallying cry. It was certainly worth the bother of cutting off the head of their king!'
'And look! Just look at that! All those points of light running about.'
'They're lighting torches.'
'Is it an attack?'
'An attack, you call it! The general assault! There's been nothing like it ever before! To launch such an important operation in the middle of the night!'
'To arms! To arms!'
Sounded at first by the sentinels who were covering the flank of General Prszbyzewski's column, the alert ran from south to north and from west to east, right into the depths of the Allied centre and left, like a rejoinder to that strange effervescence of cries and lights that roused the greater part of the French army. There sprang to light first ten, then twenty, then a hundred glowing points, at the same time as the outburst of cries, which swelled ever louder in proportion to the spread of the fires, not only along the French line, but far, far into the interior of the massive concentration of the Grand Army, whose assembled dispositions it revealed in ten minutes. A good deal more than a cordon of fire, it was a cauldron, a sea of flares, rapid, dying, relighted, that spread under the gaze of thousands of barely awake Russians, rubbing their eyes and questioning each other,

in tiers like spectators at some nocturnal entertainment on the gentle slopes of the Pratzen.

For several minutes all the Allied officers had thought it to be an unprecedented innovation: a massive attack launched in the middle of the night, for the first time in the history of modern warfare, by the French army, hence without artillery and almost without musketry. The thrust of a battering-ram of cold steel, and by torchlight. But in that case, why did this stream of lava extend so deeply into the interior of the French camp? Why was it not confined to the fringe of attackers at the risk of indicating their reserves for bombardment? The only units to remain quiet, opposite each other, a good three miles from there, were the French right and the Russian left, cut off from this blazing contagion by a wide expanse.

But now even the horses, in both camps, were seized with panic and pulled on their ropes. The chiefs of staff and the principal officers were summoned in haste. The great question was to know whether to wake Kutuzov—but in the event they did not go as far as that, fortunately for his familiars.

A considerable group of white uniforms, shaken by the side-steps and capers of their scandalized mounts, gathered at the end of the village of Blaziowitz, around the Czar's brother, Grand-duke Constantine, commander of the Imperial Guard, and Prince Bagration, commander of the right, who had arrived at full speed.

At their feet, the gunners of a drawn-up battery had lit firing-lances, ready to set grape-shot spewing from a dozen pieces. A platoon of Pavlograd hussars had drawn their sabres. Two battalions of grenadiers had already split up as sharpshooters amongst the stunted plants of a vineyard. But the Mongolian face of Bagration never for an instant lost its mummified expression. He breathed contempt for the human species, and was content to proclaim it a little further by a shrug of his shoulders and a few brief words:

'It's just a matter of reading a proclamation or something of that sort, gentlemen. There is nothing there to set a dog by the ears.'

Young Dolgoruki, more restless than ever, maintained that they were confronted with a stratagem of war:

'Napoleon is retreating, *mon prince*! And he has ordered his rearguard to make a lot of noise and light fires to deceive us.'

For a fortnight in which he had placed all his hopes on the battle, Alexander's favourite had lived in constant fear of the French stealing away. The icy wisdom of Prince Bagration glanced over him with a ponderous eye:

'You see clearly that the lights go right into the heart of their system. Do you suggest they are extending their kindness so far as to light up their retreat for our benefit? Besides, their flankers are still on the crown of that hillock, directly opposite us: one of my aides-de-camp has just found out to his cost.'

The poor boy's arm was bleeding through his bandages. He would nevertheless fight the next day well enough to receive two more balls.

Dolgoruki himself could insist no further: the inner variations in the incandescent layer, its ebb and flow, centred on a mysterious point moving within it, proved to every detached observer, even before Bagration's intervention, that there was no question of a nocturnal attack. This would have had to be launched in the opening minutes.

'It's a caprice of the French.'

'And what if it was a matter of mutiny?'

'That would be too rich. But the affair certainly shows their indiscipline. What will these flibbertigibbets be worth tomorrow in front of our granite masses?'

'For all that, we are too sluggish if they are too lively. There they were, for nearly a quarter of an hour, lit up like daylight and nobody on our side ordered fire to be opened! What nice little targets we could have had!'

But who among the Allies would have taken the responsibility for ordering fire to be opened? Kutuzov was sleeping like a log. The Emperors had not even had time to mount horses before Bagration in person came to recommend them to go back to bed. The Allied officers and men went their ways and curled up against the cold in the last scrap of the night that remained to them, a little disappointed, however, as if by a damp squib. The French lake of fire had suddenly been holed with wide black patches. 'A piece of paper, one might have said, about to be consumed.' Then, in the space of three minutes, there remained only a few lingering glow-worms. The event had lasted hardly longer than a blaze of straw, and it had died like one.

*   *   *   *

It had in fact been a gigantic fire of straw. Nobody has remembered the name of the grenadier who found himself in Napoleon's path when he tripped, his foot caught in the stump of a tree just above ground. He became, however, the spontaneous creator of the firework display. With no mischievous intent: his action had been purely utilitarian. He was indignant at the thought of his Emperor not being able to see a thing and in danger of a sprain. So, as in the Hindu fable, the poor chap made his sovereign a pauper's present. All he had left was his handful of straw: the comfort, one might say, of his last hours perhaps. Quickly he gathered it together, twisted it, struck his tinder-box, lit this improvised torch and held it as high as possible above his head.

His neighbour found it a good idea. And he followed suit, and then another. The idea went the round of the company and cleared the ground of its straw. Within five minutes, the pale and angry face of Napoleon appeared all lit up. Fifty were falling over each other with their lights.

He was furious: all agree about that. Captain Jaton: 'He seemed highly annoyed, and indicated the enemy with wide gestures in order to make them understand the danger to which they were exposing him.' Sergeant Morland: 'He immediately had the torches in his vicinity extinguished. But for every one that was stamped out, ten or twenty were lit.' Others have even maintained that he swore in his impatience.

'Silence! You will be crying out tomorrow,' Ségur makes him say. 'Think only of sharpening your bayonets!'

The officers, even without taking orders from him, had only to look at him to know his displeasure, and strove as hard as they could to limit the folly of these idiots, who were turning their Emperor into a target. A few of them used the flats of their sabres.

For a few moments longer the explosion of light was limited to a small area: the rectangular field of a regiment at rest. It was only a matter of rivalling each other in their zeal to light up the

Emperor's footsteps. But another anonymous person, an officer no doubt, was at hand to alter everything by a shout:

'It's the anniversary of the Coronation!'

On December 2, 1804, Napoleon had been anointed by the Pope at Notre-Dame in Paris. Now here it was, a year since he had been treading in Charlemagne's footsteps. They had certainly not waited for this cry to be reminded of it in the French army. Accounts of the Coronation had run through the bivouacs of the Guard all evening: more exactly, recollections of the feasting he had ordained on that occasion. Of the great day itself, the brave fellows retained chilly memories: ten hours of sentry-duty in the icy cold, some dozens of faintings, some cases of frost-bite, broken only by the passage of fairy-tale coaches full of unrecognizable Bonapartes and highly-painted women. But the issue of new belts and straps, two days before, and a double Napoleon for each man! And that banquet, the next day, in all the barracks, three kinds of meat and three of wine *ad lib*! Certainly here was a prize example of memory restoring some flavour to the thin soup and hard tack of the bivouac in Moravia. They had been so little unaware of it that, for lack of a place-name that sprang to their minds (and *nobody* among the French, apart from a few higher officers, yet knew the name of that chateau over there, behind the enemy lines, what was it called? Ostrelitz? Odzervitz? Austerlitz? Wasn't there a village too, and a pheasant-reserve?) they had already named tomorrow's battle the Battle of the Anniversary.

'It's the Anniversary! Long live the Emperor!'

The cry, naturally taken up at once by a dozen loud-mouths, changed the meaning of the illumination and provided the link between an anecdotal episode and a huge upsurge of men, of historic significance. The neighbouring regiments, where the men were beginning to wake up one after the other asking what on earth was going on among their comrades, heard the shout and completely misinterpreted it. Yet at bottom it was they who really grasped the meaning of the moment. The meaning of December 2. For them, all was clear: *'le Tondu'* had wanted to come and visit them, because it was his anniversary, and to some extent theirs. And he had demanded 'fairy-lights'. This was what happened in every fair-sized town on occasions of rejoicing, when all the windows had to be promptly garlanded with Chinese lanterns when the crowd yelled, under threat of receiving showers of stones at the panes.

These torches of straw in place of fairy-lights? A good idea. The army set itself on fire.

Five minutes later, it had 'taken fire', as one might say 'take arms', from Girzikowitz to Schlapanitz and on the main road from Brünn to Olmütz, all over this triangle of three-mile sides. The officers who had exerted themselves to halt the incendiarism took a hand in promoting the same demonstration. 'General Vandamme', Bezin noted, 'stamped up and down on the spot and shouted himself hoarse in his piercing voice, louder than his drums.' The other division commanders were converted. Two miles from there, the placid Oudinot politely asked a *chasseur* to let him have his torch, and kissed him on both cheeks. Opposite him, on the other side of the Ricka, Suchet, as methodical as ever, tried to group the torch-bearers and line them up; far behind him, Nansouty's cavalrymen unhitched their panic-stricken horses and there and then improvised a sort of illuminated fantasia. The entire Guard roared its joy. 'One could no longer hear oneself' (Coignet). 'My ear-drums were battered, but more by my own voice than that of the others' (François). 'It was deafening' (Gribius). 'It was no longer even *Vive l'Empereur!* but wild yells, ahs! and ohs! One would have said their chests would burst' (de Sivry). Of a sudden, therefore, more than 30,000 men were in a state of trance, in a fraternity that dissolved ranks and restored to these men the unity, long since lost, of the great revolutionary impulses. And the fact that this occurred at the ends of the world, in the teeth of danger, in this tumult of glowing flames, released all the sacramental longings of these men-children. Rather than the anniversary, this was the true Coronation. For the past year, the memorialists are in agreement in reporting that nobody believed in it. The ceremonies unrolled in a stiff formality in which everyone was caught up: the Emperor in his disguise, Josephine in his wake, the Arch-something-or-others of the Empire in their roles, the old soldiers in their wrath, and the Pope in his illusions. Paris sulked. Madame Mère had not come because dear Lucien was being

215

persecuted. And to restore their spirits Napoleon had to invoke the dead: 'Joseph, if our father could see us . . . '

Plenty of scenes of enthusiasm had since taken place, however: the distribution of the Eagles, the triumphal journey through Normandy, the great reviews around the camp at Boulogne. But it had always been an artificial enthusiasm, worked up, prearranged, canalized. Here the lava gushed out quite unalloyed. They were taking part in the materialization of one of those extremely rare conjunctions that have profoundly marked the memory of humanity each time they have cropped up: that of an uncontrollable popular current with the man capable of giving it issue, form and scope. They have almost always been expressed through a similar scene, brief and vivid, which raises all the participants out of themselves and gives them the feeling of having finally lived for a few minutes. The memory of it, for them, is all the more piercing in that disappointment has almost always followed . . .

The Man emblazoned: that was Austerlitz.

What became of his annoyance? His remarkable adaptability to circumstances was once more revealed. In an instant, he understood what was happening and the formidable advantage to which he could turn it. Not only there and then, when this collective intoxication was worth any number of additional issues of brandy, but for the future, with an eye to which Napoleon, since Lodi, had always kept a part of himself on show. He seized the limelight and switched on a radiant smile as he slowly advanced, protected from jostling by his familiars who formed a chain around him, pausing at every bivouac. 'He stopped at the fire next to mine to insist on drinking to the honour of the grenadiers. But he only had a sip. Never have I seen him so gay.' 'He asked me where I was on duty on the day of the Coronation. This was the first time he had addressed me and I was so stupid I did not know how to answer him. Fortunately he passed on without waiting' (Jacques Doubet).

He lingered only briefly. His course was no circular tour, and in spite of the beckoning vivats, he hardly strayed from the track that ascended to his headquarters. He therefore crossed only Vandamme's right, Oudinot's left, and half the Guard. He retained enough composure to rebuke gracefully those who

approached the ammunition wagons of the artillery too closely
with their torches. As soon as he had re-entered the lines of the
Guard, the regiments that had hoped for a visit and had watched
his progress from afar understood that he would not be coming
and stopped relighting their torches. There now spread over the
army that lightning black-out, noticed on the other side by the
Allies, reassured at last.

But before entering his hut, he turned to his aides-de-camp
and a heartfelt cry escaped him:

'This is the finest evening of my life.'

It was three o'clock in the morning.

*   *   *   *

He did not go to sleep yet: the secretaries were mobilized.
He dictated an important modification to the intended order of
battle. The illuminated ovation had not wiped from his mind
one jot of the conclusive observations he had just made.[1]

It was moreover not a matter of a radical change in the plan,
but only of a tilting of the direction of the intended attack. An
inclination towards the vertical of the tip of the battering-ram.
Two facts had forced themselves on the Emperor: the Austrians'
nocturnal attack on Telnitz, and that sound of vehicles heard
during the night, heading towards the south. Besides, variations
in the terrain, and especially the relative eminence of Stahré
Vinobrady, by concealing from him the enemy camps established to the north of Pratzen, had convinced him that the Allied
army was now divided into two blocks separated by a wide
empty space, the first in the 'cavalry plain', the second on the
offensive towards Telnitz, whereas he had expected an attack
three miles higher, towards Kobelnitz. He concluded from this
that the Allies would convey the bulk of their forces concentrated between Pratzen and Krzenowitz towards Telnitz, leaving

[1] It is astonishing that no historian of the Empire has noticed the fact, so
well brought out by Colonel Colin's study, that Napoleon changed his dispositions of attack four hours before the start of the battle. It is a tribute to
the perfect organization of his general staff, capable of instantly transmitting
this alteration, without its running the risk of creating the most frightful
confusion. Colonel Poitevin's diary is explicit: 'The movement executed by
the enemy against our right caused our dispositions to be altered at the
moment when, during the night, *Monsieur le Maréchal* (Soult) went to see
the Emperor'.

an isolated corps on the road to Olmütz. He therefore at once considered how to profit from this unusual arrangement, by throwing the Grand Army into the empty space between the abandoned corps and the rest of the Russian troops. 'Giving up the oblique line which he had seemed to adopt initially in order to profit from all the advantages of the terrain, he decided, following the position of the enemy, to present himself at an angle in order to break through their two lines in the middle, and then throw half their army, thus split, on to the lakes that jutted out to the left, and offered them no retreat all the time we held the villages.' (Taken from the Reports of the Army Corps.[1])

Thus the plan still remained a frontal attack on the enemy's flank, but the advance would be aimed more to the south and more in the shape of a fan. Saint-Hilaire's division, instead of following Vandamme's, through Girzikowitz, would attack directly through Puntowitz. Legrand's division would detail Levasseur's brigade (the 18th and the 75th of the Line) with the Corsican sharpshooters, to the front of Kobelnitz instead of in support to the rear of Puntowitz as arranged. And 3,000 men of the 4th Corps were detached *in extremis* to reinforce the defence of Telnitz and Sokolnitz, which Napoleon at last realized was virtually non-existent and incapable of pinning down the enemy units for the time necessary for his manoeuvre.

This last-minute modification demonstrates Napoleon's constant adaptability to circumstances, in contrast to the mechanical rigidity of Weirother's plan. But also the conditions of improvization and mistrust, typically Corsican, under which he made up his mind: Soult, more methodical, and Savary had reported to him that the Pratzen 'hole' was not as important as it appeared on sight. But he himself, not having located a single enemy fire in that area, proceeded to strip by half the forces that would be debouching on the plateau and would therefore risk being thrust back by a Russian resistance far more substantial than had been expected there. The empty space which he supposed to exist was full.

Napoleon knew he was running a serious additional risk there. And one may wonder whether he should not have paused longer in that scene of unprecedented enthusiasm of which he had just

[1] See the diagram of the French plan, on p. 179, opposite the Allied plan.

been the object. To the very slight degree to which he had allowed himself to be, he too had been carried away. He had just seen establish itself, between his personal destiny and the military soul of France, a perfect communion. He knew that never perhaps had a sovereign had his army so well in hand on the eve of a decisive encounter.

Four o'clock in the morning. He went to sleep. It was the hour at which most of the corps and division commanders were being woken up by their aides-de-camp between Gross-Raygern, Schlapanitz, Girzikowitz and the Santon.

CHAPTER XIV

December 2nd, from 5 to 9 a.m.

THE MIST OF AUSTERLITZ

Austerlitz came very near to bearing yet another name: the Battle of Seven O'clock. Everything took place between seven o'clock in the morning and three o'clock in the afternoon. Like every great battle involving tens of thousand of combatants on each side, its unfolding was competely incomprehensible to the ordinary soldier and to the great majority of officers, even the senior ones. In the losers' camp, even the staff officers only began to understand what had happened towards the middle of the battle, round about eleven o'clock.[1]

In the victors' camp, everybody, to be sure, possessed the key Napoleon had given in his eve-of-battle proclamation: *and as they advance to turn my right, they will expose their flank to me.* But only the Emperor and his corps commanders knew the exact location of this right, and this enemy flank to be smashed.

Understanding of Austerlitz was thus the privilege on that day of four or five men around the Man who had been preparing the encounter for the previous ten days. With him, they shared that exalted sensation of living like gods through a fateful moment of history by being able to follow it hour by hour.

For them, the battle was divided, like a well-constructed tragedy, into a prologue and three acts.

*　　　*　　　*　　　*

The prologue was the awakening; it went on from four to six o'clock for the 150,000 exhausted men, who had profited

[1] Some among them, the Emperor of Austria for example, had still not comprehended ten years later.

after a fashion from the frosty night to make some show of gathering strength. In both camps, the men for the most part were up well before the regulation calls, at the same time as their officers. The latter were anxious to have their units ready to march off quickly as soon as the order should come; the former's main concern was not to march on an empty stomach, and they drew from their knapsacks reserves kept back for the decisive day: now was the moment to eat; in the evening one would be dead or victorious.

The last camp[1] had placed opposite each other, according to the official figures, 73,100 Frenchmen with 139 pieces against 85,700 Austro-Russians equipped with 278 cannon. But there were some 12,000 French who would not in fact be able to fight: the disabled, those exhausted by the march, cavalrymen inadequately mounted, men without muskets. The Allies, on the other hand, could count on the arrival of a strong column from Olmütz, which would raise their effectives to 90,000 during the morning. It was thus at odds of two against three that the battle would in fact be fought.

Gathered in the fork of the Y formed by the two Rickas, and already overflowing it to the east, were Murat's 5,600 cavalry and Lannes' 19,200 infantry (the 5th Corps), a part of which threw out random elements to the south in order to make some kind of liaison with their right. Behind them, the 23,600 men of the 4th Corps (Marshal Soult), made up mainly of Saint-Hilaire's and Vandamme's divisions, and the Imperial Guard, reduced to 5,500 men. In reserve, immediately available, Berna-dotte's Corps mustered 13,000 men, midway between the French camp and Brünn.

Lost at Gross-Raygern, finally, Davout had at his disposal the 3,800 men of Friant's division (with a few squadrons of dragoons) and Bourcier's 2,500, who were recovering as well as they could after their march of 90 miles, and these constituted the sum total of his 3rd Corps.

Opposite, the Allied disposition was so drawn out that it already resembled the encirclement of the French army dreamed of by Weirother. To the north, Bagration had 13,700 men, in a

[1] See the diagram indicating the mutual positions at that time. On all our maps from now on stars indicate the position of the opposing Emperors.

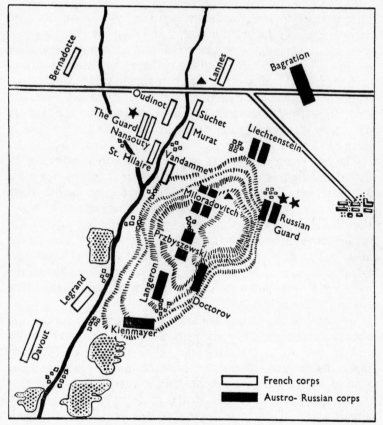

V. *The final alignment of forces*

rather remote position. In front of Austerlitz, Grand-Duke Constantine commanded the Russian Imperial Guard: 10,530 men. To his right, no one has been able to explain why almost the whole of the Allied cavalry, under the supreme command of an Austrian, Prince Liechtenstein, had encamped practically at the foot of the Pratzen, nearly three miles from the area where it would be able to deploy opposite Murat's; 5,375 men were thus clearly badly placed.

The rest of the Austro-Russian army was already strung out for the attack, in a disposition that embraced the southern tip of the Pratzen. Close by Telnitz, the Austrian general Kienmayer, a survivor of Ulm, commanded the advance guard as spearhead: 6,780 men, nearly all Austrians. Then, at the level of Augezd, were the Russian masses, on whom they relied to make their battering-ram: the first column (Doctorov, 13,650 men) and the second (Langeron, 11,700) were parallel. Further to the north, between the village of Pratzen and the Stahré Vinobrady, Prszbyzewski, Kollowrath (an Austrian) and Miloradovitch had charge of the third and fourth columns: 23,960 men, who were tangled together in a dire state of confusion.

The first picture of Austerlitz, then, is of this initial immense confused commotion of men groping about in a night made denser by the very thick layer of mist over the ground, with which there mingled the smoke from the dying bivouac fires.

As early as this awakening, a contrast distinguished the two camps: the French were almost all stamping their feet on the spot to get warm, the Russians were beginning to deliver their attack.

'The Allied left', if one can so call a confused mass of troops constantly changing position, moved off between six and seven o'clock under the command, theoretically, of General Buxhouden. A mediocre Russian officer of German origin, he owed his high rank to a Court marriage that puffed him up more than the winning of ten battles, and considerable drinking habits, even for a Russian, succeeded in making him apathetic. His role during the battle would be confined to inflicting his presence on one of the three columns of attack nominally confided to him, that of Doctorov. He, by way of contrast, was an excellent commander, full of courage and intuition, as were the two commanders of the columns parallel to his, Langeron and Prszbyzewski.

Here then were the three columns in process of taking up their positions to descend from the Pratzen plateau[1] in the direction of Telnitz. For want of a commander capable of co-ordinating their movements, they advanced almost without liaison between them, according to the inspiration of their general, and it would be so much the better for the French that they would be attacking separately instead of uniting their forces.

Before leaving camp, the soldiers took on a new lease of life

[1] To avoid confusion, when reference is made to the plateau, we shall say the Pratzen, whereas the village will be referred to simply as Pratzen.

round the fire by throwing on to it pell-mell in joyful disposal everything that would not be of any use to them: planks from the huts, benches, casks, broken wheels, etc. The batmen were busy round their officers, helping them to button up their uniforms and buckle on their belts, while handing them a few gulps of scalding tea. Opposite, one could have scoured the camp from one end to the other without finding a single cup of this beverage, whose name alone made the entire Guard wince: it was the moment for brandy and mulled wine.

At last, brief orders set the thousands of Russians already under arms surging forward. Their officers mounted their horses and gave the signal to start, as soon as one of the Austrian guides for the columns had arrived, who knew the terrain and would act as 'pilot fish' to the Russian masses lost in this ocean of thickets. The last gesture before action was the same for all, and there lay the sole brotherly link between officers and men: it was the cascade of rapid signs of the cross over the upper part of the body. It is true that the French opposite would evince a certain faith by the monotonous invocation invariably shouted each time a commander led his company on the assault: 'Sacré nom de Dieu! Forward!'

*　　　　*　　　　*　　　　*

From six to seven o'clock, there swelled and grew on the Allied side the monotonous sound of thousands of feet hammering the ground. The columns were on the march without knowing where they were going and without being able to see, because of the throng, the smoke and the mist as thick as ever, either the terrain they were abandoning or that on which they were embarking.

But what was happening suddenly? After scarcely half an hour of marching, here was the whole of the Russian left at a standstill, abruptly halted on the spot and forced to mark time without a shot having yet been fired. The mist was still so dense that the guides took bushes for trees and plains for ravines.

'What's going on?'

'Why aren't we moving?'

'Is it peace, little father?'

Jests and jeers broke out all the way down the Russian lines at a standstill over nearly three miles, where good humour reigned all the more since, by common accord, they were resolved to lay the blame for the least incident of the day on the Austrians.

'What do you expect, these Austrian canaries have led us astray!'

'Perhaps the guides have gone round the bend?'

'We ought to let them have the Virgin of Kazan, eh? She would put them back on the right road!'

In fact, this blockage in the Allied machinery was due to a colossal blunder, made by Prince Jean de Liechtenstein's cavalry which had quite simply confused Blaziowitz and Pratzen. Weirother's plan had required them to convey themselves to the Blaziowitz area, ready to debouch in the northern plain so aptly fashioned for their charges. And here they were suddenly four or five miles further south, bang in the middle of a plateau of valleys where no deployment of cavalry was possible!

The bulk of the Allied cavalry would therefore have remained in reserve all morning if one man, one of the only clear-sighted and resolute commanders on their side, had not noticed it: Count Langeron. He now rushed up, took Prince Liechtenstein's bridle and argued and stormed so successfully that thousands of men swung round over a length of three miles and made ready to resume the road already covered on their resigned mounts, whom this adventure would end by starving, for it cut out the time to give them what little forage it had been possible to collect.

The need for the cavalry to cross three great infantry corps already on the march was to block the latter for nearly an hour and would retard by as much the attack on Telnitz. Paradoxically, the French would suffer from it, for when Soult came to make the assault on the Pratzen, there would be far more men there than there should have been. But this gigantic false manoeuvre, symbol of the total confusion that reigned amongst the Allies at the highest level, completed the embitterment of the commanders and began to demoralize the men.

*　　　　*　　　　*　　　　*

Seven o'clock in the morning. The scene: about three-quarters of a mile above Schlapanitz, a little hillock from which one could see to the left, near at hand, the main road from

Brünn to Olmütz, lined with trees. Straight ahead, on the other side of the Ricka, was the plain, at the edge of which the French cavalry was simmering, and, a little to the right, the first slopes of the Pratzen.

Here stood Napoleon I.

For two hours already he had been on his horse turning this way and that between the two Rickas, in a continual torment to know whether the Russians would really confirm the movement to their right. Now he was radiant: he had just come back from Puntowitz where he had observed a quite distinct sound of cannon and horses indicating a march from left to right towards the lakes, behind the enemy fires, already almost extinct.

He was now on the threshold of the greatest glory that had ever been given to a commander in war, that of consolidating at a single stroke forty lucky ventures. The sky began to pale somewhat, in the direction of that chateau where it was said the other two Emperors were quartered: Austerlitz. But the icy mist still covered the countryside and allowed him to glimpse, like islands above the sea, only the more prominent parts of the landscape. At his feet, Soult's men were in the midst of moving slowly downwards in readiness to cross the Ricka. But they would stop in the bottom of the valleys, where they would be completed covered by the thick fleece of mist.

Mounted on a little grey Arab, almost the same colour as his redingote, Napoleon was silent, because he had a sense of grandeur and knew that no word, however well turned it might be, would be able to match what was about to happen. He was silent also because the marshals, all about him, were exasperating him by besieging him with impatient questions, like children in a hurry to run out to play.

Lannes, who had not shaved for two days, the only one to whom the Emperor still permitted the disorder and familiarity of the days of Vendémiaire. Murat, already covered with a whole bazaarful of gaudy decorations, his horse adorned with a tiger-skin. Jean-de-Dieu Soult, still, composed, attentive, affecting serenity all the more because he was quaking inwardly, certainly not from fear of musket-balls, but from fear of giving offence. Bernadotte, full of boastfulness and high spirits because he was anxious to dissipate the coldness with which the Emperor had been punishing him since Moreau's conspiracy. Davout, all the more arrogant and harsh this morning because he knew he was commanding sacrificed troops.

Such were the Imperial beasts of prey who, in descending the slope of Schlapanitz, would be heading for kingdoms, duchies, principalities, and on whom Napoleon had to keep a tight rein to prevent them from losing all by leaving a moment too soon.

To the right of the Emperor, a good faithful dog: Savary.

'What a thick mist! . . . ' the latter murmured, and had the surprise of hearing the Emperor at last reply:

'It is in our favour. It gives us time to concentrate. Moreover, as you can well see, it is inclined to lift as the day advances. Just now, it was enveloping our bivouacs so completely that you could distinguish nothing at ten paces.'

He resumed his silence, and with a gesture silenced his impatient companions. The stillness, for a moment, was impressive. It was incredible to think that so many people and so much menace could be enclosed in so small a space.

. . . And then, like pin-pricks in that padded material, came the distant sound of a few shots through the mist. One guessed that an action had begun, timidly at first, towards the lakes, in the area for which Davout had already left to fulfil his mission of sacrifice.

Great was the tension on all the faces around Napoleon. One question predominated: in the bottom of the valleys where action had been engaged there was still a thick mist; higher up it was becoming possible to see more clearly, although it was still too obscure to tell what was going on directly in front. Were the bulk of the enemy forces, as was supposed, five or six miles from there? Or, on the contrary, were they waiting for them behind the line of mist? Nobody knew for certain.

A little before eight o'clock all was still shrouded and silent over the rest of the line, when suddenly, beginning among the hills, the sun dispersed that thick mist and revealed to the French commanders the Pratzen plateau, being stripped more and more by the flanking march of the enemy columns. At the same time they noticed with glee that the smoke of the bivouacs and the haze screened from the Russians' eyes their own centre, drawn up in columns and ready to attack.

That was the touch in which God had a hand. The miracle. The sign of a lucky star: *the mist of Austerlitz,* not the sun. The latter did indeed reveal to the French the Russians on the move across the Pratzen, but this movement had been well known to them since the middle of the night. The sun of Austerlitz might have proved fatal if it had shone more strongly or too soon. The allies would then have seen the French ready to surprise them, and would have been able, if not to alter their disposition, at least drastically to curtail its deployment.

But the mist had come when it was wanted—and it had lifted likewise. As if awed by a wondrous sign the marshals gazed at Napoleon's face, which shone and held, for a short moment, happiness of a most rare kind. They were more familiar, perhaps, with the scornful sadness that was one of the main elements in his habitual expression.

A gesture of the plump little hand:

'Go, gentlemen!'

A flight of sparrows! . . .

'No, not you, Soult! Not yet!'

Jean-de-Dieu was flushed with impatience.

'Sire, I beg Your Majesty to hold me back no longer! I have 20,000 men to set in motion! . . . '

'How long do you need to climb the Pratzen?'

'Ten minutes, Sire.'

'All right, go; but you will wait another quarter of an hour. And then, it will be time.'

THE RUSSIANS SCORE THE FIRST POINT

For nearly an hour, 100,000 men ready to confront each other on either side of the Goldbach cocked their ears to the fusillade, punctuated by hardly any cannon-shots, which indicated that swords had been crossed down by the lakes. The Russian left, already 40,000 strong, was ineptly attacking Telnitz and Sokolnitz, and was held for a long time by less than 8,000 Frenchmen.

In the end, the Russians would score the point they—and Napoleon—had anticipated. But a little too well to please the latter.

It was Doctorov's column that became the first to find itself in action, but the honour of the engagement went to the advance guard of five battalions and fourteen squadrons of Austrians commanded by Kienmayer: the survivors of Ulm were burning to avenge themselves. They had been ordered to scour the plain between Augezd and Telnitz while Doctorov was descending from the higher ground. There they were, still in semi-darkness, moving down the imperceptible slope running from Augezd to Telnitz. They could see 300 yards away the thatched roofs of the village, which consisted, like all those of the region, of one very broad street (nearly fifty feet wide), lined by low houses with no upper storeys. It ran parallel to the Goldbach, flowing by to the west. When one reached the fringe of Telnitz, after the easy route from Augezd, there remained an almost perpendicular embankment to descend.

There it was that a few squadrons of Austrian hussars finished up towards seven o'clock, in order to reconnoitre the French positions. They could see to the south, on the Moenitz side, some small detachments of cavalry and some companies of infantry in front of Telnitz: besides the 3rd Line regiment, there was the battalion of Corsican *chasseurs*. The French *voltigeurs* (that is to say, light infantry, always placed as sharpshooters in front of the main body of the regiment, in defence as for attack) put up a good front and forced Kienmayer to throw in not only the hussars of Hesse-Homburg, but also 2,600 men from the two regiments of Szecklers. Cleverly ambushed among the vines, the *voltigeurs* shot down a certain number of hussars, and it was at the cost of losing half its effectives that an Austrian battalion ended by advancing as far as the ridge from which Telnitz could be seen.

This affair of 6,000 men, which was the priming-flash for the great battle, became progressively more ugly, more desperate, more noisy too, as the Austrian generals Carneville and Stutterheim threw into the assault all their available soldiers, while opposite, Generals Legrand and Merle brought in the 26th Light as reinforcements and stirred up a fierce resistance.

Two miles further down, the little village of Moenitz was strangely quiet, and its houses gleamed in the sun like brooding hens. Its isolated position in the midst of the lakes would spare it from becoming a field of carnage. A few French soldiers, too disabled for the firing line, had even got permission to heave as best they could what remained of their poor carcasses to the top of its little belfry, from where they proceeded to follow the contest as passionate spectators.

'Look at that: nature has been kind to us at Telnitz! She's provided a natural entrenchment all round, with that wide ditch that borders the vineyards! . . . '

'All the same, the Russians have got there all right . . . '

'They're Austrians, I keep telling you! . . . '

'So what, the enemy! They've got there and look like breaking through into the village any minute now.'

'You saw well enough how we pushed them back, and pretty quick too! For the third time at least!'

'The fourth, I counted.'

'Fourth or fifth!'

'Whew! What a lot they've left for dead on the ground! Just look at that carpet of white uniforms! . . . '

The infantry regiment of Szecklers had in fact left two-thirds of its effectives in front of Telnitz, dead or wounded.

That was up to eight o'clock. But at that moment the brave men of the 3rd Line regiment felt themselves endangered and almost abandoned in Telnitz: the 26th Light and the Corsican *chasseurs* had left them to their own devices, in order to go a mile further up to help the defence of Sokolnitz, which was cracking.

*　　　*　　　*　　　*

Telnitz was to the east of the Goldbach, Sokolnitz to the west. To reach it, therefore, the Allies had to cross the little river before coming upon the village, of some importance, with two streets in the shape of a T, to the north of which there stretched a park, a chateau, and finally one of those little woods enclosed by walls, known at the time as pheasantries. There was one at Austerlitz. The one at Sokolnitz was 600 or 700 yards long by some 300 yards wide.

Access to the village, over the Goldbach, would thus have been very difficult, above all for the Allied cavalry, if the outskirts had been strongly defended from the start. But Davout and Legrand were obsessed with Telnitz, where the enemy struck his first blows. They had neglected to concentrate sufficient defensive elements at Sokolnitz, and suddenly there was the slope from the Goldbach swarming with grey men, frenzied and yelling savage huzzas: Langeron's column had descended from the Pratzen. At its head, the 8th regiment of Russian foot *chasseurs* and the company of pioneers (2,000 men), forerunners of the regiments of Viborg, Perm and Koursk, hurled themselves into the attack under cover of thirty pieces of artillery which Langeron set up to batter the houses of Sokolnitz, held only by the sharpshooters of the Po, and then by the 26th Light which General Merle brought in from Telnitz in a ten-minute dash. This last regiment drew itself up in battle-array to the rear of Sokolnitz, all proud of its two cannon. This made a total of 1,800 men against more than 8,000, since the head of Prszbyzewski's column was now debouching to the right of Langeron, between Sokolnitz and Kobelnitz, and Doctorov was deploying his below Telnitz.

At this moment, the disproportion in effectives and material between the French and the Russians appeared to be verging on madness: if the latter had co-ordinated their efforts better and lost less time, nothing could have prevented the bolt of the French right from being broken open within half an hour.

General Merle and Colonel Pouget, under a hurricane of grape-shot, positioned the men of the 26th however they could. They had the drums beaten to death. Mechanically, the men levelled and fired at the Russians who appeared inexhaustibly at the brow of the slope, and hardly took the time, for their part, to fire any more: those who survived the French balls arrived to fight hand-to-hand. Two companies of Russian *chasseurs* took the chateau of Sokolnitz; what was still standing, at least. During this time, 3,000 Russians came to grips with the men of the 26th Light in the main street. It was not there, however, that the fighting was the most violent, but further down, along the Goldbach, between Sokolnitz and Telnitz. Here, the 8th regiment of Russian *chasseurs*, the Viborg regiments and that of Perm, 5,000 in all, concentrated on the right of the poor 26th Light, each man of which had to take on ten of the enemy.[1]

---

[1] 'The French,' writes Langeron, 'defended themselves with fury; our regiments [meaning the Russians] had much to suffer, but at last the three regiments and the whole of Prszbyzewski's column carried the village.'

Outflanked, submerged, the first battalion of the 26th Light had to yield a hundred prisoners and lost its two guns.

At the same moment, towards eight-thirty, Doctorov's Russian battalions had just relieved the Austrians, who were breaking their teeth on Telnitz. Fourteen thousand men began to press with all their weight against the 1,200 soldiers who remained to the 3rd of the Line. Exhausted, demoralized, the regiment ended by abandoning in some disorder the two ends of the village. The mounted *chasseurs* and the dragoons sent by Davout had to charge several times in order to cover their retreat and allow them to re-form behind the Goldbach.

Telnitz lost as well as Sokolnitz? Not yet. Setting out from Gross-Raygern, nearly three miles to the west, Friant's and Bourcier's divisions moved forward to come and make up at last an opposing mass. Rather late, it seemed, rather slowly—but what could be expected from the stiff legs of men who had covered 90 miles in two days? Spurred on by Davout, sweating on his horse in spite of the cold, Heudelet's brigade arrived as advance guard, towards quarter to nine, at Telnitz, where the Allies were venturing further only with caution. They were without artillery, without baggage train, and badly drawn up—it mattered little. Heudelet, a crimson Hercules, swept off all the men he could find of the 15th Light and the 108th of the Line into the main street of the village. Amongst them: Jean-Pierre Blaise, his eyes wide open, and with no intention of dying yet.

Their furious charge swept Telnitz from one end to the other. The Russian *chasseurs* and Kienmayer's Hungarians were thrown into disorder. The New Ingrie regiment, assailed unexpectedly, fled and threw into confusion the whole of Doctorov's column.

Telnitz retaken? No. The battles of that time were no more than fluctuations: everything depended on the skill with which the officers could regain control of a unit, rally it, and change an ebb into a flow almost in the same movement, as one reverses the controls of a machine. Heudelet had only 800 men at his disposal. This was too few to spread out in the village. As soon as the Allies realized this, they took a fresh grip on themselves and attacked the 108th from all sides. Two squadrons of hussars from Hesse-Homburg made a brilliant charge and forced the

French to debouch from the village by the north in order to make their escape.

Jean-Pierre Blaise had lived through the whirlwind without understanding a great deal about it, and resting against a wall while recovering his breath, he was already considering the description he would be sending his parents that evening:

'On the eleventh, at six o'clock, our regiment was set on the march, with only two companies of *voltigeurs* of the 13th regiment as scouts. We marched for about an hour, hearing a few musket-shots from time to time. Marshal Davout was at our head. When we had got within cannon-range of the battlefield, we heard a most terrible fusillade which took place between the Russians and the 3rd regiment of the Line, whose large number of wounded we came upon. At that moment, we were made to double our step, which did not prevent me from eating the leg of a goose that I had on the top of my knapsack, well knowing I would scarcely have time during the battle. I was right: before ordering the charge, Marshal Davout, who did not leave us although the balls were beginning to bother us, reminded us of the Battle of Marianzelle. General Heudelet placed himself at our head; we marched into battle very well until we were stopped near a ditch of such width that we could not cross it. General Heudelet ordered the colonel to have us cross over a bridge to our left. The necessity for this movement was our undoing, for the soldiers, who were burning with impatience to try their luck with this much vaunted infantry, mixed up their ranks, in spite of the good advice the officers gave us, and while battle order was being re-established, under very sharp fire, the Austrian hussars whom, in the thick smoke and mist that there was that day, we thought to be Bavarians and wounded a large number, took about 160 men prisoner, among them four officers.'

At that moment there occurred one of those tragic mistakes, frequent in military annals, so closely did the uniforms of all the troops resemble each other and so quickly did the smoke from the discharges obscure the view . . . and the mind. The men of the 108th escaping from Telnitz saw vague outlines in the mist, as thick as ever, who were bearing down on them from the direction of Sokolnitz, and who suddenly began to fire on them:

'Stop! Stop, you wretches! We're French!' yelled the officers who understood: it was the remainder of the 26th Light driven out of Sokolnitz to the south, who were wiping out the remainder of the 108th of the Line, driven out of Telnitz to the north.

'Are you mad? We're *French, nom de Dieu!*'

'The Eagle! Raise the Eagle!' cried Captain Livadot, of the 2nd company, thus halting the massacre: when the men of the 26th Light saw it being held on high opposite them, they at last understood.

But matters were becoming very serious for Davout: at nine o'clock the two linch-pins in the disposition of the French right were gone. The Allies held Telnitz and Sokolnitz.

A BLOW OF THE FIST ON THE PRATZEN

The slender gloved hand of Prince Czartoryski rested on the arm of Alexander I, Czar of all the Russias. It was eight-thirty.

'Just look, Sire, at the brisk and purposeful march of those Frenchmen scaling the plateau . . .'

'Eh, I see nothing else, *mon cher*! Have you noticed that they don't even return our fire? What would you put their strength at? Two battalions? Three? Four?'

'Several regiments at least, Sire, if not several divisions. It's an attack by an army corps.'

'But they come from a clear sky! How is it we have had no warning?'

'Your Majesty should say rather that they come from hell. This cursed mist hid their troops from us.'

The Czar and the Emperor of Austria stood in the midst of their general staffs on the Pratzen plateau, to which they had just climbed without greatly hurrying themselves, after having taken the time for a copious luncheon, surrounded by the first battalions of the Russian Imperial Guard who were taking the place of Buxhouden's three columns engaged in the attack on the left. The mist had finally cleared, except in the bottoms of the valleys where it still looked like a milky sea. Above the plateau, a winter sky of a delicate pastel blue was clear of all clouds, for the first and last time during the day. Behind the sovereigns, the enormous red disc of the sun tinged with pink the hoar-frost over all. Opposite them, in the distance, on the other bank of the sea of mist, intense activity indicated the abrupt departure of the French masses, a standing army up till now on the wooded hills that stretched as far as Brünn. To their left, in a din of wheels, horses' hooves, and the tramping of men, the tail of the last assault column for Telnitz, that of the Austrian General Kollowrath, was in the process of moving off, while the numerous infantry of Miloradovitch took up their position in turn.

Great consternation suddenly fell upon the group of large white topcoats and plumed two-cornered hats: they had expected to follow quietly the progress of the stream launched by Weirother against the left to encircle the French army—and the French army, all of a sudden, was hurling itself at the Pratzen plateau. Alexander, at the moment when he felt the hand of his Minister for External Relations on his arm, was experiencing the evaporation of his hopes, along with the last of the mist. A foreboding of Austerlitz entered into him like a musket-ball and would leave him no more. But this great crowned nobleman would pass his examination in fortitude that day with flying colours. He would remain consistently calm, courteous and even engaging, towards the bringers of ill tidings who thereafter would hardly cease to follow one after the other. As for bravery, it came of itself and seemed the natural attribute of the profession of kingship. For 200 years, even the fiercest republicans are unable to point to one who showed cowardice on a field of battle. Surrounded very shortly by balls whistling about their ears, Alexander and Francis took less notice of them than of flies, but the Emperor of Austria, for his part, was unable to put up a good front in face of the catastrophe and his sad countenance created a void around him.

*   *   *   *

'*Sacré nom de Dieu*, forward! . . . '
Issuing from the mouth of Soult, the exclamation went down the whole hierarchical ladder via Saint-Hilaire and Vandamme, the brigadiers, the colonels, the majors, the company officers.

Two hundred drums beat frenetically between Girzikowitz and Puntowitz. Like a spring compressed over-long, Soult's army corps, more than 20,000 men, bubbling with eagerness, warmed by a triple issue of brandy (nearly half a pint per man), rushed into the assault on the Pratzen. Forced at first to keep a relatively slow step, because they were pressed close together, 'like herrings in a barrel' as one of them was to remark, they assumed a faster pace as soon as they could, and then a dash, so impetuous that they not only made no reply to the enemy's sharpshooters, obedient in this to the Emperor's orders, but ran the risk of breaking up their columns, the more rapid overtaking those in front.

It was the decisive blow of the fist at nine o'clock, the end of the first act, in which one could say that the whole of the drama was played within twenty minutes.

The dam of patience that the Emperor had imposed on them having been broken, the liberated human flood divided itself into two equal streams, once through the bottlenecks of Punto-witz and Girzikowitz: to the left, Vandamme's division rushed with their eyes raised to the Stahré Vinobrady, to the right, Saint-Hilaire's division did the same in the direction of the Pratzen hillock.

The first of these little hills stood out only insignificantly in comparison with the surrounding ground, since it was reached by a very gentle slope of about one in fifty. But its profile was sufficiently characteristic to serve as a rallying point even at some distance: since his encampment, Napoleon had pointed it out to Soult and Soult to Vandamme.

The Pratze-berg hill (1,063 feet) which dominated the village of Pratzen was more important and more prominent. It dominated the whole area and was visible for miles around. Seen from close to, it was shaped like a much flattened skull-cap, laid on the plateau and standing out clearly from it. Seen from afar, it appeared simply as the summit of a hill a little higher than the others whose unbroken slopes ran down to the Goldbach.

On debouching from Puntowitz with the Pratze-berg as its point of reference, Saint-Hilaire's division had first to cross the shallow ravine that ran down from the Pratzen towards Kobel-nitz, and then to cover nearly a mile and a half of gentle incline

up to the village of Pratzen, which was situated in the middle
of a sort of amphitheatre with slopes of little significance to the
north and the east, and fairly abrupt to the south. Its church
was directly overlooked by the Pratze-berg, from where the eye
plunged into the street and into the gardens of the village.

Before the volleys of musketry, which would be at first almost
exclusively the act of the Russians and would take place in a
very disjointed way because of the effect of surprise, the sounds
of this decisive battle would be fanfares, the hammering of
drums, the yelling of frenzied men on the attack and, in the
background, the marching songs of those battalions who were
as yet unable to run. Lieutenant de Tinguy du Pouët, a nobleman adhering to the Empire, was shocked and horrified to hear
a corporal with a stentorian voice give a rendering to his section
—men almost all hailing, it is true, from the Fauburg Saint-
Marcel in Paris—of *The Awakening of Père Duchesne*:

> Arise, in the name of thunder!
> Brave warriors, arise!
> We fill the world with jingos
> By dying thus in glory.
> To hell with ancient custom
> And all those bloody fools
> Who sought to show their courage
> By dying for five sous!
>
> To the noble, in his knapsack
> We'll present him liberty.
> Let the hugger now bow down
> In name of equality!
> A thousand curses, together
> Let's draw and break our swords;
> That in the tumult all shall quake
> To liberate the world!

The formation of attack adopted by the two divisions had
been minutely laid down during the night: first, the two
battalions of light infantry in fairly loose and winding lines,
advancing by leaps and zigzags like hares through the bushes;
then, in columns of three abreast, the first battalions of the four
regiments of the Line; finally, in the same order of columns, the

second battalions of these regiments. This order had been strictly maintained by the officers during the whole of the first part of the advance. The only perceptible variation that occurred between eight-thirty and nine o'clock was in the space between the battalions, at first almost non-existent all the time they had to conceal themselves, but drawing out, as much in width as in length, as they covered the ground.

To the right, Saint-Hilaire advanced like a thunder-clap. The 10th Light, under the command of Colonel Morand, carried out a veritable point-to-point race towards Pratzen. But he was explicitly forbidden to occupy the village, so that nothing should delay conquest of the hillock. Behind this regiment, the whole division crossed the ravine without difficulty, advanced over the plain, and emerged from the mist at about the 800-foot mark.

During this time, Vandamme's division, held up slightly in Girzikowitz, found itself a little behind. The palm for speed went therefore to Saint-Hilaire. At the moment when the Allied sovereigns saw, along with the whole of their army, the men of the 10th Light pop out of their boxes like devils, the latter had less than 900 yards to cover to reach the plateau. The Allies, to be sure, still had superior forces at their disposal to set against them: the 8,000 men of Kollowrath's column, which could have been set before Saint-Hilaire, and nearly as many for Miloradovitch to throw between Vandamme's legs; this made almost two against one.

But it was too late. Kollowrath's rearguard was nearly as far from the Pratze-berg as the French. Seven or eight minutes would not have been sufficient to inform the general, get his orders and carry them out. Two Russian battalions had just enough time, one to flatten themselves to the ground in a little ravine that covered Pratzen, the other to climb to their death on the hillock. At the moment when the 10th Light had already reached the latter and when Thiébault's brigade, which followed it, had got his two regiments to defile in the outskirts of the village of Pratzen, the Russians in ambush sacrificed themselves bravely in delivering a most murderous volley. They forced General Thiébault to concern himself earlier than had been intended with the village of Pratzen, whose defenders he had hacked to pieces on the spot. Saint-Hilaire then hastened to have his division deploy over the plateau and to cover it with a battery of twelve pieces loaded with balls and grape-shot. He foresaw in fact that all the troops the Allies would be able to summon would quickly flow back towards him after the briefest of respites.

Further north, Kutuzov, whose sullenness was shot through with profound pessimism, received the news of the taking of Pratzen, which was brought to him within a few minutes by General Vodnianski. The supreme commander stood, as always at a certain distance from the sovereigns he shunned, almost at the foot of the Stahré Vinobrady. Understanding now the full significance of the great commotion that was being unloosed to his left, he prepared to mount an attack to retake Pratzen, but in a few minutes the storm of fire and sword redoubled and broke over the general staff itself: Vandamme's division had made up its lost time and saved Kutuzov the whole complicated operation by coming straight at him too and by making an assault on the Stahré Vinobrady, on which the Russians still had at that moment five battalions and a few pieces of artillery.

In a few seconds, Kutuzov, full of gloomy joy at seeing his forebodings realized, confined himself to ordaining that resistance to the French onslaught was to be offered as far as possible at all points, by having the Allied troops perform a quarter-turn to the right and thus no longer look towards Telnitz but towards the Goldbach. He spoke no word of surprise or annoyance, dabbed calmly with a silk scarf at the blood which ran down his cheek, scored by a heavy iron bullet, and allowed himself to be led off a little to the rear by his aides-de-camp, the very picture of fatalism.

Sabre in hand, and marked already, he too, by three scratches, Dominique-Joseph Vandamme, one of the best divisional commanders of the army, led his men into the attack on the Russians drawn up in battle-array, routed their first lines with the bayonet, threw the second into confusion, captured their artillery, and in his rush found that he had overshot the Stahré Vinobrady. Unlike most of the leaders of the Grand Army, Vandamme knew how to direct men under fire without ever losing his calm and almost without raising his voice. He brought to bear here all the weight of his experience: it was in 1793 that he had been made brigadier, the same year as a certain Napoleon Bonaparte. He now wheeled his division round the hill, mounted it himself with the 4th of the Line, in spite of plunging fire, and gained possession of it. He had marched for half an hour and fought for half an hour. Saint-Hilaire had marched and fought for twenty minutes in all. By nine o'clock, Marshal

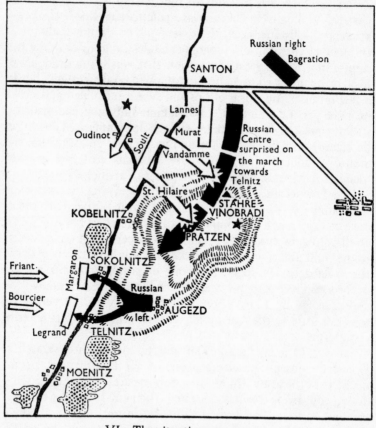

VI. *The situation at 9 a.m.*

Soult's corps had hoisted itself on to the Pratzen plateau and had thrown back the Russians and Austrians pell-mell down the slopes that led to the chateau of Austerlitz.

Informed blow by blow at half-past nine by the first young officers—triumphant about the centre, anxious about the right, and impatient about the left—Napoleon was able, at a glance, to note each point on the map of the battlefield.[1]

To the south, near the lakes, the Russians had crossed the Goldbach and taken Telnitz and Sokolnitz; they were broaching the weak defences of Generals Legrand and Margaron, but Friant's and Bourcier's divisions were beginning to come to their rescue in order to prevent at all costs the development of their encircling movement.

In the centre, Soult's troops had just shattered the Allied centre by the thrust of their battering-ram. Behind them, Napoleon, alarmed by the news from Davout, had just given orders for Oudinot's grenadiers to head to their right.

Finally, to the north, almost nothing so far; the third area of combat had not been engaged: the French left (Lannes) was not in contact with the Russian right (Bagration) and Murat's cavalry held itself ready to deploy in the plain the moment they saw the first enemy movement that lent itself to their charges.

*　　　*　　　*　　　*

One point to the left for the Russians; one point in the centre for the French; very little loss of human life for the moment; almost no artillery in action. Was it all over? Nothing was certain. Some clouds, heavy and low, were beginning to veil the sun of Austerlitz.

[1] See our diagram, 'The situation at nine o'clock'.

CHAPTER XV

December 2nd, from 9 a.m. to noon

ONE HUNDRED AND FIFTY THOUSAND MEN IN COMBAT

———————

In the second act, all that had been begun by a few thousand men over a few hundred square yards took on amplitude, implicated the whole of the two opposing armies and covered the full extent of the field of battle. From nine o'clock till midday was the time of consolidation, of exploitation, but still, perhaps, of possible reversal.

In the centre, the French established themselves on the Pratzen plateau, in spite of Russian counter-attacks a great deal more violent than they had expected there.

In the south, the Russians continued their thrust and pressed very strongly on the far side of Telnitz and Sokolnitz, but Davout held out and they were prevented from deploying, all the more since their third and fourth assault columns were blocked by Soult's offensive.

In the north, on either side of the road from Brünn to Olmütz, the French left and the Russian right waged virtually a separate battle, of great importance in itself, and this was the fresh event during this part of the day.

DAVOUT HOLDS OUT

Towards nine-thirty, a lull of sorts reigned in the neighbourhood of the lakes after the atrocious hand-to-hand fighting that had enabled the Allies to cross the Goldbach. Russians and Austrians, tangled together in Telnitz and Sokolnitz, tried to restore order among the sorely tried troops. Buxhouden drew up the regiments of Kiev, Jaroslav, Vladimir and New-Ingrie into two lines in front of Augezd; the rest of the first column and Kienmayer's units occupied Telnitz and deployed along the Goldbach, expecting the second and third columns to be able to debouch from Sokolnitz and so move forward. But the Allies had just been severely mauled by a powerful charge by three squadrons of dragoons, the cavalry advance-guard of Friant's division, which had just arrived at full speed, and they were forced to entrench themselves in the captured villages. The three defeated regiments of French infantry were trying to reassemble and dress their wounds while resuming battle formation to the west of the two settlements.

Everybody well knew that the pause was fraught with significance for the future: the Allied success would be of no value unless their cavalry succeeded in rapidly sabring the last lines of French infantry, thus opening the way into the Turas plain for the powerful masses of infantry that were already marking time to the north of the Satschan lakes.

To locate more readily the 'lines of force' of the Allied pressure in the order of the disposition, one could say that the head of Doctorov's column was thrusting out of Telnitz; the head of Langeron's out of Sokolnitz; and the head of Prszbyzewski's, immediately to his right, out of the chateau of Sokolnitz.

But at ten o'clock Friant arrived on the scene.

A hurricane. His men, utterly done in, whom the officers had had the greatest difficulty in getting to their feet with kicks, three hours earlier at Gross-Raygern, after their ninety-mile agony, had been fired by the sound of the cannon and came at the Russians with the frenzy of Red Indians. General Lochet's brigade (the 48th and 111th of the Line, about 1,200 men) rushed into the fray at Sokolnitz at the charge, carried off two flags, six cannon, cleared house after house at bayonet point and drove the Russians back across the Goldbach. His hair already greying, Louis Friant promptly got up off the body of the first of the four horses that would be killed under him that day. Almost fifty, he was one of the oldest veterans of the army with twenty glorious memories behind him: Wissembourg, Landau, Fleurus, Italy, Egypt . . . Davout relied on him at least as much as Napoleon relied on Davout. At that moment, he was the man of destiny. He ordered the 48th regiment of the Line to hold Sokolnitz and turned immediately to the left with the rest of his men to wrest the chateau of Sokolnitz from Prszbyzewski.

But opposite Sokolnitz was a military leader who, making up for his lack of experience by a certain intuition and by the awakening of a thousand-year-old heredity, played his part that day with a valour equal to that of the leaders of the Grand Army: Count Langeron. He threw all his available forces into Sokolnitz and crushed the 48th with their number. Friant sent back the 111th, who charged the enemy masses and the Russian skirmishers spread out in the plain and took two cannon from them. Langeron drew on his reserves for the Koursk regiment and drove the 111th from the houses to which they tried desperately to cling. The 48th regiment of the Line remained isolated for three-quarters of an hour in the southern end of Sokolnitz and managed to stay there by prodigies of valour under the direction of a young leader so full of initiative that he drew from Friant, however blasé, the admiring tribute, 'there's no officer as fine as him in a fight': General Lochet.

There followed a terrible struggle, swinging like a pendulum as fresh forces were thrown into Sokolnitz alternatively by Langeron and Prszbyzewski on one side and by Davout on the other. Twice, three times, the 15th Light and the 33rd of the Line regained the advantage for France. The 111th of the Line likewise returned to the charge, to be twice repulsed. The 48th held its ground by utilizing every bit of cottage wall still standing. Equal in fire power, in the valour of their leaders, and in the bravery of the combatants, France and Russia here were evenly balanced. Honours went to Davout, however, who succeeded in losing only a few patches of the ground he had just regained, by running endlessly from one point to another along this so hotly disputed line of the Goldbach, so as to increase tenfold the resistance of his 7,000 to 8,000 infantry and 2,800 cavalry against the 35,000 Allies.

After two hours of this deadly game of prisoners' base, which this time amassed some bodies on the ground, only the southern tip of Sokolnitz remained in French hands, thanks to the heroism of the 48th who barricaded themselves there. The other elements of Friant's and Bourcier's divisions re-formed to the north of the village. It seemed irretrievably lost.

Doctorov still held Telnitz, half a mile lower down.

The situation still seemed therefore to be in the Allies' favour, but in fact it was a matter of stalemate, since they had not succeeded in exploiting their victory and were still unable to debouch into the plain. Opposite them, the advance guard of Davout's corps was in the process of arriving in order to make good the losses of this fierce struggle, and a little before midday an undeniable wavering in the Russian offensive became apparent for the first time. Everything slowed down to one fusillade in half an hour. Why? Were they already short of reinforcements? Not yet: nearly 10,000 available men then in that area had not been engaged. But Buxhouden was dead-drunk, and the only man capable of forming a plan and getting it carried out in that part of the field, Langeron, had just left his troops in order to find out for himself what was happening on the Pratzen plateau, since nobody had been able to give him any reliable information about it.

LANNES VERSUS BAGRATION

A little after nine o'clock, as the sun was beginning to warm the atmosphere once more, but also to hide itself at times, two immense masses of men, hitherto inactive and separated by two or three miles of bare ground, began to move towards each other. Prince Bagration, who was undoubtedly the most deliberate and capable Allied leader, had as his essential mission to keep open access to Olmütz whatever happened and to resist implacably any encircling manoeuvre to the rear of the Allied army, in case Napoleon should want to try against him what Weirother was trying to do to Davout. To permit the possible retreat of his Emperor in the event of defeat, or the arrival of reinforcements in the event of victory, such was Bagration's task.

Lannes, opposite him, had at his disposal Suchet's and Cafarelli's divisions, first, at all costs to prevent the enemy from capturing the Santon, which one knew to be the cornerstone of Napoleon's disposition, next, to involve Bagration sufficiently to ensure that he would not attack the French centre in the process of establishing itself on the Pratzen. It was thus more a matter of a defensive than an offensive mission. But to the right of Lannes, on the threshold of that plain which Napoleon in his letters had already christened 'the cavalry plain', Murat was ready to lead into battle first General Kellermann's light cavalry, then the dragoons, and then the great heavy cavalry of Nansouty and d'Hautpoul. It was on him in principle that the task of exploiting the breaching of the Russian centre would devolve, of subsequently wheeling to the north towards Olmütz and, by enveloping Bagration, to make possible the complete annihilation of the Allied forces.

At nine-thirty it was Bagration who moved first. Having listened to the mounting fire on his left wing for nearly two hours, certain that the encirclement of the French army had begun, furious at being left without orders and without news, and completely unaware of what had just taken place on the Pratzen, he moved forward, and got two battalions of the Russian Imperial Guard to occupy the village of Blaziowitz without the least difficulty.

At the same moment, Lannes moved off, but in his case it was in accordance with received orders: he had just heard cannon on the Pratzen and knew what it meant. His 12,000 men crossed the left-hand side of the plain, almost at parade-ground pace, the kind of movement they would have been able to do at a review: in front, several battalions in lines and behind them, in the intervals between them, other battalions in compact columns, to support and protect them. To his right, the cavalry began to deploy at a jog-trot towards a vast kaleidescope of colour and magnificence that to the veterans foretold a battle like the one at Alexandria: the eighty-two squadrons of Russian and Austrian cavalry under Prince Jean de Liechtenstein were preparing to bar the way to Lannes's infantry.

The first round would therefore unfold in three movements, parallel to the main road:

The first movement: Grand-Duke Constantine's Uhlans were launched at Cafarelli's division, covered only by Kellermann's brigade of light cavalry. It was a classic attempt at a checking stroke delivered by cavalry at the advance of a great mass of infantry.

Cunningly, Kellermann drew off: the son of the victor of Valmy, placed here at one against ten, did not wait to be thrown back against the soldiers of the line, in whose ranks he would have spread confusion. He therefore left it to them to break the Russian charge. When the Allied horsemen came within a hundred yards of the French bayonets running fire assailed them and killed a large number of their horses and men. Leaving very nearly a quarter of their number on the ground and without having been able to breach any part of Cafarelli's lines, nor Suchet's, the Russians were reduced to defiling down the whole of their line and drawing off to rejoin Bagration. Three other charges met with no more success.

The second movement: Kellermann in his turn launched a cavalry counter-attack against the Russian cavalry, followed by the dragoons, and there ensued a fearful confused free-for-all, in which everybody fought hand to hand, in which men hampered on their horses needed an extra hand to cope with pistol, sabre and reins at the same time, in which all thrust and slashed, in which horses fell, dragging their riders down under them. When this tumult of horses and men over several acres finally dispersed, in accordance with the same mysterious laws that preside over the subsidence of maelstroms, the two compact masses of infantry sent forward by Lannes advanced again, still at the same even pace, over the ground covered with dead and wounded men and horses—and this was the third movement.

But Bagration knew, better than anyone else in his camp, how to place his artillery and use it: forty muzzles spewed their hail at the French. The battle reached here one of its bloody paroxysms and the height of its racket; one volley carried away the whole group of drummers of Cafarelli's first regiment, and 400 Frenchmen were killed in three minutes. But just as a minute earlier cavalry had counter-charged cavalry, the artillery of Lanne's corps hit back at Bagration's.

Lannes, for his part, had only twenty pieces at his disposal, three of which were already out of service. As usual with him, he was drawn, as if by an accurate magnet, to the spot where the enemy bullets converged. His aides-de-camp had long since given up pulling him out of danger: he chose them because they loved to share it. It was the soldiers who yelled:

'Take cover! Get out of the way, *monsieur le maréchal*! Everything's being ripped up around here, *nom de Dieu*!'

His great frizzy locks covered with powder and dust, his two-cornered hat long since gone with the wind, his collar undone, without his cloak, flushed, Lannes flew on his horse right down the line and himself positioned fifteen of the cannon that he suddenly unmasked. These were harnessed pieces: after each round, the servers whipped up the horses and moved the smoking monster. This enabled them, although one against two, to escape almost all the fire of the Russian artillery drawn, on their side, by men, and with much slower changes of position.

During a short pause, if one could call it that, round about half-past ten, the battle of the two wings seemed to be confined to this hellish exchange of cannon-balls and grape-shot. Then, simultaneously, Lannes and Bagration both judged that the moment had come to resume the assault.

Bagration, right to the north, tried to throw back Suchet and take the Santon. But Napoleon had personally instilled into the men of the 17th of the Line, on the previous day, that they were to let themselves be killed on the spot rather than yield: in spite of violent attacks by Marioupol's hussars, the Russians gained no more than 400 or 500 yards on that side.

Lannes, on the other hand, advanced his right, linked with Murat's cavalry, and ordered the 13th Light to seize Blaziowitz, whose position, in the middle of the plain and at the northern foot of the Pratzen plateau, constituted one of the keys to the day. Four companies set off as skirmishers, but made little progress before the hail of balls from the Russian musketry. All the rest of the regiment then received orders to make a bayonet charge, hurled themselves into Blaziowitz behind Colonel Casteix, whose reputation for bravery achieved the distinction of being exceptional, even in that epoch, took 500 Russians prisoner, routed a corps of cavalry and collected five cannon.

Blaziowitz was taken, but Casteix was dead.

Holding Blaziowitz, Lannes would be able to debouch massively by bringing the whole of his weight to bear on his right: he would thus cut the already tenuous link between Bagration and the Allied centre and would be able to initiate the encirclement of the Russian right. Seeing this danger, Bagration and

Liechtenstein decided to commit practically all their available cavalry in a desperate effort to push back the French left. The latter would be all the more endangered since Murat, though fully resolved to cover Lannes to the best of his ability, at that moment had no more than about 3,000 men at his disposal, whereas the Allies would be throwing in nearly 6,000.

Cafarelli's division saw swooping down on them, just as they were debouching from Blaziowitz, a body of forty Austrian squadrons. Impeccably deployed, the triple line of French fire cut short three successive charges by Liechtenstein's Uhlans and hussars, who failed to break the ranks of the infantry. But the Austrian officers ceaselessly rallied their squadrons and brought them back for a fourth time, followed by 1,000 Russian cavalry. Murat, who was with his staff on the extreme right of the battle, where everything might succeed or crack within seconds, appreciated the seriousness of the moment all the better since he found himself surrounded for an instant and was forced to free himself sabre in hand; he now called upon the formidable heavy reserve which had not yet been produced; the equivalent of the armoured knights of the middle ages, the squadrons of cuirassiers of Generals d'Hautpoul and Nansouty. They had been following Cafarelli's division of infantry. They now defiled at the trot behind them, formed up to their right, deployed there and surged forward at the gallop. The earth shook beneath the hooves of the 1,000 horses, almost giants, themselves bearing colossi swathed in steel, sabres in hand, throwing themselves upon the mass of Austro-Russian squadrons twice their strength. There now began a memorable cavalry fray.

During the brief period when the French were surging towards the Allies, across about half a mile of open plain, the batteries placed to the front and to the sides of the Russian cavalry blasted them from every muzzle, but were forced to withdraw hastily after a few volleys, for the bloody gaps they opened in the ranks of the French were immediately filled.

'Sound the charge!' cried General Nansouty, drawing his sabre. Slim, upright and phlegmatic, he held station, on a magnificent chestnut, at the edge of the first line of cuirassiers deployed over about a quarter of a mile. The clear notes spurted out to the echo, sounded by the trumpeters, themselves in full flight, who saw to the making of the sonorous rallying calls around which the charge evolved with such order that Colonel Picard, to the left of Nansouty, was unable to restrain himself from remarking:

'What harmony, *mon général*! One would have said our squadrons were drilling in front of an inspector-general!

Nansouty smiled without speaking: silent by nature, in combat he was virtually mute, and in that only exercised an attraction all the more imperious over the other officers who, while leading the fifty or a hundred men of iron for whom they were responsible, made a habit of keeping an eye open towards him, even if he were at the other end of the fray, so as to follow his orders for the whole.

He now let the carabiniers smash the first enemy line and throw it back against the second. But the latter were better commanded, by the Prince of Hohenlohe and the Russian General Ouvarov, with his long grey beard floating in the breeze like a banner above his red uniform. The cavalrymen were trained to open up so as to let their disordered comrades through—and there confronting the carabiniers were the Elizabethgrad Hussars and Chernikov's dragoons, supported on their left by the cuirassiers from Lorraine (Austrians). For a very brief instant, a sort of gigantic check delayed the impact of the two lines: it was the moment when they came face to face and when the horses instinctively stiffened in spite of being spurred. Already the French cuirassiers, led in by Nansouty and Picard, were arriving to reinforce the carabiniers and were overthrowing the enemy line, in which only a third of the combatants were as heavy and had their bodies as well protected as them. One had the impression of a clash between two different races of insects, the better formed prevailing by their weight.

In five minutes, confusion seized the Austro-Russian cavalry. That is to say, that moment, the dread of every officer, when all their men became deaf to their cries and ran, every man for himself. In a cavalry duel, this is not so advantageous for the victor as might be thought, for it provokes a crumbling similar to that of the defeated since pursuit of them is rendered very difficult for squadrons remaining in close formation.

Liechtenstein, Hohenlohe and the impassive group of Russian

officers knew what had to be done in such an event, and they did it. The commanders had only one resource: to run faster than the fastest of the fugitives. To reach, ahead of them, some feature of the ground where a stand could be made. And to rally them, with the sabre if necessary. Just such a tiny little stream was on hand in the nick of time, bridged by culverts of no significance, but sufficient to bring together the scattered cavalry. There Liechtenstein positioned the harnessed artillery pieces still at his disposal and under their cover reassembled his squadrons—re-formed as quickly as routed.

Nansouty, for his part, had no intention of venturing further and rallied his cuirassiers behind Cafarelli's division. But, carried away by their ardour, like a mass of molten metal, the 3rd Cuirassiers had been engaged too far afield, and suddenly found themselves surrounded on three sides by the Austro-Russian cavalry, in hand once again and ashamed of a passing weakness.

This was why a cavalry general dreaded nothing in one of his corps so much as excess of enthusiasm in pursuit: this was the misfortune that brought about that mysterious reversal in the collective psychology of the combatants thanks to which the initiative changed sides and came back like a boomerang on those who thought they had already won. The Prince of Liechtenstein, yelling interminable Teutonic imprecations with the frenzy of a second lieutenant, brought back two regiments of cavalry against the right of Cafarelli's infantry.

But the soldiers of the line did not give way. Their fire, however, brought down one hussar in four, and they were ready, at the right moment, to open up regular gaps to let through, at the trot, in two parallel columns, Nansouty's tireless cuirassiers, always in peak condition, always calm, and miraculously spared by the balls whistling around them.

The confrontation began again!

There were five or ten minutes more of these terrible fluctuations between the two great masses of cavalry. The French carabiniers, exhorted to maintain their time-honoured reputation by the powerful bellowings of their colonel, broke up the first Allied line. But the second line brought them back: it was the turn of the French, consisting this time of the 2nd regiment of cuirassiers, to hold out and repulse them. This appalling cavalcade, during which everyone sabred and grappled pell-mell in a whirlwind of earth, dust and powder finally dispersed, after three charges and counter-charges. Each side reassembled and drew up a balance sheet: the ground was strewn with three times as many Russian bodies as French.

Potentially, Bagration was cut off from Kutuzov and the Emperors a little after midday. It remained to translate this possibility opened up by the cavalry into practice; this, as always in military matters, would be the concern of the infantry. After Murat, it was up to Lannes.

The 5th Corps in its entirety continued to advance at a steady pace, free this time from the danger of being sabred, and made a direct attack on Bagration's infantry at whom they directed their calm and steady fire, executed by the troops, trained as well as hardened, with the utmost precision. If the pace of the French was slow, above all that of Suchet's division, it was because the Russians, on their side, formed a solid mass, bristling with muskets whose volleys, though a great deal less accurate (the young soldiers were so poorly trained that they fired into the air), were nevertheless very frequent and prevented the attackers from coming at them with the bayonet. Besides, Bagration continued to make good use of his artillery, which mowed down whole lines of soldiers. How was it Suchet was not thrown back? His two-cornered hat carried away, his arm covered in blood, his garments scorched, he advanced on foot in front of the first line of the 34th regiment; the complete serenity he emanated at that moment would be reflected in his report the following day:

'The infantry in battle endured the fire of grape-shot with the greatest calm. The Emperor's orders were faithfully carried out and, for perhaps the first time during the war, the majority of the wounded got themselves to the field hospital on their own.'

It was at this moment that at his side General Valhubert, less fortunate, had his thigh shattered by a cannon-ball and with his barking overbore the unhappy soldiers who proposed to carry him off:

'Stay at your posts! I'll die well enough on my own! There's no need to lose six men to save one!'

The engagement of the Battle of Austerlitz best supplied with men and munitions slowed up, if it did not come to an end, towards midday. That was the moment when Murat, always in a hurry to proclaim his successes, sent a messenger to the Emperor:

'Tell him that we have gained the ground and that my troops, with those of Marshal Lannes, have succeeded in throwing back Prince Bagration towards Olmütz.'

It is true that at the same moment Bagration, as unperturbed and apparently indifferent as at a chess club, hurried an emissary to the Czar:

'Inform His Majesty that I have succeeded in keeping intact the whole of my army corps and that we are only retreating foot by foot.'

The young officer had already sawed at his horse's mouth, when a brief call made him turn round again. Coming from Bagration's cadaverous face, livid, utterly expressionless, the murmured phrase was all the more pathetic:

'For the love of God and the saints, *monsieur*, bring me some orders!'

NAPOLEON ON THE PRATZEN

Having arrived on the Pratzen plateau, on either side of the village of the same name, it was Saint-Hilaire's division who, for the space of two hours, would bear the full weight of a dangerous counter-attack. Better conceived, it might have turned Napoleon's risky plan into a disaster. The other offensive branch of Soult's corps, Vandamme's division, firmly planted on the Stahré Vinobrady, would not have anything like so much trouble.

Saint-Hilaire's division landed in what the Emperor believed must be a void, according to the over-hasty observations that had influenced his plan in the night. In fact, the terrain was far from being stripped, first because there were far more Allied troops in the area than Napoleon thought, and also because the false manoeuvre by Liechtenstein's cavalry had forced the Russian infantry to stay there.

True, Doctorov's and Prszbyzewski's columns were already

engaged down below, at Telnitz and Sokolnitz, but there still remained nearby the whole of the tail of Langeron's column: Kamenski's brigade, whose general, having profited no doubt by a contagion of intelligence through contact with his chief, brought it back spontaneously at the thunderous noise let loose behind him on the Pratzen. Within a few minutes, Thiébault's brigade, which was situated to the right of the village of Pratzen, was hemmed in by an angle-iron of grape-shot and balls: opposite them, Kollowrath's Austrians, to their right, Kamenski's Russians. Three French regiments, the 10th Light and the 14th and 36th of the Line, would suffer hell there for nearly an hour.

It was Kamenski's Russians who first threw themselves upon the 10th Light, scarcely drawn up, shouting frenzied huzzas. A large number of officers and men were killed or wounded within a few minutes. The troops, crushed by numbers, retreated.

The 36th of the Line, for their part, hung on longer, thanks partly to a sort of human volcano, Major Perrier, seized with a delirium of death: half naked, bloody, transported with rage, he waved about in front of his men and threw himself into the midst of the enemy armed only with his sabre. While he lived, his battalion held. Not for long: two balls laid him low for ever. The men retreated, as if released from harness.

. . . But they were landed with the adjutant, Labadie, that is to say with the principal officer in each regiment charged with assisting the colonel and taking his place if necessary. It was as if the spirit of his dead comrade Perrier had just been reincarnated in him. He wrenched the flag from the man who was carrying it, and advanced upon the enemy under a hail of balls and grape-shot fired at thirty paces.

'Soldiers! Here is your line of battle! Let the brave follow me!'

Captains Raoul and Duhil needed no repetition. The two of them were filled with sublime madness. Behind them, the entire regiment resumed the offensive and regained the 200 yards of lost ground.

Towards ten o'clock, however, the situation of Thiébault's brigade became virtually desperate, when Kollowrath's Austrians attacked them from the front, after they had already had the greatest difficulty in holding against Kamenski. A curious thing, these Austrians had been left as rearguard, because their regiment consisted of invalids and recruits, who had never been under fire. But an excellent commander, Czech in origin, General Jurschek, led them into battle, full of courage and spirit. This was the moment when the whole French line around Pratzen seemed ready to crack, under the mass of cross-fire. Saint-Hilaire, not yet hailed by Ney as the bravest of the brave, who stood sword in hand at the most exposed spot, himself seemed to weaken. He asked Thiébault whether it would not be wise to retreat, and it was one of his colonels, Pouzet, commander of the 10th Light, who for once proved to be more reckless and perhaps won Austerlitz by his roar:

'We retreat, General? If we stop for a moment we're lost! Give the enemy no time to count us! Let's at them with the bayonet!'

'You are right, forward!' replied Saint-Hilaire, and sent all the available men back into the heart of the furnace with a frenzy so demented that even the Russian lines, of proverbial solidity, were shaken.[1]

The respite Saint-Hilaire's division gained from this sudden spurt by the 10th Light enabled Thiébault to receive decisive help in the form of six twelve-centimetre pieces, the whole of the 4th Corps' artillery, which Marshal Soult, dismayed by the situation, sent him at top speed.

Half an hour later, Soult in person was astride his horse in the middle of the terrain, cleared at last of Austro-Russians (live ones, that is . . . for their dead covered it abundantly). Hat in hand, Thiébault was giving his account of the use he had just made of this invaluable reinforcement. With his oily voice, hairy hands and bloodshot eyes, Thiébault that day deserved more than ever the nickname Butcher-General which had been

[1] The majority of military historians have not given this final spurt the place it deserves in the story of Austerlitz, always on account of a perspective deliberately Napoleonic, which sees the matter as won from the moment the French set foot on the Pratzen. But if Thiébault's brigade had wavered at that juncture, Saint-Hilaire would have been thrown into disorder, the whole of Soult's corps breached by the flank, the plateau retaken by the Allies and the latter given time to recover by recalling their left. Colonel Pouzet deserved well of the Empire that day.

bestowed on him by his many enemies. He had the reputation of systematically seeking to shed blood—and had just had his fill. His account conveys an unusual degree of complacency, even for that epoque of coarseness: [1]

'Your cannon arrived in the nick of time, *monsieur le maréchal*! I at once ordered Colonel Fontenay to have all the pieces loaded with grape-shot and balls. "That will sink them!" he retorted. "My word," I said, "if they can stand it for ten minutes it will suffice!" I then had the laying of the pieces checked, so as to fire at ten or twenty fathoms . . . I had ten cartridges of grape-shot and ten cannon-balls placed beside each piece in order to fire more quickly; I myself repeated the advice to the troops to aim well before firing and *to aim for the men's belts* and for the centre of the platoons, so that not a shot should be wasted. Then, having been occupied in this way up to the last minute, I allowed those formidable masses to approach to the intended distance and my pieces, abruptly unmasked right down the line, began one of the most destructive volleys that have ever been made . . . '

Soult, though he was no choir-boy, signalled to him to be brief. But Thiébault exulted:

'You may conceive my satisfaction at seeing each of the cannon-shots open up a large square hole in the regiments, and these four regiments that were assailing my three battalions break up into fleeing masses! In preventing a conflict, which we were in no fit state to resist, I saved my brigade ("Here's a man," thought Soult, "whom neither modesty nor sensitivity can suppress . . . ") and the whole of the advance guard!'

'I will report to the Emperor . . . ' said Soult dryly as he moved away.

The contest, however, was not yet won for the French in the centre, on account of that elegant and energetic fellow who was exerting himself between the lakes and the Pratzen plateau between ten o'clock and midday, as if the European quarrel was his own—which it was—Count Langeron.

'At nine-thirty,' he himself recounts, 'Lieutenant-Colonel Balk, who commanded two squadrons of the regiment of St

[1] It can be found word for word in his *Mémoires*.

Petersburg dragoons, had me informed that French columns had been seen climbing the Pratzen hills. [Langeron was at that moment in front of Sokolnitz, consolidating its occupation.] Knowing that Kollowrath's column should have been on that side, and not having received any order from Kutuzov, I thought Lieutenant-Colonel Balk had taken the Austrians for the enemy, though the direction he had seen them take seemed to me extraordinary and I sent to have him make a more accurate reconnaissance.

'A moment later, Count Kamenski sent to tell me that the French had actually occupied the Pratzen hills in strength, that he had made a right-about turn with his brigade, that he had reascended the ridge and that he had very strong forces in front of him.

'It was difficult for me therefore to understand what had happened and how the enemy came to be behind us. I left General Olsufiev to continue the Sokolnitz attack and went to join Count Kamenski. By then, he had already deployed his brigade, with his back to our columns, and at 200 paces from him, the enemy had also deployed two or three brigades of infantry (it was, as we know, Saint-Hilaire's division) who outflanked ours and occupied the very camp we had just left.

'Down below, in the direction of Austerlitz, to the right of Count Kamenski, I saw a few battalions who were faltering and appeared to be in retreat; I sent to them for information and was told that they were part of Kollowrath's Austrians who were withdrawing and were being pursued by the French.

'It was eleven o'clock.'

What Langeron does not say is that at that moment he realized that the technical superiority of the firing of the French infantry was inflicting considerable losses on the Russian foot-soldiers and that, in order to extricate them, he ordered, and himself led, a bayonet charge on Thiébault's scarcely established brigade. A fierce infantry free-for-all ensued, after which it was necessary for both sides to reassemble, without having gained ground. During this time, Langeron hardly had leisure for self-admiration, while the bearing of the soldiers of his adopted country won his esteem:

'In spite of their slight propensity for war and the effect a quite unforeseen attack in their rear must have had on them, in spite of the effect the sound of cannon must have produced in them, which many of them were hearing for the first time, they were to bear up admirably for nearly two hours and, in those two hours, more than half of Kamenski's two regiments were laid low.'

All the courage in the world, not Langeron's any more than that of the moujiks, would have sufficed now to uproot Saint-Hilaire's division from the Pratzen. Thiébault had just been reinforced by Vare's brigade (the 43rd and 53rd of the Line). The struggle would be very hot until half-past twelve at this point, between 6,000 Frenchmen on one side and 6,000 Russians and 5,000 Austrians on the other. Langeron, once again, in the complete absence of orders from headquarters, behaved like a true commander-in-chief. He decided to return to Sokolnitz and send back to the plateau a large proportion of the troops who were engaged below. It was much too late.

During this time, Soult's left, that is to say Vandamme, consolidated the occupation of the Stahré Vinobrady and deployed to the north of Pratzen, not entirely without difficulty, but with relative ease, if one compares his situation with that of his neighbour Saint-Hilaire. He had opposite him, however, not only part of Kollowrath's column, but Miloradovitch's nine Russian battalions, amounting to nearly 5,000 men. The latter did indeed attempt to deploy to the north-east of Pratzen: they were crushed and dispersed in less than half an hour. A few commanders performed prodigies of valour, but here they were not followed by their troops. General Repninski tried to keep the first Novgorod battalion in the firing line all on his own, but collapsed wounded by three musket-shots. His unit at once retreated. General Berg did the same with the Little-Russia regiment, until he was wounded and taken prisoner. Whence came the disproportion between Saint Hilaire's difficulties and Vandamme's advantages? The two French commanders were of the same merit and found themselves before manifestly equal effectives on equivalent terrain. The explanation seems to lie in the fact that if it was an incompetent, Buxhouden, who was in nominal command of the Russian left, he was compensated for well and truly by worthy subordinates, Langeron, Doctorov and Prszbyzewski. On the other hand, the Russian general who was actually in control of the resources of the Allied centre, at that crucial moment, was a booby all the more dangerous in that he raised a lot of dust and gave the impression of activity.

Mounted on a splendid English horse, a very fast runner, General Miloradovitch came and went at great speed in the midst of the balls and shot. From the little hillock where the Czar, golden eye-glass in hand, was observing the scene with the same slightly irritated detachment as he would a badly staged ballet at the Opera, all eyes were on him alone. He fascinated the officers of the general staff and the Sovereign himself.

'He's a hero . . . ' murmured Alexander to Dolgoruki. 'Ah, *mon cher*, I should like to be able to do as he does! . . . It is sometimes a bitter duty for an Emperor not to be able to die . . . '

Always between the soldiers and the enemy, Miloradovitch swore, roared, stormed, waved his sabre and fired shots at random from an enormous pair of silver pistols.

'Have you noticed that he never goes out of the Czar's sight?' breathed Czartoryski, too shrewd to be taken in by this clumsy performance.

'What is far more serious, Excellency, is that he is completely taken up with his pantomime,' replied General Intzov. 'He hasn't given his men an order since the morning!'

'A hero . . . ' said the Czar thoughtfully, once more.

Even if he had been a military genius, Miloradovitch would have been unable, by himself, to wreck 'the blow of the fist on the Pratzen' any more than, on his own, Langeron could have prevented the destruction of the Allied left. The fact remains that, for lack of a commander worthy of the name, the conquest of the north of the Pratzen by Vandamme came up against only two spasms, instead of the numerous convulsions that Saint-Hilaire found himself having to contend with.[1]

[1] The Russian historian Danilevski, who has done his best to rehabilitate Miloradovitch, notes with precision:
'Miloradovitch performed prodigies of valour to hold his position and give the Austrians time to reassemble behind him. But, in spite of his heroic efforts, he was uniformly repulsed. In his turn, he reassembled his detachment behind the Austrians. The latter, riddled with cannon-balls and shot, weakened

The first spasm, as we have seen, had been almost instinctive and disputed the Stahré Vinobrady fiercely from the moment the French reached it.

The second was delivered without conviction between eleven o'clock and midday: half of Kollowrath's Austrian forces (about 2,500 men) who still lined the foot of the Stahré Vinobrady formed themselves into a square and tried to set up a living wall to prevent Vandamme from going further. The latter then attacked the Salzburg regiment with the 4th of the Line and the 24th Light, the first from the front, the second by the flank. These two regiments climbed to the attack with determination, and without firing a musket shot smashed this strong line of at least six battalions and cut it to pieces. The cannon remained in their power and practically the whole of two Russian regiments were destroyed.

The Pratzen plateau was definitely in the hands of Marshal Soult.

*　　　　*　　　　*　　　　*

Midday. Several witnesses mention the biting cold at that hour; first, because they were exhausted, famished, at the end of their strength, but also because a sharp wind had begun to blow from the east and the sun hid itself more and more frequently. Would it rain, would it snow? On either side, in both camps, the great leaders passed a hand over their brows and tried to take their bearings, to find out how they stood. Berthier sent Napoleon a concise account which makes it possible to see the battle as a whole at the end of the second act.[1]

What emerges above all is that the situation seemed in general static; no significant arrows indicated the direction of any movement by the great corps facing each other, who were hanging on where they were and taking a sort of breather before the final resolution.

[1] See our diagram, 'The situation at noon'.

within a very short time by the loss of 2,388 men, gave way and swept off in their flight, in descending from the hills, the remainder of Miloradovitch's detachment.'

This tends to show, in passing, that accord no more reigned, *a posteriori*, between the Russian and Austrian historians than in the combined general staffs of the two Emperors.

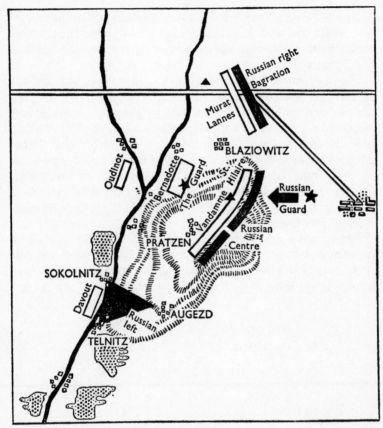

VII. *The situation at noon*

In the south, the Russian left, as massive as ever, occupied a triangular area on the Goldbach from where it could still debouch through Telnitz and Sokolnitz, still in its power, if Davout were not presenting an insuperable barrier, and if it were not already being preoccupied by the presence of the French at its back.

In the north, on either side of the road to Olmütz, Lannes' infantry and Murat's cavalry was forcing the Russian right under Bagration, intact, to retreat step by step, but had already achieved the valuable result of virtually cutting it off from the rest of the Allies.

In the centre, Saint-Hilaire and Vandamme, having passed beyond Pratzen and the Stahré Vinobrady, were exerting a cross pressure on the Russian centre hanging on to the last slopes of the Pratzen, to the east.

The star that indicates Napoleon's headquarters had moved: as early as half-past eleven, he had repaired to the Pratzen plateau and would convey himself to the top of the Stahré Vinobrady, in order to regulate the last act of the battle. With him, the full Imperial Guard and the whole of Marshal Bernadotte's 1st Corps were in the process of taking up their position to constitute, if they should be needed, an additional manoeuvrable mass. Behind them, again, Oudinot's grenadiers remained ready to move towards Napoleon or towards Davout, according to need.

Ah, if, however: there was one arrow! In a desperate effort to reverse destiny, the Russian Imperial Guard, who had left Austerlitz that morning and had hardly fought up till then, would engage some of its finest regiments in a desperate charge.

CHAPTER XVI

December 2nd, from noon to 3 p.m.

'MANY FINE LADIES WILL WEEP'

The contest was over: from the moment the Russian centre was thrown back from the Pratzen, the Allied attempt to break through the French right lost its point. Napoleon was therefore certain of victory. But the three hours of fighting that were yet to take place would decide what sort of victory it was to be. Total? Decisive? Putting an end to the war by the annihilation of all the Austro-Russian forces—or only partial?

It was with such considerations in mind that all that remained of strength and courage, on either side, would be thrown into the scales. The French to secure a collapse, the Allies to avoid it. And all decisions taken after midday would be made in this light.

The rupture of the Allied front accentuated the division of the terrain into three quite distinct sectors of operation:

The duel between Lannes and Bagration continued in the north, around the road to Olmütz. The Russians made a last effort to re-establish a link with their centre. Lannes prevented them from doing so, but, except for a brief moment, did not succeed in seriously disturbing their retreat.

In the centre, the bulk of the French troops established themselves firmly on the Pratzen, in spite of a desperate charge by part of the Russian Imperial Guard, made more to save face, it appeared, than to alter the state of affairs now set up. And Napoleon gave the decisive order: he caused the bulk of his forces to carry out the quarter turn that condemned the Russian left—but released the right.

In the region of the lakes, the Allied assault columns, who were to have opened up a conclusive breach that morning, were caught in a vice of fire and steel. Thanks to the valour of their leaders and the courage of the Russian infantry, part of them would succeed in escaping, whereas the rest would be captured or killed. This last episode would constitute the most spectacular outcome of the Battle of Austerlitz. Napoleon would not fail to exaggerate it accordingly, almost inordinately.

THE RUSSIAN RIGHT ESCAPES

The last fluctuation of the struggle in the north took place towards one o'clock. Prince Bagration certainly had no illusions about the general outcome of the battle. Kutuzov, or the Czar, had succeeded in sending him a message telling him of the pulverization of the centre and enjoining him to hold the road to Olmütz at all costs so that the greatest possible number of the retreating troops would be able to reassemble there. As a good tactician, Bagration decided to attack in order to be able subsequently to retreat: he launched his right against Suchet's division, towards the Santon.

Towards one o'clock, Lannes sent an urgent message to Napoleon:

'A formidable line of infantry and cavalry has just been drawn up on the Rausnitz plateau, in front of the centre of my army corps . . .'

This 'plateau' was no more than an undulation, scarcely more noticeable than others, situated on the road to Olmütz shortly after the point where the road branches off to Austerlitz. The fight would unfold at the level of this fork, located to the south by the village of Holubitz and to the north by a staging post bearing the name of a village situated a mile and a half higher up towards the mountains of Moravia: Posoritz.

Suchet, in his report to Lannes the following day, did not miss the opportunity of paying him a compliment . . . He was not unaware that Lannes, for his part, was preparing a report for the Emperor:

'Some columns of Russian infantry approached by the main
road and moved upon our extreme left. It was then (at very
nearly one o'clock) that you ordered that fine change of front,
advancing the right wing. By the precision and rapidity with
which this was executed, the enemy line was immediately
broken, and his columns thrown back on the left, though without breaking up.'

In other words, Lannes applied on the scale of his army corps,
and in the opposite direction, Napoleon's manoeuvre for the
whole battle: Bagration attacked him on his left, he thrust at
the right and the centre. This could have been the start of an
immense outcome: if the Russians had ventured too far forward
and remained caught on the hook of the Santon, Lannes and
Murat would have been able to advance along the road to
Olmütz, and then wheel round and encircle Bagration, driving
him back to the north-west. That would have been the end of
the Russian army.

But, on the one hand, Bagration was to sense the danger
immediately, recall his endangered right, and present a solid
front to the French offensive. And on the other, Lannes and even
Murat were to show a strange feebleness, for want undoubtedly
of more formal and more explicit orders from Napoleon. The
latter, completely preoccupied with crushing the Russians at
grips with Davout in the south, was apparently to have no
interest in what his left was doing, at the cost of reacting
vigorously, but too late, when he realized that half his initial
plan was compromised.[1]

The French cavalry, still quivering after the clashes of the
morning, was about to be launched to disengage Cafarelli:
d'Hautpoul's curassiers charged the columns of Russian infantry,
came up at first against sustained fire from well-formed squares,
but managed to break through at the second attempt, and seized
a flag, six cannon and numerous vehicles.

Bagration then massed his cavalry on his right and prepared
to have it charge in its turn, far more massively, in order to

[1] In this momentary aberration lay Jena, Eylau and Friedland: a whole
useless war. This was what Russian historians would christen 'the miscarriage
of Austerlitz'.

allow the withdrawal of his regiments who were abandoning the Santon, and in order to retain possession of the road junction to Austerlitz. Once again and for the last time Murat, too, concentrated all his available men and horses, who this time would be equal in number to the enemy: the light cavalry and Walther's dragoons, plus the cuirassiers. With that incomparable feeling for offensive tactics that was his prerogative, Murat succeeded in delivering his thrust first, and forestalled the Russian charge by several minutes. This showed remarkable capacity, first of intuition, and then of execution, when it was a matter of grouping, deploying and launching at the gallop, under a deluge of fire, 2,000 men already exhausted and sorely tried by very violent engagements.

The 4th Hussars were the first to give battle, then the whole of the brigade of dragoons under General Sébastiani, one of the most detested commanders in the army, for his consistently vinegary temper that burst out in shrill screechings. Sébastiani now atoned at one blow for three or four years of torture inflicted on his men in the tilt-yard, by falling in front of them all, wounded by a ball. General Roget, who was following him with his brigade, took charge of the four squadrons and repulsed the enemy cavalry, caught at the moment when they were gathering their impetus. One pursuing the other, the two bodies of cavalry defiled from right to left between the two masses of infantry, and regrouped to the north, at the foot of the mountains of Moravia. The duel was now engaged between the foot-soldiers: Bagration had his regiments advance, with fixed bayonets, upon Lannes, uncovered. The latter recalled d'Hautpoul's cuirassiers, who made an about-turn, took Bagration's right by the flank and managed for a moment to unsettle it with the terrible impact of those hundreds of steel-clad men arriving full tilt and sabring the serried lines of foot-sloggers.

Lannes had gone to the Santon to exhort the men of the 17th Light, who had been exposed to fire almost without remission all morning, to be patient. It was there that he received an officer from Suchet, telling him of one of the finest results of the day:

'Victory, *monsieur le maréchal*! General Suchet has sent me to tell you that he has brought up the whole of his division behind the cuirassiers. The enemy had formed into squares, firing all the time. Our battalions advanced on this mass at the charge, and crossed bayonets. We were almost held up for a moment by our own cavalry, who hadn't managed to make much impression on them. They slowed us up. But before long the 34th, the 40th and the 88th resumed their strenuous efforts and at last! at last we broke through a whole section of the Russian squares. We laid more than 2,000 there dead on the ground! We captured sixteen cannon! The prisoners are being counted . . . '

This was in fact the only moment at which Bagration's infantry faltered. At three o'clock the whole of the cavalry plain was in the hands of the French, including the road-fork to Austerlitz. Passing beyond the Posoritz post, the 30th and the 17th of the Line advanced towards Olmütz on either side of the main road, the cavalry in front of them. Three other regiments held all the area to the left, between the mountains and the road. Disdainful, but pale, slightly wounded in the thigh, Prince Bagration reassembled his troops a mile further on, towards Olmütz, under cover of the last pieces of artillery he still had at his disposal, placed so judiciously that they slowed down the French advance. This had been taking its course rather slackly since Murat's order to suspend pursuit and call a halt. It was he who was in supreme command, above Lannes—and this time he was committing the exact opposite of the mistake that had made him throw himself thoughtlessly on Vienna a month earlier . . . perhaps just because Napoleon had so stunned him by the vigour of his reproaches at that time and had dinned into him the fear of going too fast and too far.

He had at his disposal however a formidable array, almost intact: behind the cavalry, Suchet's division on the left, on the main road; Cafarelli's division on the right, linked to Soult's corps and beginning to advance towards Austerlitz. The men were tired, certainly, and hungry, but beside themselves with joy and ready to go on for at least another two hours. Why did Murat not see that in letting Bagration withdraw, he was providing a life-saving refuge for the two Emperors and for all the Russians who might escape from the disaster?

A general so covered in powder and mud that he looked like a negro and that his uniform, all torn, might have been that of a sergeant, came dashing up to the staging post at Posoritz, where Murat had just set up his headquarters. It was Cafarelli, one of the great tacticians of the day. He was mad with rage and waved his arms in all directions:

'Where the bloody hell is Murat?'

The aides-de-camp, who were already enveloping the latter in an almost monarchical atmosphere, presented him with a scandalized front.

'His Serene Highness has gone in person to reconnoitre the enemy positions towards Rausnitz. But if you wish to see General Belliard . . .'

This was Murat's chief of staff, his military good angel, the only able strategist in his entourage, a sincere and reliable men, moreover. Cafarelli hurled himself upon him as at a Russian square to be broken:

'Belliard! At last, my good, my brave Belliard, do you understand all this? I have just detailed a few companies of the 13th Light to cut off the Russian fugitives who are decamping from the Pratzen like rabbits! . . . I have taken Krzenowitz, where the enemy left me three cannon! Our skirmishers have already crossed the stream and are spreading out to the rear of the hills! I found myself in front of a tattered screen of Russians who were merely trying to draw out their lines to deceive me as to their true strength, while their vehicles defiled behind! I felt a formidable booty within reach of my hands. I assembled two battalions of the 51st, I made ready to launch them into an assault on the hills, and to have them supported on their right by the 13th . . . Think of it! I might have laid hands on the Emperors' carriages . . . And do you know what I received then? No, really, do you know?'

'Lannes' order to fall back,' said Belliard, as jovial as ever. 'The battle is over for you. You should take a wash at the nearest fountain.'

Cafarelli exploded:

'Jesuit! False friend! Lannes' order! I rushed off to the Marshal, of course: he was a thousand yards away. I thought he would devour me quite raw when I asked him his reasons. "Go and see Murat," he told me. "You know very well I am under his orders. Would Lannes bring to a standstill a fight three-quarters won? . . . " I hurried here . . . and was told that "His Serene Highness" was taking a stroll somewhere or other.'

Belliard took him by the hand and spoke to him as to a fever patient:

'It's just as well you didn't see Murat in the state you are in. It's not worth the penalty of ending your finest battle under close arrest. Are you capable of listening to me, yes or no?'

Cafarelli made a gesture of disgust.

'Do you take Murat for a coward? His intention had certainly been to continue to press the enemy, and seize the hills of Rausnitz and Austerlitz. But you must have heard the violence of the fusillade towards the lakes? Some formidable things are happening down there! It looks as if they are being chopped into mincemeat. We have one explicit order, just one since noon, for the Emperor has lost interest in us, it would seem: preserve communications along the roads to Brünn, Olmütz and Austerlitz. And what if His Majesty should need cavalry units on his side? Where would he draw them from if we gallop off into the blue? When Murat decided to suspend his advance so as to remain within reach, and sent the same order to Lannes, I myself clearly saw his eyes full of tears! Of course, now that he is being prudent for once, you are all against him . . . Eh! Where are you off to?'

'To lie down,' replied Cafarelli, as he lurched off with his ungainly walk. One suddenly recalled, for the first time during the battle, that he had a wooden leg.

Firing stopped at that moment (4.30 p.m.) down the whole line in their sector. Lannes and Murat, arms grounded, sent messenger after messenger to elicit orders from Napoleon.

Was it up to Murat, at that moment of the battle, at that turning-point in the European war, to 'elicit orders'? Where at that moment was 'His Majesty', whose silence was petrifying the commanders of his left, what was he doing, what was he thinking?

'AH, JUST AS HE GETS THERE!'

Napoleon had kept his word: he had not exposed himself to fire. His role up to the last third of the battle had been far more passive than on the majority of the other days of glory. He had been content to look on at the evolution of the clockwork mechanism he had wound up so perfectly. His main service in the morning seems to have been to restrain the impetuousness of his marshals, who would have spoiled everything by unleashing the offensive too soon.

After sunrise and the departure of Soult, he had performed the routine functions of an army leader, by haranguing the regiments of Bernadotte's corps. In one way or another he had passed the time and waited for definite news. Around him there had of course been the usual mounted group of couriers, of aides-de-camp: those of his marshals, the corps commanders or his own, arriving dusty, covered in mud, the mouths of their horses frothing, all proud, sometimes, of a fresh wound to show. But they had succeeded each other more to give their news than to ask for orders. No reinforcements demanded at any point, except by Davout at the beginning of the morning; no reserves to throw in; no changes of front to carry out. The Emperor had scarcely had to consult his maps. He had sat on his horse almost the whole morning, had moved slowly to the left of Soult's corps, and had then advanced towards the Pratzen plateau at the head of his reserve. A little after midday, he rapidly climbed the Stahré Vinobrady, which Vandamme held firmly, and which was the best observation post for following the whole of the battle.

At that moment he was engrossed by the most highly coloured episode of the day, though of only secondary strategic significance: the charge of the Russian Imperial Guard.[1]

At first it was a matter of an infantry charge: four complete battalions of the Russian Guard, about 3,000 men, debouched from Krzenowitz and attacked Vandamme's division, to the north of the Stahré Vinobrady, under the orders of the Czar's own brother, Grand-Duke Constantine. They were magnificent men, giants of over six feet, clad in white and green: the

[1] If the majority of those describing or commentating on Austerlitz, beginning with Gérard, have considerably exaggerated it and have made of it one of the pivotal episodes of the battle, it is undoubtedly because Napoleon himself was excessively impressed by it, rather as if he personally had crossed swords with Alexander. It was also one of the few moments of the day when he influenced events by his direct orders.

Semenovski and Preobrajenski regiments, whose presence at the right time in certain squares of Moscow or St Petersburg had sufficed to overthrow this Czar or that Czarina, and have a successor proclaimed. They were insanely brave, and this would cost them dear. The Grand-Duke directed them to attack with the bayonet, but such was their enthusiasm, they began their dash too soon, 300 paces from the French, and reached them out of breath. Luckily for the latter: the impact of these giants was as redoubtable as that of cavalry. The first ranks of the 24th Light and the 4th of the Line, whose murderous fire did however sprinkle the ground with bodies, were thrust back and routed.

But the second French line held everywhere: the attackers were at the end of their breath. The infantry of the Russian Guard, kept remarkably well in hand by its commanders, withdrew in good order towards Krzenowitz.

At that moment Vandamme's regiments thought they were clear and the episode was all the more quickly forgotten since a very important order had just reached the division: they were to make a quarter turn to the right, leave the Stahré Vinobrady where Bernadotte's troops were about to relieve them, descend to the south to help Saint-Hilaire, still hard-pressed towards Pratzen, and take part in the crushing of the Russian left. It was a matter already under way for all Vandamme's forces, except the two regiments that had just been delayed by the infantry of the Russian Guard: the 4th of the Line and the 24th Light, their battalions drawn up in columns and already containing sad gaps, were isolated in the middle of the Pratzen plateau when they saw, swooping down on them, six squadrons of Russian cavalry!

Behind the infantry, which had just been repulsed, Grand-Duke Constantine was leading in person all that was available of the cavalry of the Imperial Guard.

*　　　*　　　*　　　*

Vandamme was far from suspecting the storm that was about to burst on his division. He had just heard of the defeat of the Russian Foot Guards, and believed himself all the more firmly established round the Stahré Vinobrady since the Emperor was in the process of climbing it. Marshal Soult had already preceded the latter and was methodically sweeping the horizon with his glass, from the summit of this incomparable lookout point. It was thus he who first became aware of the danger. Vandamme had at last sat down on an overturned wagon and was consenting to have a quick dressing or two applied to his minor wounds, when an aide-de-camp from his corps commander came galloping up:

'*Monsieur le maréchal* sends to inform you, *mon général*, that a small enemy column seems to be debouching from Krzenowitz; it is undoubtedly a further part of the Russian Guard that has hitherto remained in the general reserve. He requests you to detail a battalion to watch it.'

Vandamme thought, quite naturally, of that regiment of his that had been most delayed in the plain, the 4th of the Line, and despatched in his turn one of his aides-de-camp:

'Captain Vincent!'

'*Mon général?*'

He was almost a child: those attached to the division commanders, always taken on very young as a privilege, were the laughing-stock of the officers exercising a regular command, who called them 'the generals' page-boys'. Vincent, rosy-cheeked, beardless and reckless, was no exception to the rule.

'Go to the Colonel of the 4th of the Line . . . '

'Do you mean to Major Bigarré, *mon général?*'

Vandamme checked him with an impatient gesture. He knew perfectly well that the titular colonel of the 4th of the Line was Prince Joseph Bonaparte, the Emperor's elder brother, and that the whole army was seized with wild laughter whenever he pretended to assume his rank effectively. This only occurred on parades, three times a year. For the moment Joseph was in Paris, where he considered himself indispensable to the Council of Regency. The adjutant, Major Bigarré, who therefore exercised actual command of the 4th of the Line in his place, was in full flow to the south, about half a mile from the division, when he saw Captain Vincent come galloping along:

'General Vandamme directs you to take the head of one of your battalions personally and to go and reconnoitre an enemy column that is threatening your rear. My mission is to accompany you till contact is made, and then report back . . . '

The first battalion, quite naturally, found itself detailed to make a half turn and advance to the edge of the plateau, preceded by two officers: Bigarré, moustached, athletic, already covered in scars, his chest bespangled with the stars of the cross, and Vincent, who could almost have been his son.

'Not so fast, now! You'll go and get yourself killed like a pheasant!' cried the first to the second—in vain. Captain Vincent spurred away and galloped beyond even the line of scouts. Unit commanders all dreaded the outbursts of these 'staff greenhorns' anxious to wash away weeks of mockery with a show of rashness.

Vincent thus discovered the considerable mass of cavalry on the reverse of the slope, and returned full speed to Bigarré making desperate signs.

'The head of the column to the left! Quick, you lazy buggers, quicker!' yelled the Major, who sensed a terrible threat and had the presence of mind to keep his battalion marching along in columns in separate sections, so as to have them ready to form a square. Then he in turn galloped forward, joined Vincent and went back with him to the steep edge overlooking the two reverse sides of the slope.

'*Nom de Dieu!* What's this bearing down on us!'

'I have a strong impression, Major, that it's the whole of the cavalry of the Russian Imperial Guard. They're coming at us full trot . . .'

'They're forming up on the plateau, at extreme musket-range. My unfortunate first battalion will have to bear the full weight of their first charge! I have only time to . . .'

And Bigarré returned to his men at full speed:

'Form a square!'

'Look out, Major, look out!' cried Vincent, as he himself returned at walking pace! 'They're unmasking six pieces of light artillery which are about to fire grape-shot, and we . . .'

The young officer fell, riddled with bullets.

*   *   *   *

'Hurrah! Hurrah!'

The staccato Russian cries tore the air like bursts of artillery fire. Grand-Duke Constantine, brandishing his sabre, stood up in his stirrups and turned towards the flower of the youth of his country that perpetually bewildered face in which all the sombre heredity of the Romanovs seemed to have found refuge. The beauty, the intelligence, the charm, had been bestowed on his two brothers: Alexander, the Czar, and Nicolas, the younger brother; to him, their father had bequeathed a face all bumps, the hands of a gorilla, the gait of a peasant, and that disquieting gleam in the depths of his eyes. Twice already, it was whispered, he had strangled valets who had failed to do his bidding fast enough.

Interminable nights had seen him prostrated before icons, begging with sobs to be forgiven for the debaucheries into which he had plunged himself since the morning. But today he was washed free of all hesitation and ready to die in a sort of ecstasy: he was transfigured by the joy of danger, which rendered him almost handsome.

'For God, the Czar, and Russia!'

Behind him, a thousand glittering horsemen, whose white uniforms contrasted with the black of their mounts. Every one of them was the scion of a noble family; many possessed domains vaster than some French departments and had in their train, even in the army, whole squads of retainers. But the moment of truth was at hand when all that counted was sheer courage. The clinking of arms and the sound of hooves was added to the rattle of the fusillade, rudely cut by cannon-shots, on the slopes of the Pratzen. Striving to maintain their line while gathering speed, the Horse Guards of the Czar, the pride of all the Russias, entered the gathered host through a volley of heavy pieces where the denser smoke of the cannon-shots swirled like grey serpents. Already, opposite them, the flashes of the French bayonets were confronting them with a prickly wall. On their thousand-rouble horses, released from gaming, chattering and idleness, the hundreds of fine young men followed the Grand-Duke, himself in cavalry helmet and jacket, and no longer uttered more than inarticulate cries according to how far they were carried away by the collective frenzy.

Two regiments of cavalry concentrated their assault on the first battalion of the 4th of the Line, to take advantage of their isolation. Bigarré had flung himself on his horse into the middle of the scarcely formed square, to stand or die with them.

'Courage, men! Keep calm! Above all don't fire without orders! Wait till you have them on the muzzles of your muskets!'

Indeed, the first Russian charge was sharply broken by the accuracy of a formidable volley of musketry at point-blank range, executed as if on manoeuvre. But a third regiment arrived before the French had time to reload their guns.

'On your bellies! Look out!'

The deadly tornado crossed the square, going and coming pitilessly. More than 200 men were sabred. It was a butchery from which there rose a chorus of cries and groans.

'The Eagle! Save the Eagle at all costs!'

The little god of shining bronze that had become for the past year the symbol of a battalion's honour—and not one of which had yet fallen into enemy hands — twisted in the hands of Sergeant-major Saint-Cyr, who received a dozen wounds on the head and arms before letting it be taken. A Russian officer seized it and bore it off, provoking a roar of anguish from Major Bigarré who till then had uttered not a cry under the twenty-five sabre cuts that disfigured him and gave him the appearance of a bloody fiend. By his side the battalion commander Guy and ten other officers lay dead or wounded. The first two assault regiments, re-formed during the charge of the third, returned, sabred what was left of the completely shattered 1st Battalion, and went on in the same dash to rock the other battalions, which had not received the order to form a square in time. Already the Cossacks, the grenadiers and the cuirassiers of the Guard were joining the cavalry and were breaking wave upon wave, beyond the 4th of the Line, on the 24th Light, who had committed the mistake of deploying instead of closing ranks in face of this numerous cavalry. For a brief instant, those taking part in this bloody affray had the impression that 2,000 or 3,000 French infantrymen were about to be thrown into disorder, massacred and crushed by a slightly superior number of Russian cavalry remarkably led and armed. Was the outcome of the battle once more at stake? Behind this wedge that the Russians had thrust afresh on to the Pratzen, would Kutuzov be able to debouch some infantry to exploit the breach, regain a footing and, who knows, cut off Napoleon, Soult and Davout from Lannes?

In reality, no: behind the Russian Guard there was nothing. The only bodies of Allied infantry still more or less intact were those of Bagration, who was retreating before Lannes and Murat two and a half miles to the north. Even if this desperate charge had gone further, it could not have been validly exploited. But Napoleon was not even going to let it gather its full virulence.

*   *   *   *

The Emperor, even without the help of his glass, could see barely two miles from his lookout point a sort of whitish tidal wave breaking irregularly amongst the ranks of his infantry. He was not the only one: all the general staff were shuddering around him.

'The Russian Guard is cutting up Vandamme!'

Napoleon smiled: since the start of the battle, he had sensed the growing ill-humour of his Guard, not in action.

'Bessières!'

'Sire?'

'Take the cavalry of my Guard forward to support those brave fellows.'

Bessières and his aides-de-camp dashed across the great bodies of infantry in whose midst the Emperor at that moment stood, and who were proceeding in close columns by battalions: Oudinot's grenadiers, still not in action even after a series of marches and counter-marches, the whole of Bernadotte's corps, and the infantry of the Guard. The thousands of jealous men yelled their cheers and cries of envy at seeing the squadrons of cavalry set off one after the other, advancing in two lines 500 yards from Napoleon.

Bessières, always methodical, and very economical with the lives of the men, made the mistake of sending too few at first. He called to one of the best cavalrymen of the army, Colonel Morland:

'Take two squadrons and charge, Colonel.'

The locality in which the affray would develop, a very shallow basin, ensured that thousands of helpless spectators biting their knuckles would see this first charge of the French Guard end in catastrophe: Morland and his *chasseurs* clashed against the infantry of the Semenovski regiment, providing a screen

between them and the Russian cavalry. They broke through—
but were brought to a standstill when Prince Repnine led a
crushing charge against them with the Horse Guards.

'Good God, ours are retreating!'

A point to the Russians. Overwhelmed by the grape-shot and
the fusillade, sabred at odds of four to one, the *chasseurs* of the
Guard retreated in good order. In the midst of their platoons,
two of them were propping up a great bloodstained puppet:
Colonel Morland had been mortally wounded.[1]

Bessières at last understood. He despatched, one after the
other, General Ordener with three squadrons of mounted grenadiers, and then Prince Borghese, Napoleon's brother-in-law, with
two others of *chasseurs*. Finally, he had the whole of the horse
artillery deploy. But even before these men came into contact,
the Russians saw advancing upon them, coming from Girzikowitz, a vast foaming of foot-soldiers in squares: Bernadotte
had taken the initiative of detaching Count Drouet d'Erlon's
division from his corps. Three regiments of fresh infantrymen
were firing on command and mowing down the Russian Guard
under a carpet of shot.

Caught between Bernadotte's infantry and Bessières' cavalry,
what would the Horse Guards do? Uplifted by sacred rage, they
chose death on all sides. As if multiplied tenfold by the force of
despair, they attacked at the same time both the soldiers of the
line and the cavalrymen. Two of Drouet's squares were broken,
their men forced to lie down and curl up between the legs of the
horses. Ordener's grenadiers, now on equal terms, came up
against unleashed demons who broke short their charge. A
strange equilibrium was established for a few minutes in the
plain, in the midst of an indescribable uproar and under a
funereal greyness: the overcast sky where daylight was already
fading, the smoke, the whirlwinds of dust . . . The combatants
no longer shouted and the trumpeters forgot to sound: some
hundreds of men were reduced to the insensate hoarseness of
cavemen, who no longer thought of anything but killing. The

[1] A touch of macabre humour: his body, preserved in a barrel of rum, was
sent to Paris for ceremonial interment at the Invalides. When the cask was
opened three months later, it was found that the process of preservation had
developed in a monstrous manner the growth of brave Morland's moustaches,
which reached to his knees.

sabres clashed, producing on occasion enormous sparks. It was a duel of giants, the tragic set-piece to the terrible firework display, a private meeting of France and Russia.

An order from Napoleon would tip the balance. A quarter of an hour earlier, dissatisfied with the clumsiness with which Bessières had made his riposte, he had turned to his aide-de-camp Rapp, an Alsatian, thickset and placid:

'There's some confusion there. Go and put it right.'

Rapp had taken two squadrons of *chasseurs*, and one of Mamelukes. He intervened with this conclusive weight, and manoeuvred cleverly so as to drive back the Russians from the side of their infantry, who no longer dared to fire for fear of killing their own men.

'*Vive l'Empereur!*' cried Rapp, rising in his stirrups, his eyes popping out, with all the sudden impetuousness of people calm by habit. He let himself go so effectively that he outstripped all his fellows and arrived in the thick of a group of Russian cavalrymen overjoyed at their slice of luck: to take prisoner one of Napoleon's aides-de-camp!

'Surrender!'

Six sabres were pointed at him.

'Never!'

Rapp was prepared to fall, pierced already by two minor thrusts, when a furious charge of *chasseurs* led by Captain Daumesnil forced his assailants to withdraw precipitately.

'You've been carried away like a second lieutenant!' his rescuer reproached him as he embraced him. 'My word, you're well decorated to go back and see the Emperor before having yourself dressed! Many would envy you those two buttonholes . . .'

Around them, the situation had been brutally resolved. Having ventured too far forward into the midst of fresh French arrivals, the Colonel of the Horse Guards, Prince Repnine, and 200 of his men were taken prisoner. All the artillery of the Russian Guard was captured. More than 500 dead covered the ground. The remainder of the Russians, led by Grand-Duke Constantine, promptly withdrew towards Krzenowitz, which Cafarelli had just evacuated, and from which Bernadotte would dislodge them when he decided to: much too late for the

Emperor's liking, who would reproach him bitterly before long.

For the moment, Napoleon exulted as much as if he had himself passed his sword through Alexander's body.

'Many fine ladies will weep tomorrow in Petersburg!'

He rubbed his hands, but nevertheless reproved the Mameluke Mustapha, who apologized for only handing over a standard when he had nearly seized the Grand-Duke in person.

'Ah! If me catch Prince Constantine, me cut head and me bring it to Emperor . . . '

'Hold your tongue, you barbarous wretch!'

Already Rapp was coming forward, wounded, covered in blood, for a scene that all considered worthy of the great painters. It was he who led Prince Repnine to Napoleon as prisoner. The Emperor, as usual, divided his attention between victor and vanquished, restored to the latter his sword, and turned, with the gaiety of an incorrigible child, to the twenty or thirty witnesses of that moment that embodied the winning of the battle.

'The day is ended, gentlemen. We have them. The Allied centre is broken for good. The Pratzen hills are definitely in our hands. It only remains to reap the reward of our plans.'

All faces turned in the same direction as his own. Farewell to the north, where Murat and Lannes were beginning to be demoralized, for lack of orders. Farewell to the east, where the Czar, swept along by the rout, might perhaps have fallen into the hands of the French if only they had thrust more vigorously towards Austerlitz.

Faces to the south: the lakes shimmered, a long way below, in the midst of a cannonade and rattle of musketry that was showing no sign of slackening.

'An order to Bernadotte to occupy the Pratzen plateau in our place. As for us, gentlemen, we will go at last, with all Marshal Soult's corps, the Guard and Oudinot's grenadiers, to relieve once for all poor Davout. Forward against the enemy left!'

Twenty-five to thirty thousand men made a half turn to the right and proceeded to roll down upon half the Austro-Russian army caught in a trap. From this moment on and radiating from this central point, the rest of the battle would be no more than a series of fragmentary scenes.

As he set out on the road that led to the southern tip of the Pratzen plateau, Napoleon called for a draught of brandy and had a bumper poured out for Rapp, in his own goblet of gold, before insisting that he had himself attended by Baron Larrey. Then he dug in his spurs and without hurrying led his staff into the midst of the human flood he had just diverted, singing a tune of his youth:

Ah, just as he gets there . . .

HALF-PAST TWO: BUXHOUDEN

General Count Buxhouden, nominal commander of the Allied left, was strutting about on a hillock to the south-east of Sokolnitz, in the middle of a group of dismayed officers, a little more than a mile from the violent cannonade whose sound sometimes drowned the remarks being exchanged around him. Fanagorie's grenadiers and the Perm fusiliers were crowded on to a few acres of ground in tight clusters in which the French cannon-balls were beginning to trace their bloody furrows more and more frequently. Close by the greatcoated officers, the regimental field hospital was taking on the aspect of a gipsy encampment from which not even the caravan with its smoking chimney was missing. But all around it bodies were laid out in two distinct groups: those that writhed and groaned, still alive. And, somewhat more densely packed, the dead, no longer even loaded on to carts. Where would one take them to?

The saddest part of this scene was undoubtedly the expression on the thousands of faces turned towards the great men: all the infinite patience of Russia. 'Why aren't we going on? Is it true we may have to retreat? Have the French really outflanked us, then?' Pleasantries no longer rippled down the line; instead a sort of smiling melancholy had settled over the mass of men.

Langeron came along at that moment, exhausted and furious — he had had no food since the evening before — but still haughty and correct in spite of the tears in his uniform and the capers of the temporary mount he had borrowed from a Cossack. He had taken the time to pass a cloth over his face and have his hair-knot powdered. He went straight to Buxhouden.

'In the name of God, what are you doing here still, *monsieur?*

How is it you haven't yet ordered your three columns to retreat?
Haven't you seen, from where you are, what has just taken
place before your eyes? I tried to get two Koursk battalions back
on to the plateau, to ease the pressure from the French a little:
they found themselves faced with I don't know how many
thousands of enemy troops![1] In a moment, I saw them—and
you too!—surrounded, dispersed, sabred by the cavalry, blasted
by the artillery. One half were killed, the other taken. The
cannon and flags are lost. Do you want the whole of your corps
to suffer the same fate?'

Buxhouden came to a standstill. His chin, projecting into the
air in martial indignation, bore witness to the profound contempt
he had for this émigré poltroon:

'Now, Monsieur de Langeron, how very precipitant! Are you
forgetting that I have taken Telnitz and that I still hold it?'

The fuddled voice, the reiterated syllables, caused Langeron to
outface his chief. A minute was enough for him: the purplish
tinge, the dull eyes, the over-rigid bearing testified that General
Count Buxhouden, dead drunk, remained on his feet only
through force of habit. An Austrian officer, white with anger,
Captain Jurczik, all constraint cast aside, burst out to Langeron
almost under the poor man's nose:

'He's as soused as a pig, and has been since eleven o'clock this
morning! Can't you see?'

The émigré spoke to Buxhouden as to a little child:

'Telnitz, but that's ancient history! Everything has changed
since nine o'clock this morning, and you are still there? We
have the French at our backs, do you hear? At our backs! We
are being taken in the rear!'

Buxhouden gurgled a laugh of commiseration:

'*Mon cher ami*, you see enemies everywhere! . . . '

Langeron's voice cracked like a shot from a gun:

'And you, *monsieur le comte*, you are no longer in a state to
see anything!'

At that moment, an officer from Kutuzov's headquarters
arrived like a bolt from the blue: he brought an order from the
commander-in-chief, issued *three hours* earlier, less than four
miles from there . . . The order to withdraw. Buxhouden, hag-

[1] The whole of Saint-Hilaire's division and Levasseur's brigade.

gard, bowed mechanically and clicked his fingers, which his entourage at once interpreted. The officers left in all directions to try to extricate the Russian columns from encirclement.

'It's about time!' murmured Langeron. And before he himself took the head of his regiments for the retreat, he unburdened himself to that congenial Austrian, Jurczik, whose face seemed already shadowed by death.[1]

'Our centre has already completely evacuated the hills, from the road to Olmütz as far as Augezd. What is still more serious is that the initiative seized by Bonaparte and the surprise of his attack on the Pratzen, by upsetting our plan, has broken our generals' resources. Their morale has not been destroyed: I saw them continue to fight valiantly. But they have become stupid! They don't know what to do. They are no longer in a state to make any arrangements. You will see: some of them will sell their lives dearly without budging. The others will try to get out of the mess as well as they can.'

'Defeat is certain, then?'

'The rout has begun.'

HALF-PAST TWO. LET NO ONE ESCAPE!

'Ground arms! At ease!'

The clattering of muskets to the ground and the happy hubbub of the pause ran all the way down Thiébault's first four battalions, which had arrived at the southern tip of the Pratzen plateau, after a rapid march delayed hardly at all by the stray Russian elements eddying about: some hundreds of fugitives picked up in passing.

Two generals, almost in rags on their horses, ploughed through the battalions in the midst of cheers, followed by a group of their aides-de-camp, half of whom had an arm in a sling or a bandaged brow. Saint-Hilaire and Vandamme had come together for a short moment, at Soult's request, to agree on the movement to crush the Russian left, which was now confided to them.

There they both were, on the highest spur of the Pratzen on

[1] He got himself killed an hour afterwards, in the rearguard, deliberately it was said.

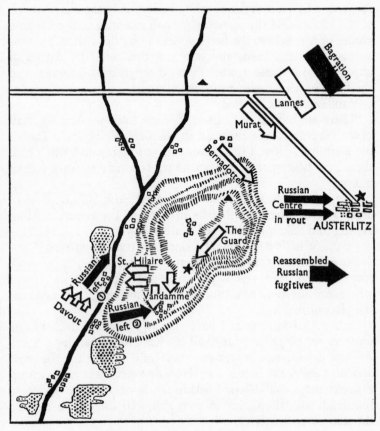

VIII. *The situation towards 3 p.m.*

1. *Part of the Russian left encircled*
2. *Part of the Russian left in retreat*

that side: a slight escarpment before the slope that led down to the Goldbach.

'We're in for a fine time!' exclaimed Saint-Hilaire—who had his arm in a sling, broken in three places—'There's a confounded ring of them!'

Under their eyes stretched a sea of men, covered in smoke, from the chateau of Sokolnitz as far as the market town of

Augezd, with its completely white belfry. Only the clear patches of the lakes holed the immense greyish assembly, ringed with a border of fire; below, the fierce volleys of battles still in progress against Davout's men, and now, on this side, the flashes of improvised fusillades against them, through a panic reversal of the Russians threatened with encirclement.

Vandamme was worried.

'There are too many of them. We are too few. And we shall never manage to get them all in the net. Well! . . . There's not a minute to lose. I shall leave you, to join my division, which should be here within half an hour. You may be sure I shall hurry.'

'We are clearly in agreement,' replied Saint-Hilaire. 'I shall order a right turn.[1] I will take in the rear the enemy holding Telnitz and Sokolnitz. Pinched against Davout.'

' . . . What's left of him! I think it's time we arrived!'

'As you wish! Caught between Davout and me, they won't cost us much. As for you, you come and take over the ground where my division is stationed at the moment, the south of the plateau in short.'

' . . . And as soon as I have regrouped, I shall descend due south to cut off the retreat of all the Russians remaining around Augezd. I have the impression that Soult has left me the most difficult task of the battle . . . How do you expect me to set up a sufficiently solid barrier within an hour in front of those thousands and thousands of men still well under control? In the state mine are in . . . '

The two divisional commanders looked at the soldiers around them with grounded arms. Good men, of good morale: but a certain slackness of the body spoke volumes. Some of them were obliged to sit down on the spot, their buttocks in the mud.

'They have had nothing in their stomachs since the meal at five o'clock this morning. And their knapsacks are half empty. You well know that units in the state they are in are no longer reliable in battle. It is enough for the wind to change or a malingerer to cry out, and there's panic . . . '

'What about them, do you think they are any better off?'

[1] To understand what follows, see from now on our last diagram: 'The situation towards three o'clock'.

replied Saint-Hilaire, indicating the Russians. 'Come on, let's make haste! It looks as if they are going to show their hand!'

Formal regroupings were taking place in the four or five square miles of men, stagnant up till now. Undulations, whirlings of cavalry indicated that a general order to evacuate had been given: more than 20,000 Russians were setting out in the general direction of Birnbaum and Austerlitz, jostling each other in the passage through Augezd.

CHAPTER XVII

'I AM PLEASED WITH YOU'

Marshal Davout jumped off his horse, stumbled through the rubble of the half-demolished chateau of Sokolnitz, and holding out both his hands, rushed towards General Friant, standing amidst the devastated park. For 1,000 yards on either side of the Goldbach, the fusillade was as lively as in the morning: for more than seven hours, they had both lived on the edge of that lacerating cordon of explosions.

'General Friant, I congratulate you. Since this morning, with a handful of men, you have defended yourself against 15,000 to 20,000 Russians, and now, not content with not having given way, you are driving them out of the village!'

Friant, smiling and weary, anxious about discipline as at the end of a parade, almost came to attention for his methodical report:

'At midday, as soon as I saw my regiments of the left thrown back beyond the Sokolnitz stream, I considered it necessary to strike a decisive blow. I concentrated my efforts on the tip of the village. Having withdrawn the 33rd from my extreme left, I introduced it between the 15th Light and the 111th. Then I joined the 15th. I threw them at the little culvert and debouched them north-west of Sokolnitz, while the 33rd, wheeling to the left, fell on the enemy flank which was defending the salient. On seeing this, I had the charge beaten in all the regiments. The 48th, which was still holding out in the south-western corner of Sokolnitz, regained some ground, supported to their left by the 111th, the 3rd and the 108th. These were the sharpshooters of the Po who had taken the chateau at that moment. And now you can hear the 26th Light moving into the assault for the crossing of the Goldbach.'

'The enemy?'

'For the past half-hour, he has been withdrawing down the whole of the line, but not without a very brisk delaying action, as you can hear.'

An incredible event: Davout smiled.

'In other words, you haven't heard that the bulk of our forces are descending from the Pratzen to relieve you! It hasn't been enough for you to hold out at odds of ten to one from seven o'clock to midday in impossible conditions, but you have had it in mind to attack at a time when you still had the full weight of the enemy strength on your hands!'

Friant smiled, a malicious gleam lighting his greying arch-angel's head:

'Have we got to be satisfied with this dirty work we've been loaded with all day?'

Davout's bitterness had already returned:

'Do you think they will consider our taste in the matter? It is Soult who will gather by the armful the flags we thrust upon him. And it is Murat who will lead the pursuit. I am accustomed to this role of scavenger or sluice-man. My job hasn't changed since Abukir.'

He was back on his horse again.

'But, for the honour and the pleasure, well, we'll give it them! I shall order Bourcier to support you fully. Send into action all the battalions that have been re-forming below Telnitz. The general direction of your attack: from south to north, towards Kobelnitz. Do you hear that redoubling of fire, over there? Our centre is descending from the Pratzen. We've got to seize the Russians by the waist and prevent them from disengaging before they've been caught in the trap.'

Friant followed him, his mouth a grim line:

'We'll do what we can. But at the moment I have more than 300 dead and 1,700 wounded.'

'Let me know before tonight those you recommend for the Cross.'

One man propped up against an oak, and comfortably seated on a pile of dead leaves, heard this passing phrase with profound satisfaction. It was Jean-Pierre Blaise: the campaign had ended for him in a 'lucky wound', the dream of every soldier. Two of his toes having been smashed by a stray ball, he had applied the first dressing with great care himself and was waiting patiently for the stretcher-bearers, a meal, the Cross and the quarter-master-sergeant for the letter to his parents.

HALF-PAST THREE: THE MORT

The Polish general Prszbyzewski threw upon the brave men who surrounded him the look of a captain whose ship is going down. The mort was sounding. Hell was let loose. How many centuries had passed since the morning, when these same men had thrown themselves into the assault with hurrahs enough to bring down the walls? Now, here they were crowded amongst the debris of wagons, overturned by maddened horses, crushed under the wheels, almost killing one another in their panic, no longer listening to their officers, trampling on the wounded and the dead. Here were those he had led forth to capture the army of the Usurper: the fusiliers from Galitch, Butirsk and Narva, the regiment from Azov and the one from Podolia, the company of pioneers from Wyrubov, all jumbled together . . . Their great-coats in holes, their shakos and caps long since lost, their muskets thrown away to make flight easier, they were no longer any-thing but collective panic. Was it in order to end in this terrible hour that he had loyally served the Czar on every battlefield for ten years, exposed to the coldness of his cronies and friends in Warsaw who had remained in the reserve?

'Will you permit me to take the few companies we can still officer, and attempt an escape towards Moenitz?' asked his adjutant, General Wimpfen.

A German in origin. An unshakeable rock, whose scrubby moustache underlined the immobility of his wooden features. Prszbyzewski shrugged his shoulders:

'You really have some left?'

Wimpfen pointed to the end of what had been the main street of Sokolnitz; a chaos of stones and smoking beams with lunatics running about in every direction.

'More than 500 men. Olsufiev and I still have them in hand, but not for long . . .'

Every ten seconds, now, a cannon-ball fell, a shell exploded, and traced its furrow through the confusion, spattering the neighbourhood with blood.

'We are caught in an angle-iron; there is nowhere you can get through. Already the French are almost bold enough to come to hand-to-hand fighting . . . '

Prszbyzewski pointed to the Eagles and the tricolour flags that were drawing a pitiless circle around them in the distance, at the point where the grey and dirty sky joined the earth in fury. His column was the only one to be completely trapped. In a hurry to liquidate it so as to turn back towards Doctorov's and Langeron's units, whom they guessed to be in the midst of escaping, Saint-Hilaire, Legrand, Levasseur, Thiébault and even Oudinot, who had come to the rescue from Pratzen, were throwing a dozen regiments at them.

'Well, if you think . . . Go! Good luck, my friend!'

It did not last long; after barely 200 yards, Wimpfen and Olsufiev, followed by their wild horde, armed with cold steel, came upon General Boyé's dragoons, whom Saint-Hilaire had launched in a conclusive charge and who were about to sweep Sokolnitz from one end to the other. The encounter, the last organized battle in the sector, was of a terrible violence. In a minute, a hundred dead, a hundred prisoner, and the rest scattered, every man for himself. Prszbyzewski, himself forced to take sword in hand and retreat, surrounded by a few faithful officers, on to a little ridge that overhung the Goldbach, saw Wimpfen from afar, overwhelmed by a host of French dragoons, defend himself like a lion, fall from his horse, his shoulder stained with blood, cut his way free on foot, with the help of five fusiliers from Narva who came to his rescue — and eventually fall again, wounded afresh, into the hands of the French.

Prszbyzewski himself had only a few minutes more of liberty. His long and haughty face creased with a thousand little wrinkles, of irony, care and disappointment, assumed the light smile he adopted at desperate moments. Keep the flag flying! He watched, not without amusement, the keen race that was being run in Sokolnitz by two or three unbridled groups of Frenchmen for the honour of capturing him.

'Tally-ho! Tally-ho!' he murmured.

General Lochet was sweeping along a battalion of the 36th, bayonets before them, and was ploughing through the crowded mass of the last combatants. Wild with joy at having one of the great enemy leaders within his grasp, he was already shouting:

'Surrender!'

But a whirlwind thrust him aside: Colonel Franceschi, of the 8th Hussars, at the head of a dozen men, unscrupulously took advantage of the superiority of a few good horses in a fray, and did not hesitate to use the flat of his sabre on the French foot-soldiers to clear them out of the way more quickly. Very courteously, he saluted Prszbyzewski:

'You are lost, *mon général*. What is the good of sacrificing further brave men?'

At Prszbyzewski's side, Generals Stryck and Selekov raised their pistols. One could still die . . . 'elegantly'. But the Polish nobleman felt all the weariness of the day descend upon him. And he noticed that a few hundred of his men were still firing behind bushes or sections of wall. To save their lives, at least, from these others! To preserve them for the Czar, for Russia— or for Poland, who could tell?

'Very well, gentlemen. Have them cease fire in all my column.'

And he tendered his sword to Colonel Franceschi.

'*Merde!*' cried General Lochet, who had lost his big game by less than fifty yards.

FOUR O'CLOCK: DOCTOROV SAVES WHAT HE CAN

'The French have just occupied Augezd, general! We are surrounded in Telnitz!'

Captain of *chasseurs* Davidov, a great hop-pole as panic-stricken as if disasters were flocking about him by the hundred, was writhing his arms in front of Lieutenant-General Doctorov, commander of the first Allied column. The Captain had passed through the meshes of the net that had just strangled the third column and arrived, the very embodiment of disaster, in the middle of a corps as yet in very good order. The regiments of Kiev, Jaroslav, Vladimir, and New-Ingrie, drawn up in squares around Telnitz, were so many living fortresses with walls fearfully pitted, but still sound. The panic had not spread there.

'And General Prszbyzewski has just laid down his arms!'

'Well, that won't happen to me,' said little General Doctorov mildly, without raising his voice, but in such a tone that he restored to calm the great rascal who overtopped him by a head. 'Langeron has just let me know that he has managed to get through, with half his column.'

'Through Augezd, general! Through Augezd! Every outlet is now closed to us to the north of Lake Satschan.'

'Never mind about that. We shall get through to the south.'

'To the south? But there's the lake at Moenitz!'

'There's a dike between the two lakes. I'll have all who can defile there—and in good order.'

Doctorov's voice became hard and rough. His eyes flashed. There emanated from this little man, suddenly, an inner force that banished doubt and fear from all his entourage. Within a few minutes a stream of orders, composed, precise, rained down upon the four corners of his unit:

'Generals Kienmayer and Nostitz will cover us between Telnitz and the lake, with what remains of the Austrian forces. We ourselves will proceed to concentrate all our artillery—more than twenty-five pieces, gentlemen! And some of the largest calibre!—on the rising ground that affords us a natural bulwark below Telnitz. Draw up the troops in three lines: the cavalry first, the artillery second; the infantry third. During this time, all those not needed in combat will defile over the dike.'

All the Russians were already obeying without saying a word. But the Austrian cavalry general, Stutterheim, more independent—and sacrificed by this arrangement—pointed out:

'Before 3,000 or 4,000 men at most have managed to cross by the dike, the others will be hacked to pieces where they stand. By this device, you sacrifice half your column!'

'You mean I save half of it. We have no choice. Would you rather lay down arms?'

HALF-PAST FOUR: FIRE ON THE LAKES

'That's slack! That's far too slack!'

Napoleon lowered his glass and looked around him to find a

victim for his bad temper. At that moment, he was far from being the conquering hero. What held sway over him was irritation, nervous tension, the disappointment of a spoilt child before a hollow plaything: his victory was dwindling in extent suddenly, and he was too shrewd not to sense it.

He had just arrived at the chapel of St Anthony, or the Augezd chapel, at the south-eastern edge of the Pratzen plateau. It was on that side that the slopes were most precipitate. They were broken halfway up by a terrace that immediately overlooked Augezd, where the piety of the Moravians had raised, as a votive chapel to St Anthony, a granite sugar-loaf of vaguely Romanesque appearance. There the Emperor had joined Soult and Vandamme, who still had at their disposal only five battalions without artillery and had been brought to a standstill by the unexpected outbreak of Doctorov's fire. Under the Emperor's eyes, 10,000 to 12,000 Russians were making an imposing show of force, whereas he had been looking forward to a pursuit without hitches. Now, he had just been informed of Lannes' and Murat's passivity. He knew that Bagration's forces would be able to reach Olmütz. The escape of the Russian right could only be compensated by the complete crushing of the left. Spurred on by his harsh reproaches, Soult had just had the 3rd division of dragoons charge on Doctorov's left to cut him off from Sokolnitz. But, before the Emperor's eyes, General Boyé and his men had just grappled with the last sacrificed squadrons of the Austrian cavalry—and had been fairly briskly shown the way back to the first slopes of the Pratzen. Napoleon could not get over it. Had one ever seen defeated men show so little respect for the game?

'That's dreadfully slack! The dragoons weren't thrown in wholeheartedly! It is inconceivable to press home a decisive charge so feebly!'

'The Russian artillery is still impressive, Sire,' murmured Soult.

'A fine affair! The remains of a battery! Ah, there you are, sir!'

An unhappy colonel of dragoons arrived at that moment to give an account of his division's tribulations. The Emperor did not even let him open his mouth:

'Return at once from whence you came! And you will tell the general who commands you, on my behalf, that he is nothing but a coward! General Gardane!'[1]

'Sire?'

'On consideration, go yourself and take command of the dragoons. Charge at their head. Clear all those Russian pieces within twenty minutes. And break these people's last squares for me.'

Soult, too, sent all his available aides-de-camp to speed the Allied collapse. Each minute that slipped by deflated the victory. The day was declining. A fine and sticky rain hastened the onset of night and seemed moreover to hold all the smoke of the discharges and fires. Napoleon stormed the more violently since he felt in his commanders and in the men that abrupt depression that follows a victorious battle. The impression of having gained all at a single stroke was so strong that nobody—except him—could any longer see the need to do anything.

But here came Colonel Franceschi, radiant, who conducted General Wimpfen, quite downcast on a stretcher, to the Emperor as prisoner, and told him of the capture of Prszbyzewski, detained for the moment amongst his men for the counting. Napoleon cheered up, offered Wimpfen a glass of his celebrated Chambertin and had him commended especially to Baron Larrey. Meanwhile, the massive arrival of Vandamme's troops changed the face of things: in less than a quarter of an hour, the 46th, the 57th and the 75th of the Line and the Corsican sharp-shooters, finding fresh inspiration in Soult's voice and the Emperor's vigorous gestures, defiled uttering war-cries on either side of the little chapel, passed through Augezd at the double, went for Doctorov's regiments again in front of Lake Satschan, and finally rounded up all the Russian forces that were there. Boyé's dragoons, humiliated to the very core, had not waited for General Gardane before setting out again, unmasking in their turn six pieces of horse artillery of the Guard that Bessières had just sent them, which battered the heroic Austrian cavalry—and they gained possession of Telnitz.

Restored to serenity, Napoleon grimaced again on seeing through his glass some three miles away, and out of reach, the

[1] One of the oldest of the Imperial aides-de-camp.

long line of Russian infantry that Doctorov was successfully defiling over the Moenitz dike, and for whom some thousands of others had gained the necessary time by letting themselves be cut down where they stood.

But on bringing his gaze back to his feet, he saw with his naked eye the picture he had dreamed of an hour earlier: left to themselves, without orders, the remains of Langeron's and Doctorov's columns, 5,000 to 6,000 men, were milling about and had no idea where to head for. A few Allied officers calmly sacrificed everything to the saving of the artillery: the twenty-five pieces which to the end had barred the way to the French, hitched to the last available horses, were in need of a miraculous solution if they were not to be captured. It was in the hands of God! The only way out was to turn them on to the ice of Lake Satschan, which the twilight bathed in a leaden colour giving a false idea of its thickness. With this example before them, a confused flood of fugitives set out like sheep on to the vast empty space.

'They're mad!' everyone was shouting round the Emperor. 'The poor devils will drown! The surface of the lake is already full of cracks!'

'A few of them will get across all the same! . . . '

'The guns will never get over. Look: two have already been swallowed up.'

'Not one of them will escape,' said the Emperor.

All around him then fell silent, as they understood the order he had just given in person to the battery of twelve pieces Soult had had lined up in front of the chapel. A mixture of horror and excitement gripped all those martial figures by the throat. The pieces, in an instant, vomited a shower of projectiles on to the surface of the lake.

'With *red-hot* balls!' Napoleon had stipulated.

THE VICTIMS OF THE LAKES

'Come on my lads! Courage! You don't want to leave your fine pieces to these enemies of Christ? Only half a mile to go and we'll escape them!'

Major-General Prince Orussov tried every possible resource, from gentleness to violence, to wring the last drop of energy from Doctorov's gunners. The latter had entrusted him with the mission of saving all he could of his artillery—and it was he who, as a last resource, had launched the confused convoy of harnessed pieces, that procession of horses, men, wheels, caissons and gun-carriages, on to the huge expanse of ice.

From afar, it appeared smooth. From near, it was merely a blackish marsh where reeds held in the ice emerged in tufts and accentuated the unwholesome aspect of the stretch of water. The Austrians and French would have recoiled, but the Russians were accustomed to dubious ground. Their interminable half-seasons when everything was mixed together, sky, earth and water, were known as *rasputitsa*: the season of bad roads.

One after the other, pushing, pulling, helping each other, the gunners got their pieces on to the slippery crust—and at first things went fairly well. The officers, brandishing their whips, saw to the proper spacing of the cannon. The head of the column covered over 200 yards, and it was true, the safe shore was less than half a mile off, the gateway to Austerlitz, the open place where Doctorov had promised to draw up and wait.

'Stop all those people from coming! They're mad! The ice won't hold!' cried Orussov.

It was inevitable: the foaming mass of abandoned infantry assumed one direction; as soon as the fugitives realized that the ice was holding under the guns, they hurled themselves in hundreds on to the lake, and even some of the cavalry took their chance there, two squadrons of the St Petersburg dragoons, a hundred Cossacks from Issayev!

'All the same, one can hardly fire on them . . .' exclaimed Orussov, who certainly had a mind to.

In five minutes, the weight of the artillery had been increased tenfold by the immense ragged mass. In front of the General, a first crack: the ice gave way under the weight of a fugitive who found himself immersed to the waist. Another by his side, yet another, a horse engulfed suddenly to the belly, which reared neighing to death . . .

'If only that would frighten them!'

Those who were near the crack did indeed waver; the leader of the piece that formed the head of the convoy pulled with all his might on the reins to stop his horse. But behind them the crowd was pushing irresistibly. More than a thousand voices were now yelling:

'Come on! The ice is holding! Faster! Why are you slowing down, you vermin?'

Another crack, ten, twenty — and the yells changed their tone: it was terror that predominated. At that moment—yes, only at that moment—did the whistle of the French cannon-balls draw nearer, and a rain of crackling and smoking projectiles burst on the scene of disaster. They accentuated it; they amplified the horror of it; but they did not cause it: the ice would have cracked in any case.

It now gave way in whole sections, and General Orussov was himself again, half drowned amongst forty men floundering in the mud and icy water.

'Don't lose heart, men! Hold fast! We're within our depth everywhere! Get back to the bank! Every man for himself now, and may the Virgin protect you!'

'Leave the horses! They can't get out, not them!' cried General Stutterheim at the same time. 'But the men, yes! Every man who doesn't panic!'

About 2,000 men spent a quarter of an hour in that vast paddling pool . . . They were within their depth almost everywhere, it was true: the water never reached higher than their shoulders. But the mud made them slip and drew them down treacherously; the cannon-balls fell thick and fast and completed the destruction of the remaining pieces of ice of any size, which might have served as rafts; the shock of the water, searingly cold, gripped their exhausted bodies; the gunners were entangled in their lines and straps—and a few of them, wild with frustration, died still trying, against all common sense, to drag their pieces out. However, the panic was almost less than a moment earlier: now that it was a collective struggle against an element they were familiar with, the Russians helped one another, gave each other a hand, pointed out the firm ground, and hauled each other on to the bank, where they were promptly collected, half frozen, by the French.

From the chapel of St Anthony the spectacle was all the more impressive in that the night, drawing on very rapidly, blotted out details and let the imagination magnify the drama. It was an ants' nest that had been stirred up, a hive that had been flooded, a disaster where men were reduced to the state of crushed insects . . .

One could no longer see, from the French headquarters, anything but a blackish mess from which rose a single confused roar made up of a thousand heartrending cries. And the latter became unbearable to all ears, for one suddenly became aware that firing had stopped almost everywhere—except for the nearby battery with its red-hot balls.

'All right, stop!' said Napoleon, mistakenly convinced that it had been his artillery that had broken the ice. 'That's cooked their goose. See that as many of those brave men as possible are fished out.'

And so, at five o'clock, firing ceased on the battlefield of Austerlitz.

When Vandamme's men, almost ashamed of such an addition to the carnage, arrived at the shores of the lake and made a decent attempt to hold out a hand to the poor wretches, they found that the Russians, in an extraordinary upsurge of collective vitality, had fished one another out fairly effectively. About 2,000, almost naked, were taken prisoner; more than 500, seriously wounded or dead, lay on the steep bank. Lake Satschan retained thirty-eight cannon, 130 horses, and 200 men.[1]

---

[1] The Bulletin of the Grand Army, drafted by Napoleon himself, would quite simply add two noughts and proclaim 20,000. It was one of the most notable examples of exaggeration in a military balance sheet. 'The question of the Austerlitz lakes' was completely settled in 1908, after scrupulous study, by Colonel Colin, who can hardly be suspected of severity towards Napoleon. Apart from the fact that these 20,000 men *could not* have been there, since Doctorov and Langeron had only left behind them at that time and in that place 4,000 to 5,000 men at the very most, a whole series of irrefutable witnesses are available: General Suchet, four days after the battle, had the job of draining the lake and dragging it to recover the Russian cannon. Some Austrians were present. The consensus of their reports, both military and civilian, confirms the virtually complete absence of human bodies in the lake, where, in order to drown, a man would have had to be already wounded or sick, since he would have been within his depth everywhere. One must remember that it was more a marsh than a sheet of water. The 200 drowned which it seems reasonable to concede to the unlikely legend—against which, moreover, Russian historians have always protested—had been pulled up on to the bank by their comrades during the evening of December 2nd, and were absorbed into the charnel-houses of Augezd along with those killed by musket-ball, cannon-ball or cold steel.

FIVE O'CLOCK: ALEXANDER I

'What is this village called?' asked the Czar wearily.

'Hodiegitz, Sire. It is the place appointed by Prince Kutuzov yesterday as the rallying-point behind Austerlitz, in the event of the battle being lost.'

'Mikhail Illarionovich certainly anticipated events more than Weirother . . . ' murmured the young sovereign, very pale, his cheeks hollow, his eyes sunken, and his gestures as stiff as an automaton's. He had not spared himself for hours and hours past in his exertions to take the place of his panic-stricken generals, to halt the stampede of the regiments, to try to understand what was happening, and stem the tide.

Now night had fallen completely and thrown its cloak of compassion over the shame of his army. It was raining hard. The troops, rallied somehow or other during the passage through Augezd, were marching along, exhausted, in the utter darkness, preserving a gloomy silence. Hodiegitz was crammed with wounded and sick, looters and equipment. It had been hard to find the room in which the Emperor now sat, taking his bearings by the gleam of a miserable candle—almost alone with all that remained of his suite and staff. He had by him only his physician, Wyllie, his equerry, Jaehne, a courier and, as his sole aide-de-camp, Czernichev. Not that the others had abandoned him: but they were all on missions, to the column commanders engulfed in the catastrophe, in search of news, or at the head of regiments that had lost their commanders.

'Do me a further service, Czernichev! Find Kutuzov for me, for the love of God!'

The commander-in-chief was not far off: at Wazan, less than four miles away, in the middle of the Imperial Guard, still in good order, and the remains of Miloradovitch's division. He, for his part, had sent out messengers in every direction to find his sovereign—but such was the confusion of the overcrowded roads that they were not to meet until the middle of the night.

The Czar pondered, his elbows on a rough table, his head between his hands:

'Prszbyzewski's column, completely destroyed;

'Doctorov's and Langeron's columns, two-thirds lost;

'Miloradovitch's corps, slashed by half and still in almost complete disorder;

'The Guard, very sorely tried, but in good order;

'Far to the north, Bagration's corps, exhausted and reduced by the battle, but still capable of making a valiant rearguard.'

His eyes full of the sight of the poor wretches scattered over the ground whom he had had to abandon, Alexander questioned his physician:

'What do you think our losses must amount to?'

'Less than might appear perhaps, Sire: a lot of still able-bodied men have gone astray and will rejoin their units . . . '

'And so?'

'Ten or fifteen thousand in all[1] . . . '

'Has my carriage been recovered?'

'No, Sire. It is to be feared that it has been destroyed or captured.'

'Where is the Emperor of Austria?'

'He is waiting for you at Czeitsch, nearly eight miles from here, in order to consult with you and Prince Kutuzov.'

Alexander raised his head and his familiars were struck by the strange brightness of his eyes, which held large tears. But it was not the prostration of an effeminate: he had shed none of his dignity, even at his most dejected. A sort of mystic exaltation sustained him: his lips kept moving. He was praying.

'To horse! Let us go to Czeitsch! I will take home to Russia all the brave men that are left to me . . . '

*   *   *   *

But the hardships of the battle, disappointment, and the cold and rainy night made him ill after a few miles. He would spend

[1] It is difficult to estimate the total Allied loss. The only accurate figures are those for prisoners taken by the French. These would include, in the days to come, eighteen convoys of captives passing through Brünn, giving a total of 9,767 Russians and 1,686 Austrians. The latter would acknowledge having had a little over 4,000 killed. The Russians never gave precise figures for the number of theirs and the figure put forward by Napoleon was quite unrealistic. In cross-checking the state of the regiments and in following them during the retreat, one arrives at the approximate figure of 11,000 Russian dead. It would seem that one is coming very near the truth therefore in saying that the all-round losses of the Allied army, including prisoners, was in the region of 27,000 men, that is to say, a third of the effectives in action.

the night on straw, in a peasant's hut, in the village of Urchitz. Only after three hours sleep would he be able to remount his horse, and the two Emperors would not be united, with Kutuzov, until the middle of the morning of December 3rd. Then it was that they would set in motion the arrangements for the retreat and take the decisions, sad and necessary, to save at least the essentials:

'The Austrian cavalry will provide a screen for the retreat of all the re-formed elements of the Russian army, who will make an abrupt change of direction and march off towards the east, while the French believe them to be on the road to Olmütz, to the north.

'Bagration will take command of the rearguard: he will have them cover thirty-eight miles in forty hours. Sustenance will be obtained from whatever may be found along the way. No stop will be made anywhere. Stragglers, the wounded, and those suffering from inanition will be left where they are. Hungary will be reached in four days, Russia in ten.'

But what if the French should unleash their cavalry, almost intact, at this retreat? What if they should try once again to outflank their route, to cut off their retreat by one of their damned forced marches, rendered all the more rapid by the wings of victory? By pressing home their advantage vigorously, from December 3rd, they would be able to sabre 10,000 men a day!

There was only one way out: the Emperor of Austria would effect 'a mission of sacrifice'. His country in any case was abandoned and deprived of all resources. The Russians would not have reconstituted their forces in under a year. The whole land was at the discretion of the conqueror.

Austria would make peace. Her Emperor would go and request it in person. Already, on the evening of December 2nd, in order to moderate the French pursuit (which the Allies could not guess was so sluggish), Francis II sent Napoleon one of the most meritorious combatants of the day, the brilliant commander of all the cavalry.

'I WAS AT THE BATTLE OF AUSTERLITZ'

'Sire, Marshal Bernadotte sends me to advise you that Prince

Jean de Liechtenstein has arrived at our outposts and solicits an audience of Your Majesty . . . '

Napoleon smiled absent-mindedly and looked at Bernadotte's aide-de-camp who stood before him. The atmosphere in the main room of the posting house of Posoritz, to which the Emperor had just returned after a three-hour inspection of the battlefield, resembled that of a laundry. All the officers had wet clothes which were steaming in the heat of a crackling fire in the vast fire-place.

'What does he want?'

'To arrange an interview between his Emperor and you. Austria is asking for an armistice.'

'Tell Bernadotte to treat the Prince well and to give him a meal. Then to spin things out. I will receive him, but in my own time. Not before tomorrow morning. Berthier!'

'Sire?'

'Write:'

'No. 514 . . . ', the Chief of Staff noted scrupulously on his register, before recording the instructions, which came five hours too late, and could not be carried out by any means before the next morning: night and weariness rooted the victorious army to the ground.

'Order to Prince Murat to pursue the enemy.

'Order to Oudinot's division to take up position at Rausnitz.

'Order to Marshal Lannes to follow the advance of the cavalry with the remainder of his corps.

'Order to Marshal Bernadotte to pursue the enemy along the road from Austerlitz to Goeding.

'Order to Marshal Soult and to Marshal Davout to pursue the enemy.

'The same order to Generals Klein and Bourcier.'

'Lebrun!'

'Sire?'

'Leave for Paris at once. You will give the first news to those gentlemen. Have the cannon fired at the Invalides. The flags will follow. I wager the stock market will show a remarkable recovery! You will deliver this letter to the Empress:

' . . . I have defeated the Russian and Austrian army commanded by the two Emperors. I am a little tired; I have been camping for eight days in the open air by fairly cool nights. I shall rest tomorrow at the chateau of the Princes of Kaunitz where I count on sleeping for two or three hours. The Russian army is not only beaten, but destroyed. I embrace you.'

His eyes were troubling him. Constant brought him at that moment, to bathe them, a warm lotion of diluted rose-water. Around him was the happy throng of all who wanted to share the incomparable moment with him: 'The finest of his victories!', the cry was already being raised on all sides. He was becoming convinced of it, more slowly than many of those present, but finally he relaxed somewhat and accepted the day as it was. Only an obstinate furrow remained on his brow, behind which the phrases of the Bulletin and the Proclamation that he would dictate during the night were already running. *'Never was field of battle more horrible . . . '*
'The losses? A first estimate?'
'Theirs, Sire?'
'Ours.'
'Not 2,000 killed in all. 7,000 wounded without doubt.'[1]
' *. . . This will not surprise military men, who know that it is only in a rout that one loses men . . . '* Napoleon was dreaming, and confiding snatches of his song of victory to the admirers beside themselves with joy and exhaustion who formed a respectful semi-circle around him. *'This day will cost tears of blood at St Petersburg . . . ' 'It will take three days to evacuate all the enemy wounded through Brünn . . . Their heart bleeds!'*
'Savary!'
'Sire?'
'You will make your arrangements so that my interview with Francis II shall be given a military character. I want it to strike the imagination of the men. I shall receive him at my bivouac, by the side of the road, and we will seat ourselves on two tree-stumps, by a fire lit by my grenadiers. For the rest, we shall see about that tomorrow with Prince Liechtenstein.'
He was silent for a moment. Was he already seeing himself

[1] The exact figures, checked with the help of the state of the corps: 1,305 killed; 6,940 wounded; 573 prisoners, for the whole of the French army.

shaping 1806 in that end of 1805? Tomorrow would see him enter the society of Kings. The Emperor of Austria at his bivouac! Was he already distributing the crowns of the Great Empire? Westphalia to Jerome, Naples to Joseph, to Louis Holland . . . But behind that glittering scene there was the ransom of December 2nd: the Russians defeated, but not crushed; Alexander, Kutuzov and Bagration on the way home with 40,000 men. Prussia would not declare war this month, that was certain! But in six months? Did he see himself next winter at Saint-Cloud, opening the anniversary ball—or in the snow-drifts of Poland, at Warsaw, not far from Eylau?

'*May much spilt blood, many misfortunes, fall at last upon the perfidious islanders who are the cause of it! May the cowardly oligarchs of London suffer the penalty of so many evils!*' . . . Did he have a presentiment that the last victim of Austerlitz would be William Pitt, whom the news would kill? He rose, walked up and down, and then went towards the door of logs, which was hastily opened before him. A gust of icy wind ushered into the smoky room all the hardship of the night. The rain was turning to snow. The picket of *chasseurs à pied* of the Imperial Guard who watched over the inn presented arms, without great enthusiasm: the Foot Guards had not been in action, and only the surgeon Maugra had been wounded in giving his services on the battlefield.

'They're crying with rage about it!' declared Napoleon, highly delighted. 'I shall put it in the bulletin. Bessières!'

'Sire?'

'The details of the losses in my Horse Guards?'

'The *chasseurs* lost Colonel Morland, Sire, Captain Thervay, two N.C.O.s, nine corporals and *chasseurs* killed, seventeen officers and forty-two cavalrymen wounded; 153 horses out of action.'

Under their eyes, on the bare slope cluttered with debris, four or five fires fed with the endless litter, the huge pulsating mass of men, filthy, bloody, garrulous, happy—alive. And kept at a distance by the *chasseurs*, with fixed bayonets, the assemblage of captured Russian officers, removed from the company of their men.

'Why is one of them shouting so much?' asked the Emperor

indignantly. 'I certainly hope no one has done him any harm!'

His head bare under the rain, he walked towards Sergeant Heuillet, who was in charge of the sentinels, an old acquaintance.

'Was it you who beat the charge at the Lodi bridge?'

'I was fifteen, Your Majesty, when I first served you!'

'What's the matter with that Russian who's making such a noise?'

'It's a cavalry-major of artillery, Sire, a man hardly older than me. He keeps demanding to be shot at the top of his voice, because he prefers death to captivity.'

'Does he speak French?'

'My word, Sire, more than me, I should think.'

'Let him come here.'

'He's a madman, Sire . . . '

'Let him come!'

The madman drew near, a child, a proud wounded angel. All pink and blond, he was the embodiment of the unhappiness of defeat. The whole of outraged Russia wept and made moan in him.

'Sire, have me shot. I am not worthy to live, I lost all my artillery!'

'Calm yourself, young man. One may be beaten by my army without dishonour!'

It was said in such a tone, with such force, that the young man was silent, saluted, and decided to live. Napoleon I went back into the posting house at last, relaxed, eased, sure of himself. Flashes of style were passing through his mind, and preparing to run into the bronze of History. He pinched Sergeant Heuillet's ear as he passed:

'I am pleased with you . . . '

And scarcely before the fire, he called a secretary:

'Draft for the proclamation! "*Soldiers, I am pleased with you* . . . " You have, on the day of . . . '

He hesitated for only a short moment, remembering his letter to Josephine: 'I shall rest tomorrow at the chateau of the Princes of Kaunitz'. Was it not there that the Czar had stayed yesterday?

'You have, on the day of Austerlitz, fulfilled all that I had expected of your intrepidity. You have adorned your eagles with immortal glory. An army of a hundred thousand men, commanded by the Emperors of Russia and Austria, has been, in less than four hours, either cut off or dispersed . . . '

He stopped, reflected once more, and put off till the next day his account of the battle that had held at one and the same time his luck and his folly, his genius, his limitations, his greatness, and all that those first years of the nineteenth century contained of nobility and coarseness, of progress mingled with barbarity. One can say all that one likes, after all, and even, in the course of a century and a half, the civilian historian, who prides himself on accuracy. It was he who won. It is from him, across the varying colours of his commentators, that December 2, 1805, has taken and kept its tone—inimitable, alas! It is always he that one hears:

'It will be enough for you to say: *"I was at the Battle of Austerlitz"*, for one to reply: *"There's a brave man!"* '

CHAPTER XVIII

NEAR VIENNA, ON THAT DAY

On December 2nd, at the end of the morning, as on every day, a man of the same age as Napoleon I was walking in the country around Schönbrünn; he had been living in the village of Hetzendorf for a few weeks now. He was short, unprepossessing, with a face ruddy and ugly, covered with pock-marks, so swarthy that the children nick-named him 'the Spaniard', his black hair hanging down in abundant locks. But his body was athletic and thick-set under the jacket of dark-grey shaggy material and trousers of the same, which gave him a slight look of Robinson Crusoe, accentuated by his hairy hands, very strong, with spatulate fingers. The peasants as they passed greeted respectfully the most celebrated musician of the capital, but kept their distance: his Rhineland dialect was hard to understand (he would never be Austrian except by adoption) and the sudden turns of his execrable temper were incomprehensible; except to shrewd observers who noticed, in the folds of his ears, cotton-wool moistened with a yellowish liquid.

Ludwig van Beethoven had already been deaf for five years.

He had just spent a long time sitting at his composing, haunted by the wonderful themes of the 5th and 6th symphonies, which he was writing at the same time: the victory of man over destiny, the reconciliation of man with nature . . . but he was also working on the 4th piano concerto, and on the violin concerto . . . At last he had risen abruptly, and gone to his basin to cool his fiery head with several jugfuls of water. Cursorily dried, his hair still dripping, there he was marching his smouldering dreams with long strides across the desolate countryside.

'As the leaves of autumn fall and wither, so has hope of being

306

cured, at least to a certain degree, been drying up for me . . .
Even that proud courage that often animated me in the fine days
of summer has vanished . . . O God! let me know *one day* of
pure joy! For so long already has the inner echo of true joy
been a stranger to me . . . '

It was three years since he had written that to his brothers in
the famous *Testament of Heiligenstadt*, taking a vow never to
commit suicide, whatever might happen. But today, all seemed
once more in question. He dwelt on those phrases one by one
with an emphasis all the more despairing since he had had to
renounce a cure infinitely more precious than that of the body.
'The immortal well-beloved', Josephine of Brunswick, had left
Vienna, fleeing before the French troops; and he now knew that
she would never marry him. The young woman's family had
scotched their engagement. How could a Hungarian noble-
woman marry a Court musician, in other words a valet, a
descendant of a Dutch wine merchant? . . . Josephine! . . .
She alone could have healed him. She alone could have reached
him, immured in the depths of his prison, the most elevated and
the most anguished soul the world had ever bruised. She alone
could have given a gleam of true joy to Ludwig van Beethoven.

She is present in every note of *Fidelio*, his opera, the great
work of 1805, which had just been a complete failure, on
November 20th, at the Vienna Theatre, before a sparse audience
in which French uniforms had predominated. She was Leonora,
the sublime young woman, rescuer of her husband, in defiance
of the infernal tyrant! It was she who suddenly appeared at the
darkest corner of the fortress, enabling Beethoven to deliver to
the whole world the secret of a conjugal love he would never
experience: 'Freedom is inseparable from Love'. It was she whom
the choir of prisoners acclaimed in tones already presaging those
of the 9th Symphony:

> All hail the day, all hail the hour
> So long desired, yet scarce believed,
> When Justice with Mercy reconciled
> Appears at the door of our tomb!

The stroller paused and absent-mindedly turned his ill-shaven
face to the north, from whence came the stinging rain, the

winter, the harshness of life. It was said that a decisive battle would take place over there one day soon. Who knows? At that moment perhaps . . . He shrugged his shoulders. What would it hold to compare with the struggle that was going on in his own heart, out of sight of all men? He was deaf for ever. He was alone for ever. Josephine had refused him. Vienna had cold-shouldered his opera. And these French, these imbeciles who had made his heart beat faster ten years earlier, had understood nothing in *Fidelio*. Why had they not felt that it was they who were the prisoners? . . . Why had they not recaptured the spirit of '89 at that moment when, all chains torn away, the song of the new epoch burst forth? Why had they not recognized that music for the taking of the Bastille? This was what happened when a liberty-loving people delivered themselves, tied hand and foot, to an adventurer! Beethoven had refused to disturb himself to see Napoleon march through the streets of Vienna. He would never see him.

'Did he not die in my eyes on the day he made himself Emperor?'

Come! He must return to his room in indescribable confusion and lunch on a piece of salami, within the four walls of a prison sealed up for ever by the desertion of Josephine of Brunswick. But what was he growling now between his teeth, the mad, the forlorn, the defeated Ludwig van Beethoven, of December 2, 1805? . . .

'I will seize destiny by the throat. It will certainly not succeed in overcoming me completely.'

Voreppe,
March-October, 1960

BIBLIOGRAPHY AND ACKNOWLEDGEMENTS

I should like to express my thanks to M. Rieunier, secretary-general of the *Bibliothéque Nationale*, who facilitated my access to the indispensible works of Colonel Colin on *The Campaign of 1805*. It is on them that I have based my military reconstruction, consulting on the Allied side:

The *Mémoires* of Langeron

Relation de la Campagne de 1805, by Danilevski

La Bataille d'Austerlitz, by Stutterheim

Der Krieg 1805, by Schönhals.

Colonel Colin's works were published anonymously in the *Revue d'Histoire rédigée à l'état-major* in 1907 and 1908. It is these more particularly that finally settle the famous 'question of the lakes'.

I have also drawn on the *Mémoires* and *Souvenirs* of Maret, Savary, Bourgogne, Coignet, Thiard, Ségur, Marbot, Fain, Fouché, Mollien, Gaudin, Suchet, Jomini, Mouton, Bernadotte, Soult, Davout, Drouet d'Erlon, Thiébault, Czartoryski, Barrès, Driault, etc.

I have used—prudently—the *Bulletins de la Grande Armée* and the *Correspondance* of Napoleon.

I have referred to the basic historians many times, to Thiers, Madelin, Georges Lefebvre, Sorel, Emile Tersen.

I thank the latter most warmly for his advice, as also my friends Brigitte and Jean Massin for having helped me to reconstruct Beethoven's day.

The *Lettres de Grognards* by Fairon and Heuse, the *Soldat impérial*, by Morvan, and *Napoléon et la Garde impériale* by Lachouque have helped me in reconstructing the life of a soldier in the Grand Army.

THE REPUBLICAN CALENDAR

At the time of the Battle of Austerlitz the Republican calendar was still in force, though it was discontinued shortly after, on December 31, 1805.

There were twelve months each of thirty days, with five extra days (six in leap years) to complete the year. They ran as follows:

Vendémiaire	Sept. 22nd to Oct. 21st
Brumaire	Oct. 22nd to Nov. 20th
Frimaire	Nov. 21st to Dec. 20th
Nivôse	Dec. 21st to Jan. 19th
Pluviôse	Jan. 20th to Feb. 18th
Ventôse	Feb. 19th to Mar. 20th
Germinal	Mar. 21st to April 19th
Floréal	April 20th to May 19th
Prairial	May 20th to June 18th
Messidor	June 19th to July 18th
Thermidor	July 19th to Aug. 17th
Fructidor	Aug. 18th to Sept. 16th

The calendar was reckoned from September 22, 1792, though it actually came into force on November 26, 1793.

There are various complications in connection with leap year, the most important being that Year VIII of the Republican calendar was reckoned as a leap year, though the corresponding year in the Gregorian calendar, 1800, was not. This means that subsequent years in the Republican calendar began on September 23rd. In the above table therefore all dates from the beginning of Year IX on September 23, 1800, are advanced by one. The date of Austerlitz, December 2, 1805, thus becomes Frimaire 10, An XIV.

INDEX

311

INDEX